Solving Single:
How to Get the Ring,
Not the Run Around

G.L.
Lambert

to Candice

Sparta Up

G. L. Lam

XoXo

ISBN: 0615863833
ISBN-13: 978-0-615-86383-2

Cover Design by Yittie Benedict

Viceroy Publishing
340 S. Lemon Avenue, Suite 1937
Walnut, California 91789

For more information visit:
SolvingSingle.com

TO MY WIFE, THE QUEEN OF SPARTA

CONTENTS

INTRODUCTION

There is no such thing as a man who cannot fall in love. Show me a man who refuses to settle down, and I will show you a woman who can make him go to Zales tomorrow. All women are created equal with the power to enchant and inspire men, but instead of honing that power, it becomes buried under a mountain of insecurity and anxiety. Young women raised consuming over sexualized media think that power over men comes from sex appeal. These ignorant girls serve their vagina on a platter, convinced that lust will lead to love. Older women frustrated that they are still single, bitterly attempt to compete with this sex first generation by being overly submissive and compromising. As a result, the 21st century man is oversexed and spoiled, which has made him less romantic and more entitled. This gold rush for relationships strips power away from women lowers standards and makes gods of the most average of men. The modern man does not stress over how to keep a woman and make her happy. Bookshelves aren't filled with relationship advice for guys because the male species is currently winning. I hear women angrily point out that men aren't doing their part to retain a good woman. This is true, but what incentive do men have to improve? When iPhones are in high demand, does Apple honestly listen to complaints from those who are standing in line? If the product were so flawed, you would get your ass out of line and go buy a Samsung. Only when the market collapses and the gold rush ends will men reevaluate their ways. As long as women continue to compete and compromise, there is no reason for any man to change.

Many women follow propaganda created by other females who are in more screwed up relationships than their own and stereotype men into simplified categories like "player" or "mama's boy." Few women are experts on men because they have zero understanding of what really motivates the average male beyond what they've seen on *Sex and the City*. Being submissive will delight a man, but it will not make him value you. A pretty face catches his attention, but beauty alone will not keep him content. Sex drives a man, but it will never control him. Any woman can charm a penis but few can charm the man attached to it into caring about her once his erection diminishes. Love and commitment are not impossible things to get from men if you project the right image, demand a certain level of respect, and value yourself as a woman more than the thought of one day being his wife. This book is not about pleasing a man; it is about regaining your power over them.

The core lessons found in this book were taken from a blog I created a few years ago called, Black Girls Are Easy (BGAE). The title is deliberately misleading. No woman is easy sexually. Some have lower standards, but it's always her choice. The "easy" I was focusing on was a tongue-in-cheek way to take on the stereotypes of the African American female. The media consistently showed black girls as one of two things, eye rolling ghetto queens ready to rip a bitch's weave out or as humble church-going victims of circumstance ready to sing for America's votes. Black women are far more diverse, and aren't this difficult group of women. Black girls are easy to understand, easy to relate to, and most importantly, easy to love if you take the time to get to know them intimately. Attention grabbing title aside, the content of BGAE was inspired by the lack of power I saw in various females in my life. It was insane how these beautiful, smart, and talented women were allowing themselves to be victimized in the name of love.

The women I knew personally and the majority that I observed publicly had become so thirsty for commitment, marriage, and a general sense of being wanted that they sold themselves cheap, submitting to any man who seemed halfway decent. Black, Latino, even Caucasian men raised in the 80's and 90's are unique and play by a different set of rules. This is the second MTV generation that grew up on a diet of Snoop Dogg and Nas, not Poison and Whitesnake. This generation had a certain swagger and outlook that transcended race and class, and seemed to be an enigma that no one wanted to dissect romantically. Being from that cloth, I decided to shed some light on how the so-called hip hop generation thinks.

He's Just Not That Into You may be the bible for cosmopolitan women who come across the Tucker Max types, but it's useless when dealing with the Chris Browns of the world. Steve Harvey found success in trying to teach women to think like men, but the men he exposed were from your parents' generation, not the evolved males bred in the 90's. The Lil Wayne or J.R. Smith types chew up these Steve Harvey women because they see through that Ninety-Day Rule shit. Having grown up in the wild streets of Baltimore and partied my way through college in Philadelphia, I am the epitome of the 80's baby who knows how to use a woman's desire for love against her. My way with women was the result of an understanding of the things they were into and a feel for what they wanted. My father and mother divorced before I could even walk. This resulted in me being raised by a single mother who wasn't even old enough to drink. I grew up immersed in her world of gossip, feminine pop culture, lust for love, and distrust of men. By the time I hit college, being a straight man able to relate with women on many levels made me immensely popular. However, I was still a man, and I used that connection to have sex…a lot of sex. Once I matured and found love, I felt it my duty to make up for years of manipulation by shooting straight with my female friends.

That advice turned into my BGAE blog, where I laid my thoughts out to anyone who dared listen. I used profanity like rap songs and references that my generation would automatically understand. As you will read, my sense of humor is more *Def Comedy* than *Monty Python*. I find that humor helps when trying to get the message across, especially when dealing with subjects that can make those entrenched feel embarrassed. Any slang used is not meant to alienate or offend; it's simply me being real. While I could have toned the language down, I felt no need to insult my audience in order to appeal to the more conservative ilk. You've all heard profanity before, so get over it.

What makes me the expert? There are hundreds of thousands of relationship blogs and columns; I came out with no fanfare or promotion and spoke from the heart. I had no loyalty to the man code, didn't care about exposing my own wicked ways, and felt no need to sugarcoat the truth in order to spare a woman's feelings. I laid it out, and people responded to my candor. Within a year, the readership grew and the website hit extraordinary numbers. Hundreds of thousands of people were responding to my advice because a man being brutally honest is rare. Two years after the start of the blog I signed a deal for a TV show with Lionsgate, began receiving dozens of requests to speak at college campuses, and a demand for this very book. I may not be a traditional expert, and my words aren't cosigned by the big O, but the proof is in the results. I have personally helped countless women in confidence, from award winning actresses to soccer moms twice my age, and I would love to help you as well.

Throughout these pages, I will use certain examples or scenarios that lean toward black culture in order to drive my point across, do not let that take away from the core lessons. This book isn't strictly for black women; it's a guide for all women who struggle with love. This player epidemic isn't contained to black men; it encompasses the modern man, as the majority of those under the age of 35 use the same tricks. This book is a system that will serve to point out the mistakes all women make, clearly show how they can regain their power, and what to look for when selecting the perfect mate. I hope my words are able to inspire those who are at their lowest and reinforce the resolve of those whose belief in love may have wavered.

PART ONE:
WHAT KIND OF WOMAN ARE YOU?

"It is not only the most difficult thing to know oneself,
but the most inconvenient one, too."
– H.W. Shaw

1

THE WIFEY TYPE

How do you keep a man? The ignorant or ratchet answer would be to give him the best sex he's ever had. Women who think that are still single and are currently figuring out what dress to wear to the club this weekend. Women who have locked down men, not for six months but years, brought something to the table much more powerful than good sex. You think you're pretty, you think you're smart, I bet you think you are the most interesting woman on the planet. How do men view you? Let's go deeper than the physical qualities. Do men think you're smart? Do men find you interesting? Are you classy in his mind or just another basic broad he's run through? Take a moment to think about the last guy with who you were seriously involved. What did he like most about you? If it was something as minute and superficial as, "my smile" or "the way I rode it," then you have no clue about the interworking of that man. Any kind of success is reliant on knowledge. It's not good enough to go along for the ride and be happy because you have a connection; you need to get into his head. Are you the type of woman he can spend all day talking to in order to create a connection deeper than the physical attraction or are you simply Pussy?

When I use the word "Pussy," I am not referring to your vagina. By Pussy, I mean that your only value to that man is to satisfy his physical needs. You are not his soul mate; you may not even be a good friend. He sees you as a tool, and your job is to make him comfortable. Pussy isn't just the ho or the slut, she's also the girlfriend who he has no intention of marrying or keeping around past a year. Men love Pussy, but they do not marry Pussy. A man may show Pussy off to his friends. He may even buy Pussy gifts. Occasionally, Pussy gets to come out of the house for a nice dinner. Sometimes accidents happen and a man may even get Pussy pregnant, upgrading her to the "Baby Mama." Despite all of these acts, a woman must not assume that he views her as something more. The proof is in the commitment. If you are the friend waiting to be the girlfriend or the girlfriend waiting to be the wife for longer than you feel is necessary, he's not figuring things out; you may just be Pussy. A man will lull you into a sense of comfort where, despite the obvious red flags, you become content with the little he does for you. Ignoring your position as Pussy keeps your feelings from being hurt, but in the end, it causes more damage because you're essentially agreeing to be a placeholder until he's had his fill. All men see women as Pussy initially, but after a few conversations or days spent together, they will decide if she is indeed more.

THE FACTS OF YOUR RELATIONSHIP

Does he take you out? If a man thinks of you as his girlfriend or potential girlfriend, he would not hide you away from the world. There is one type of woman I call The Relationship Girl. Relationship Girl is so happy to have a man in her life that she will take anything he spews at face value. Money, time, and transportation become the top excuses as to why he can't do something for you or with you. Car's broke can't come over. Money's low can't go to that movie. Putting in a lot of overtime at work can't see you until late night. Some of that may be true, so you swallow it. Be sensible; that's what con artists do. They use parts of the truth to make their lies seem more believable. No matter how much you like him and want the relationship to work, you have to disregard all the excuses and accept the fact that this man is most likely using you. Stop being the "drive thru ho" who he orders a value meal for, then quickly races back to his apartment. Start being the woman who demands to sit out in public and share a meal. Let's say your guy friend is on hard times and he's trying to keep his head above water financially. You may think that you can be his drive thru ho because you're considerate of his money problems. Wrong! As a poor college student, a man will dig through seat cushions for change in order to take a girl he really likes out for a nice time. This means if there is a will there is always a way! No one who actively dates is financially limited to the point where he can't buy a pair of movie tickets. It isn't about not having money to treat you, it's about not wanting to spend money treating you because you're not worth it. Why are you making excuses for that kind of man? If he can't take you out to Red Lobster it's not because his paycheck is short this week; it's because he doesn't want to bother with feeding the cow he's already milking! If he has money to buy a $59.99 PS3 game, he can scrape up a few dollars to take you to a restaurant that doesn't have pictures on the menu. Your girlfriends are single and fine dining, and you're taking Wingstop to go. You're not winning because you have a man, you're losing because you have a man who keeps your ass on Dracula duty, buried in the house, only coming out when it's time to buy condoms and blunt wraps. Think about your relationship from that standpoint and honestly determine if you are being shortchanged.

Have you met his family? I'm not talking about the friends he chills with, but his actual family. Tagging along to hang around while he plays video games with his boy's isn't the same as an invite to Thanksgiving dinner. Has this man's mother laid eyes on you? Meeting the parents is not be as big as it was in the 1950's. It's no longer a declaration of marriage, but it can mean that he thinks enough of you to get his family's approval. I remember sneaking this girl into my mother's house when I was around twenty years old. She was a pretty girl whom I'd had sex with a few times before, but I had no intention of making her my girlfriend or even dating her. She was Pussy, and I needed a place to take her in order to utilize her skillset. As we crept up the stairs, we were startled by a "Hello." My mother had been in the basement and caught us ascending the staircase. Now I had to introduce Pussy to Mom. I was pissed because this girl was as dumb as a brick. I knew my mother would only need a few questions to figure out she wasn't the sharpest tool in the shed. As soon as Pretty Pussy stammered trying to remember her own name, I knew I was in trouble. My mother asked how she was doing, and the girl stood there as if she were asked to name elements from the periodic table. If I actually cared about that girl, that exchange would have taken place at a dinner table. Any man can call you his "Girl," but if he's truly thinking about taking it further, you will meet the people who are most important to him. Being in the car and waving "hi" or seeing someone for a minute in passing is not an introduction. Stop being smuggled!

What do you talk about specifically? "We spend all night on the phone talking, we have so much in common," bitch please. Do you know how many hours I've spent on the phone with girls who I couldn't stand? I've stayed up until 6 a.m. more times than I can count, and it wasn't because the girl was interesting; it was because I wanted what was in-between her legs and was putting in the proper amount of work to get it. Take away the gossip, the TV show talk, and the flirting. What did we talk about really? We both like the same colors...wow. We both randomly know Chauncey the stick up boy...incredible. Spending twenty minutes saying, "Did you miss me" and having a back and forth on who missed who more becomes played out. The number one question a man wants to know is, "When can I see you?" Why is that? Because you are Pussy, and men can't get Pussy over the phone. You may think that he is calling to check on you, but it's merely small talk before he attempts to schedule your next visit.

Play to your strengths when showing a man what you bring to the table, but don't front like you're someone you're not. Stop pretending as if you visit cnn.com before you visit mediatakeout.com. That's a quick way to get exposed. It's okay to be into basic things so long as you're able to put together a sentence and have a conversation that consists of more than a shoulder shrug whenever he asks you about subjects you aren't familiar. If I ask, "So why didn't you like *Black Swan*?" Please don't respond with, "That was some white people shit." That is not a movie review, that's a woman with poor analytical skills who tuned out as soon as she realized the film wasn't a comedy. There's keeping it real, and then there is keeping it real ignorant. You want a successful man with a profession, not a thug with a parole officer, then get on that level. In order for a non-goon to see you as Wifey, you must expand beyond ratchet topics of conversation that fail to create a real dialogue. There are more important things in life than leaked pictures of Chris Brown's dick and *The Real Housewives of Atlanta*. If he wanted to date a woman with the life experience of a 17-year-old, he would have become a gym teacher or a stepfather. If you feel comfortable with those subjects, use them as a crutch initially, but a few weeks in you have to show him there is more to you than chitchat. Stop being afraid to ask questions, research things you don't understand, and upgrade your level of conversation. Have a desire to be the best dressed at the party and the most interesting. For those women who are educated and well read, do not be afraid to show it. A good man isn't intimidated by brains; it challenges him and more importantly, it captivates him. The problem with Pussy is that she's not challenging, that's why she'll never make it to the next level. Showing him that you are his equal, as well as his superior in some respects, proves that you are not the average girl.

Your Vagina Does Expire

You were in a relationship for three months and then he started to act differently toward you. After much debate, you ended it. Did you really break up with him or did he sabotage the relationship after your vagina expired? Yes, the vagina version of pussy has an expiration date. It expires exactly 3-4 months after you two first have sex. The more you smash the faster it expires. It's not milk; you can continue to enjoy a vagina after it has long expired. However, no matter how good that expired pussy still feels, it will never be at that same level of enjoyment it was when he considered it new pussy. As a wise man once said, "There's no pussy like new pussy, and that's how a nigga feel[1]." Being extra freaky or dating during the winter months may buy you an extra two months of that new pussy smell, but that's it. No matter if your relationship lasts four months or six months, a man will show signs of cabin fever unless you have something real that keeps him tied to you. If you two have been arguing after months of seemingly perfect romance your boo isn't bi-polar, he has become stir-crazy. He's tired of your pussy and he's ready to move on to the next girl. Not a lot of fellas can say this verbally because they don't want to be mean, and few even have the awareness to realize this is why their girls have gone from irresistible to an irritation. A cowardly man confronted with expired pussy sabotages the entire relationship until you get the hint to move on. By making up fake arguments or doing something he knows will cause a divide, he ensures that you break up with him. This saves him the trouble of explaining your flaws, keeps his reputation intact, and still leaves the door open.

Your ego may rebuke this with, "I still make him cum. I'm not expired." While your vagina still stimulates his penis physically, you don't stimulate him mentally. Any man can tell you that sex without that mental excitement he gets from exploring something new isn't the same. He may come back to hit it after the relationship is over, but don't take that to mean he's realized the error of his ways and now sees how great you truly are. Sex is a habit, and no junkie stops cold turkey. He will come back for the feeling, but he's not coming back for you—you're played out. All pussy expires, but the brain stays fresh, so that's the tool you need to utilize in order to keep your relationship exciting.

There is no such thing as "Marry Me Pussy." No matter how good you think your shot is, there has yet to be a vagina built that can make a man throw a ring on your finger. Personality, charm, charisma, those things are greater than pussy. If you want to keep a man, not just have someone to roll around in the bed and eat

---

[1] Lyric taken from the song "Oochie Wally" as performed by Nas & Bravehearts.

lemon pepper wings with, look in the mirror and ask, "Would I want me?" It's like a job interview. The strengths are obvious and often exaggerated. The weaknesses are hard to figure out. It's not because you don't have any, it's because people rarely take a serious look at what's wrong with them. Do not use sex as a crutch. No matter how many tips you get from studying porn or reading Zane books, sex is never going to keep a man at your side. Let's say your pussy has expired, he's acting differently, and learning how to perform a blowjob with a Halls in your mouth only brought you a few extra weeks of happiness. The first step in changing his perception of you is to know your strengths and weaknesses by answering the following questions.

ARE YOU BORING?

No man wants a girl who sits around saying "I'm bored." If you are a bored female that means you are boring. I do not care how pretty you are, no man wants to waste time with a boring chick that always needs to be entertained by the most basic shit. "I'm bored, nobody's calling my phone today. I'm bored, nobody's texting me. I'm bored, nothing's on TV." He's bored being with you because all you do is seek attention. Your vagina may be wet, but your personality is dry! You have to be proactive and spontaneous to keep a man's attention after the first few "getting to know you" months are finished. A pretty face alone doesn't impress the average dude who's been around the block, he's fucked J-Lo's, and their pussy feels the same as J-No's. What's the secret that will make you a must have? Personality! If a guy gets your number because your body is banging and your weave is straight out the bundle, he has high hopes. The physical is on point, now let's see what else she has going for her. When you go out with this guy and all you do is giggle or sit looking at the menu searching for something to say, you lose points.

You could have been Wifey, but now you're Pussy because you weren't engaging. What could have been something real will become about sex, because on your back is probably the only time you're entertaining. Maybe you're boring because you're nervous around him. In the later chapters we will go over what to say when you first meet a guy, as well as first date tips, but for now focus on making him feel relaxed by being relaxed. He's so fine, he's so funny, and he's so confident—hop off his dick and make him hop on your clit by being just as mesmerizing. Control your date shakes and act as if you've been around sexy and intelligent men before, then fire back with you own personality. Fear of not measuring up is a Pussy trait! How will you ever get a man to see you as more if you don't see yourself as on his level? Having the nerves and anxiety of a ninth grader will get you fucked over every time. I call this The Groupie Effect. You're so in lust and in awe of a new guy because he's everything you've wanted. You forget to be the woman you are and transform into a 13-year-old at a One Direction concert. Screaming on the inside and zombified on the outside, sitting there on dumb duty, giggling, barely talking, happy to be in his presence. Get a grip and stop being dick whipped before you even sample the dick. Ignorant women don't turn men off, but awkward women do. As long as you can make him smile and flirt your ass off, he won't care if you think Rome is in France. Stop trying to be overly impressive and just be yourself! You can teach geography, you can't teach personality.

ARE YOU FROM EARTH OR MARS?

Many positives I hear women claim as unique are ordinary. *I do this, I do that*…who cares what you do, I want to know who you are. Having a job, going to school, riding dick good, those things you are listing as extraordinary are as common as being blonde in Sweden. It's commendable that you're doing things to better your life and your vagina is moist enough to make him cum, but men expect that, it's not game changing. The woman with the sharpest wit doesn't have a problem getting a guy to call her first. The woman who can get it hard with a few words turns him on more than the one who has to put it in her mouth. Basic men get open off basic things. That's why most women have no problem attracting losers. When you're aiming for a man who's already winning and not thirsty for your vagina, you have to step your game up. Men love when something different walks in the room and respect when she takes the conversation to a weird yet intriguing place. After a few weeks of being around a girl like that, a man won't say, "Let's see what happens," he will recognize her rarity, lock her down, and commit!

If you are tired of the dating game and want something deeper than nine inches and a text message, then it's time to get serious and understand how men view you. If you two have been together for a while and you aren't getting the results you think you deserve that means he doesn't see you as special. Don't blame him for missing the boat, shoot the flares in the air, and make him take notice that you're not a boat he should ever miss. If you want a man to see you as a Game Changer, you have to work constantly on setting yourself apart. You can't be like "We are not the same, I am a Martian" and step out dressed like the Forever 21 mannequin. You're just like the last four girls he's been with and he will treat you just as average. When you go out on dates, have something fun to say instead of trying to be "fake deep," and push the conversation in directions that you haven't taken it before. Stop thinking about what turns guys on, and focus on what engages them. If you were a painting, would a person stop and look or glance and keep it moving? If your life was an episode on *Dateline*, would someone put the remote down and watch or switch because it's dry? How you talk to a man, interact with a man, and captivate a man is like a marketing plan for a relationship. Coming with cleavage showing and ass out gets his dick's attention, congratulations you're Pussy. Coming with a unique view of the world, a fun vibe, and positive attitude are things that hold a man's interest for longer than a nut. Make him feel as if you're the type of woman he can raise children with, not drop children in. They say that beside every great man there is a great woman. Define what makes you great. History doesn't remember women who could do it with no hands. It remembers women who could do it with their brains. Stop telling him that you're different from the rest and show him how different you truly are.

2

The Bottom Bitch

Before Jay-Z was GQ man of the year and husband of the all mighty Beyoncé, he was Shawn. Like most men with ambitions to be more than some "local nigga," Shawn needed two things to succeed in life: confidence and drive. Our mothers tell us that we can do anything, but it's another female that takes our confidence to the next level—The Bottom Bitch. The Bottom Bitch is the reason an ordinary man walks with a strut and the reason he doesn't fear rejection from other girls. By treating him like the center of her universe, The Bottom Bitch raised his confidence and created his swag. No matter what happens in a man's life, how broke he is or what other girl breaks his heart; that Bottom Bitch will be there to pick up the pieces. Bottom Bitches are chicken soup for the ego, and because of them, men are able to hold their heads high at their lowest moments. The funny thing about The Bottom Bitch is that once a man gets to that dream destination, she's the first one to go. In "Song Cry," Jay-Z raps of a girl who was always there for him: "A nigga had very bad credit you helped me lease that whip…" The song goes on to tell of how once the money came, Jay went for the girls that used to call him ugly and forgot about the one that loved him despite the camel features. That's the life and death of a Bottom Bitch.

It's *Pinocchio* without the Disney ending. You help create a man only to watch him cut the strings and walk out of your life for greener pastures. Someone once asked me if being called a Bottom

Bitch should be taken as a compliment. Its origin comes from the world of pimping, where a pimp's top worker earned the title of Bottom Bitch by taking on the most responsibility and being his closest confidant. In a fucked up way it's a term of endearment in the world of prostitution. In the non-pimp world, it still means he loves you, appreciates you, and needs you. However, it also means that your relationship with him has a time limit. No matter how much a man loves his Bottom Bitch, she's McCarran International Airport, a layover stop en route to the bright lights of a bigger city.

Can a man settle down with his Bottom? Sure, if he fails at life then he'll settle for her, have kids, and maybe even marry her. The key phrase is "settle for her." A man who settles will never truly be happy, and even if you get that hard-earned ring, he will always be on the lookout for his fantasy girl. The Bottom Bitch isn't the foundation of which a house is built; she's more like training wheels. You need her to hold you up, but once you get your life in order she has to go because all she will do is slow you down. Some girls run around proclaiming that they are his Bottom because they think it means they're his main chick. You're not a main chick—you're a gas station. To be called a Bottom Bitch is far from cute and if you take pride in that then you're beyond basic. Furthermore, being a main chick is just as disrespectful. The very presence of the term "main" means that you have never been good enough to make him monogamist. The line between loyal woman and Bottom Bitch tends to be blurred, mostly due to a female refusing to accept the worst-case scenario. Let's look at some of the more obvious signs.

ALWAYS AVAILABLE

For a man, there may come a time when the girl he actually likes breaks up with him. He will need someone who can restore his confidence, vent to, and have sex with while in that slump. Look no further than that girl who has always loved him. Many men attempt to go back to ex-girlfriends, but BB's are more than an ex they are support systems. Don't get it confused, a Bottom Bitch's love isn't unconditional; it's based on one thing: one day they will be together because he said so! The two things guys learn as kids are how to do Ryu's Hadouken[2] and how to fool girls into thinking they are exclusive without actually saying, "I go with you." It's the oldest trick in the book. Men make up all kinds of excuses as to why you're together...but not really together. This leaves them free to talk to the girls they really want without being labeled a cheater. At the same time, these men never have to worry about their Bottom Bitches dating anyone else because these women are loyal to that promise of "one day we'll be together." If a man treats a girl who's not his girlfriend as if she's the love of his life, she will wait for the title forever! Sounds silly, but you'd be shocked at how well it works for most men

Randy has been seeing Anita since they were in 10th grade off and on; they're like best friends with benefits. In Anita's mind, now that Randy's out of the military and has a decent job, he's going to be with her like they talked about through the years. Randy needed Anita back when he was a little dusty boy whose mother was on crack. Anita brought him lunch, paid his school dues, hell she even taught the fool how to give girls orgasms. Randy fed Anita the "I want to be with you baby, but my money's not right" lie. It's one of the easiest lies to pull off and generally dictates that the reason you two are not together isn't because of love, it's because he wouldn't be able to treat you to the things you deserve as his girl. Lies! Did his money not being right stop him from having unprotected sex with her every chance he got? Hell no. Despite that excuse, he still got boyfriend privileges without the girlfriend hassle. Now that Randy's grown and making good money, Anita thinks they'll finally be together. Ha! Randy doesn't need that safety net of a Bottom Bitch now, so he stops coming around to see Anita. Next thing you know Randy gets some girl at work pregnant and Anita's hurt like hell. Why

---

[2] Ryu is the central character of *Street Fighter II*. Mastering his simplistic move set is usually the first step in learning to play the game.

did he do that to Anita when she was his best friend and lover? Anita was never his real girl; she was being used since day one. Randy sold his Bottom Bitch a dream, and because they had so much history and love between them, she bought it. If you are my girlfriend, that means I love you. If you are my Bottom Bitch, that means I love you for what you can do for me.

LOYAL TO A FAULT

I received an email from a woman describing how her man was caught having sex with another woman. She laid out the details of the affair, then asked how to best get revenge. I told her to leave him. In typical brainwashed fashion, this woman replied that technically they weren't together for her to leave. While she claimed him as her man, they were only exclusive in her head. This is another trait of being a Bottom Bitch: phantom commitment. This girl was in an invisible relationship and expected all women to respect something that they didn't know existed. That's how blind a Bottom Bitch is to reality. Everyone in your community knows that your so-called man has been dicking you down for years, but when other women ask him, "What's up with you and that girl?" he responds, "We're just friends." The next thing you know, you're trying to fight a girl over a dick that doesn't even belong to you. Beating that rival girl up in the parking lot or Facebook bashing her isn't going to change the fact that he doesn't think you're worth claiming.

I don't care how many times he's said, "I love you," Bottom Bitch isn't a relationship status. You have no say in who he sleeps with because you are not partners. The key ingredient a man looks for in his Bottom Bitch is weakness. No woman is that stupid to let a person treat her like dirt constantly, but weak ones possess the key trait of easily forgiving infidelity. A man keeps his Bottom Bitch in check with ass kissing and lame promises because he knows that she isn't strong enough to reject his lies. After the fight is over, he will go over to her place, tell her how that rival girl didn't mean anything, then guilt her with, "You're going to let that ho come between us?" She knows he's full of shit, but she doesn't want to lose him, so the game continues.

Let's check in with Randy and Anita years later. Randy now has a baby and hasn't talked to Anita in months. However, he's now grown sick of his baby's mother and her expired vagina. Randy is stir-crazy and wants something new. He could go out and hunt for something truly new, but guys are lazy, so Randy goes back to the past for easy refurbished sex. He calls Anita; she doesn't answer. Instead, she paces in her apartment wondering why he's calling after all this time. Anita is secretly hoping that the mother and child both died in a tragic accident and Randy's free to start a new life with her. Sad delusional Bottom Bitches. Anita calls Randy back thirty minutes later and he begins to tell her how much he misses her. They talk about the old times, how he made a mistake, and needs to see her again. Anita has a boyfriend, a selfless man who doesn't cause her any stress; in other words—she's bored. Next thing you know, Randy's hitting that again and telling her how he's going to leave his baby's mom, all she has to do is be patient. Months pass and Anita's pussy is still being used as a timeshare. To top it off, her boyfriend knows that she's cheating. Anita's so confused, but anyone looking from the outside in realizes that Randy is hustling her. Anita's living foul and breaking her boyfriend's heart because she can't let go of the person she invested so much in back in high school. Despite having a good man in her life, she would still rather hold on to Randy and be treated like a Bottom Bitch.

That type of scenario happens all the time. New men who come into the lives of these weak women rarely break the Bottom Bitch spell because no matter how toxic that old relationship was, she's become accustomed to being the victim and loving it. As long as he keeps making excuses and promising that they will be together, she will remain loyal, and he will continue to exploit her. No matter how superior the new man in her life seems, he loses out to the past. A Bottom Bitch will always be a Bottom Bitch because she never realizes she's a Bottom Bitch in the first place. In her mind, she's wifey, always one day away from getting that ring on her finger and a return on that initial investment. That day will never come. Bottom Bitches aren't Bonnies waiting for Clydes, they're sponsors. Beyoncé was never Jay-Z's Bottom Bitch, she wasn't around to put cars in her name and warm up his cup-o-noodles on those cold winter nights when he came back from hustling. While some other chick was boosting Shawn's ego and telling him that Fu-Schnickens flow was hot, Beyoncé was focusing on laying her own strong foundation and achieving her goals. In the end, Jay went for an independent woman with the same ambitions that he had. Meanwhile, that sweet naïve girl from 1988 who put her man first became just a distant memory. Bottom Bitches are a necessary evil for men. All guys need a pat on the back, good sex, and a few dollars when coming of age. For your sacrifice and devotion, he will always have love for you, but that doesn't mean he was ever in love with you.

BREAK FREE

Being a Bottom Bitch is not cute, it's not sexy, and you have to accept that your loyalty will not lead to a reward. You are devoted to a man who will never value you the same way. Good times come when he's vulnerable and nice, it looks as if he's ready to give you his all, then bad times return, and he reverts to his asshole ways. Get off this bi-polar ride; it's never going to stabilize. Stop trying to mold him and stop trying to appease him. He will never give you what you want because you aren't what he wants. Real men don't want enablers they want partners, and that Bottom Bitch mentality means that he will never respect you as his equal. Embrace the truth of your situation. You've been holding him down for years, but what has he brought to the table besides false promises? He says that he loves you, yet you are still his "baby," not his wife. Stop asking, "Why doesn't he see me for the great woman I am," and understand that you allowed a 50/50 partnership to transform into an 80/20 dependency. His smooth talking and bomb sex didn't force you into this position. You created that monster by putting way more into the relationship than you should have. If you keep settling for the bottom, how the fuck are you going to make it to the top?

3

Single Mama Drama

How do men genuinely feel about dating a woman who has one or more children from a previous relationship? It scares the hell out of them. Most women are quick to point out that they don't need help and aren't looking to find their child another parent; they simply want love. That may be true, but if this budding relationship becomes serious, being a stepfather comes with the territory. There is no way to separate the life of romance from that of motherhood. Mother by day means mother by night. Any man who is down for you has to be willing to embrace this. In the beginning, you can sneak around, never introduce your new man to your child, and keep it contained, but that only lasts a few months at most. No matter how lonely you are, neglecting your child to go to Six Flags with your new boo is messy. Dropping your little rugrat at Granny's house every time you want to get sex is trifling. However, with the rate of single motherhood at an all-time high[3], many moms date under the cover of "Don't Ask, Don't Tell."

A child is seen as baggage, especially when you're under 30. With the help of babysitters and family members, young moms

---

[3] Based on the US Census Report released on May of 2013, which states that in 2011, 62 percent of women between ages 20 and 24 who had recently given birth were unmarried.

project this single carefree image and manage to pull it off—initially. For men, finding out the morning after sex that a woman has a kid because you trip over his toys has become a legitimate occurrence, not just a joke. These ladies know that the notion of "I don't mind a woman with a kid" is seldom true, so they would rather hide their baby than scare a man off. The harsh reality is that most guys see a woman with a child as handicapped. When dealing with a younger mother with a kid under the age of twelve, guys will assume the worse: her time will be split, she won't be able to chill on short notice, and the dad who is co-parenting will still be around. It sounds like a headache. Guys project this love of MILFs, but when you're 27 with a 5-year-old, you're not that fantasy MILF; you're a bitch with a baby. Nevertheless, this perception can change if you're honest from the start, show them you're not a statistic, and are ready to scrutinize these men before you bring them home.

I've come across two types of single moms, the ones who are honest with men, "I do have a son. He's 3-years-old. The father and I aren't in contact. Take it or leave it." Then there are those who try to hook a guy with pussy and bomb personality, and then surprise him with the child. "We can't go to Vegas that weekend; that's my son's birthday party…Oh, I didn't tell you I had a son? My bad." You would think all women would take the honest route, but those who are upfront are in the minority. To understand why single moms lie, you have to remember what they go through when they attempt to be honest. It's not that men don't like dating women who have kids, it's that they don't like being in a relationship with them. As long as he is not a real part of that kid's life, dealing with a single mom is the same as dealing with any woman. Once things get serious, most men begin to distance themselves because they fear committing to a family. Girls who have found this out the hard way change their method from telling the truth to withholding it, in hopes that the blossoming relationship won't stall out so fast. By surprising him after he's comfortable, she thinks the odds of him sticking around will increase.

You can't trap a man. No matter what situation you put him in and no matter how difficult you make it for him to leave, no man can be made to stay. A guy who loves children and is smitten by you won't give a damn if you have a little girl. He's hanging around not because you didn't give him a choice, but because that's his character. On the other hand, a man who wants nothing to do with that lifestyle will still leave no matter how much he's falling for you. In his mind, no pussy, personality, or emotional attachment is worth being a makeshift family man. While withholding your child may make sense the first time you meet a person, it is information that you should volunteer on the first date. If this man thinks you may be the one, he needs to know early on if it is a two-way relationship or a three-way relationship. Not only are you saving yourself weeks of dating a man who is going to jump ship regardless, you're giving him time to soul search before you grow on him. Clear your mind of this idea that no man wants someone else's kids, that's bullshit. Men recognize when a woman is from Mars, and a Game Changer who brings all of those unique and must have characteristics will be seen as a blessing regardless of her mom title. There are men who claim they wouldn't get involved with a single mom, then someone who looks like Draya Michele and talks with the wit of Chelsea Handler walks into the room, and he could care less about her parental status. Regardless of how you think he will react, be totally forthcoming. In the end, it is a choice you have to be courageous enough to let him make.

MEETING THE KID

I've only dated two women with children. One I knew had a daughter, the other I didn't find out had a daughter until after we had sex. The thing I respected about both women was that they didn't make me meet the kid. Meeting a child is serious; it says, "I'm going to be around." I had no intention of going over, bringing toys, and pretending to like those kids just so I could keep running up in their mother, and those girls knew it. As a single mom, you have to be a mother first and a romantic second.

Ensuring your child grows up in a stable environment where guys aren't walking in and out of their lives is more important than you getting dick, going on dates, or auditioning Mr. Rights. Once you let him know that you have a child, keep the dating between you two for the first few months. Men who are only after sex look for advantages that will get them in the door faster, so beware of fake super dads. If you tell a guy you have a son, it often becomes "I'd love to meet him" or "Hey, I brought this for your little man." That person is trying to win you over by showing you that he is a daddy type. That prick isn't a daddy type, he probably has kids of his own he doesn't see. He's using your soft spot for your child to get into your bed.

Keep the romance one on one. Thank him for showing interest, but lay the most important ground rule: *I don't introduce anyone to my child unless it's serious*. He may pretend as if he's hurt that you don't see him as serious enough to meet your child, but don't fall for those crocodile tears. Honestly, dating for a month or two isn't serious enough to risk your child being let down when that favorite "uncle" stops showing up. If a man is serious about you, then he will accept the situation and continue to date around your schedule until you are comfortable enough for that introduction. You have to test him in order to make sure he is unquestionably into you, not just your vagina, before allowing him to bond with your child. If he is patient and proves worthy, then slowly bring him around.

WHY HE DOESN'T WANT YOUR FAMILY

You two have dated for months. You introduced him to your child and suddenly he's changing on you. It happens. Sometimes no matter how diligently you prescreen a man, he will flip on you. The problem is that most men aren't prepared to deal with the bad side of being a parent. I've combed some Barbie doll hair in my life, and I'll sit and talk about Iron Man for hours. However, when that stuff becomes a part of your daily life, it's not as fun. The attitude, the acting out, the cries for attention, those are things parents have to put up with, but when it's not your kid—fuck that. Freedom vs. Family is at the heart of the dilemma. When a man begins to feel as if he can't come and go as he pleases, that dread of being caged will set in, and his attitude will shift. Being caged in with a woman is distressing enough for most men. Add a kid and he's finding all kinds of excuses to avoid coming over unless it's a late night booty call. The responsibility of being a stepfather is heavy, and most men aren't ready to handle it, so they run back to the carefree life they understand.

Another reason men fall back is jealousy. Men are attention whores; they want women on their schedule or not at all. When a guy tells you that he wants to see you and your response is "I don't have a babysitter," or "I'm spending time with my prince," it pisses him off. Your child isn't another man, so why should he feel threatened? Males are possessive! He may be on the phone telling you "Cool, tell little man I said hi." What he's actually thinking is, "That's why I don't fuck with bitches who got kids; they can't do shit." Men are babies and babies hate on other babies, especially when they want your titty in their mouth. You cannot play his attention game. I was in the room when a friend of mine put the guilt trip on this girl because she couldn't drive him to a concert. He made her feel so low then added some jealousy of his own by hinting that he may have to call his other female friend to give him a lift. She caved in and left the baby with god knows who, so she could cater to his ass. Be better than that. No man comes before your child. You are worried that no other guy is going to be as good as the last one who accepted you and your seed, but remember that you're not damaged goods. The moment any man starts mistreating you or showing signs of jealousy, he becomes replaceable. Stop crying about finding another dude as if it's climbing Mt. Everest. You found this one and you can find another one. If he can't play his role in you and your child's life, have the balls to show him the door.

EVERYONE HATES BABY MAMAS

It amazes me how much hate is thrown at women who have children out of wedlock. Mistakes happen, and being horny or in love can lead to some crucial ones when raw sex enters the picture. Single mothers have gone from being applauded in our society to being punch lines. With so many teenagers having children, the world seems to think that only sluts from the ghetto or trailer parks get knocked up. You know your circumstances, so don't concern yourself with the hate you may see on the internet or the gossip someone may pass along to you. Being strong and confident enough to raise your child is more important than defending those, "bitch, where's your baby daddy" taunts. Entering into the dating world, this slander will amplify, but it's essential to keep your cool.

The first person to bring you down a notch may be the guy that helped make that baby, aka The Baby Daddy. Baby Daddies are complex and vary, and I won't spend too much time on them. Some women have great experiences with the father of their child, and the dad does take care of his child regardless of his relationship with the mother. Others want nothing to do with either mother or child and end all communication. Then there are those fathers who think that because they have a kid together, her vagina is still his property. When attempting to date, this type of Baby Daddy will ruin you. A huge reason men are reluctant to get into a relationship with a single mom is the threat of the child's father coming and going as he pleases. Men are territorial, and no one wants another dog marking his tree, but when a kid's involved, he can't demand that you cut the father off completely. Some confused and extremely cruddy women can't resist that Baby Daddy sex. These women eventually wreck a new chance at love for an old spark that will never rekindle, thus giving other moms a bad reputation.

Rival females are another obstacle standing between you and love. Insecure single women are always looking for an edge over the next chick. There aren't enough quality men to go around, and in their minds, they have to eliminate all competition. Having a child automatically makes you an easy target. "Oh you playing daddy to that ho's kid? You know she only got pregnant to get on welfare. Watch your pockets." I've seen it with my own eyes; a hater will smile and play with the baby, then talk shit about the kid and mother as soon as they walk away. To women who don't have children, your child is not a miracle of life; it's more like a scarlet letter. "Girl, guess who's pregnant? Yup, her old freak ass letting dudes hit raw." They don't know the circumstances of how you got pregnant or why your relationship with the father ended; they just want to judge and sabotage. The moment a woman like this sees that you are dating a friend of hers or a guy she wants to get with, she will get her Johnny Cochran on and argue her heart out as to why single mothers aren't worthy. Some men listen and nervously find an exit, other men ignore. Recognize this hate and don't stoop to their level. You are someone's mother now; you should have more class than she does. Don't knock on a door wanting to fight or take to the internet posting your own slander.

The final hurdle is the hate from parents, which is sometimes the toughest because you can't ignore them the same way you can a hater. A man who begins to date you seriously will have to introduce you to his folks. Fathers usually understand. Ironically, a mother will be the biggest critic of her son getting into an already made family. Understand that the stereotypes of gold-diggers looking for men to support their family have been around forever. Older women who grew up around low class women are familiar with the games some females play to land a husband for her and a father for her child. You aren't good enough for her son because you had a child out of wedlock, end of story. Show patience and poise. Don't get into an argument with your boyfriend's mother trying to prove her wrong. Sit back and win her over with kindness. If you're dating a true mama's boy who begins to distance himself because his mom doesn't approve, thank her. You have one child you don't need another. A true mama's boy who can't make his own decisions would have been a burden anyway—good riddance.

RUNNING BACK TO THE FATHER

This sounds like too much work, right? Meeting a man, interviewing him, keeping your guard up, all while trying to raise a kid on your own—it's overwhelming. So why even bother, just run back to the man that got you pregnant, and do anything to make it work. Be strong! Do not let the daunting task of finding a man who will want you as well as your child, cause you to relapse into the arms of the father. There is a common practice where a woman will grasp onto the only man that's in her life, say fuck trying, and settle for the devil she knows. Your child's father seems like the perfect answer, but if the two of you are not together, understand that it's for a reason. Either he didn't want you or you didn't want him, it's that simple. The problem with some single mothers is that they can't handle a platonic relationship with someone they were that close to, so if they are having trouble in the love department, that old option once again looks desirable. Maternity didn't turn into matrimony, doubling back and lowering your standards won't change that now. "But we have a child together" is not proof that you are soul mates; it's become an excuse to act desperate. If you two couldn't get on the same page during those initial nine months and beyond, then you shouldn't force it because you feel lonely now. Save the "his son needs him" bullshit. Everyone knows who's really crying for him to come back, and it's not the one in the diaper.

I understand the want to make the traditional family work, and if you think the chances of you and your child's father getting back together are realistic, you should not be dating in the first place, you should be trying to rebuild. If you are dating other people, I assume you have come to the realization that the two of you aren't right for each other. Therefore, you have to be strong enough to keep your legs closed and limit your interaction to short visits when he picks his kid up. There is no reason for him to be lounging in your house or taking you out. Those things give you hope, seduce you, and lead to more poor decisions.

YOU WILL BE OKAY

There isn't a trick that will make dating easier for single moms. Getting to know new people in general, sort through their lies, and make a real connection is difficult for everyone. Your road will be a little tougher, but not impossible if you set your standards from day one. Some men see women with children as loose, and will weasel their way into your life because they expect it to be an easy smash. In "man logic," the fact that you gave birth to another man's child means that you have given up all self-respect, and will sleep with whoever buys your child a new Elmo. Some are successful because there are tons of women who give it up to the first man who doesn't mind that she is a mother. Having the baby, compounded with being lonely because you can't find a decent man can be a blow to the ego. It will lower your self-esteem and make you devalue yourself if you allow it. Think of yourself as a role model as well as a mother. If your child were to see a video recording of your dating life, would he or she be able to hold their head high and say, "Mom didn't take shit," or would they turn the recording off because you came off as some desperate thirst bucket?

I recognize how romantically tiring being a single mom is in this world. Few men show you attention, and you spend your free time taking care of a child who doesn't understand why Mommy's upset all the time. Mommy needs dick, Mommy needs to be told she's beautiful, and most likely Mommy needs love. Nevertheless, Mommy also needs to be strong enough to do without until the right man comes along. The world is filled with endless fool's gold. The more desperate you are for affection, the easier it is to turn a blind eye and settle. When it's just you, maybe you can afford to fuck up with a loser or an abuser, but your child's life could end up defined by the man you bring into the home. Love will come, but you have a more critical task presently. Focus on your child, hold your head high, and have the strength to go without a man if necessary.

Of Hos & Housewives

Women are quick to classify other women as hos, but no woman ever admits to being a ho. A lot of you allow yourselves to be treated like hos, and then put your blinders up as if you're exempt from that label. If you do ho shit, no matter how special or different you think you are, you are a ho. Let's take a moment to understand the ho as a living breathing human being, and not just the derogatory term for a woman who sleeps around. The ho is not the bad guy. In her mind, she's just getting what's due. Maybe the public school system or Mommy and Daddy failed her, and now she's trying to come up on something that will make her life easier. Prostitution, after all, is the oldest profession in the world. In this modern world, the role of the ho has evolved. The label isn't as cut and dry as the exchange of money for services; the 21st century ho has become much craftier.

No longer is the money put on the dresser while the man lets himself out. Today's hos look for "tricks," those males willing to spend to enjoy, whom they can latch onto and suck dry for years. It can be a short-term hustle where she gets a dinner and drinks, or a long-term hustle where she becomes pregnant and has the child support to live off. Other times the hustle can be so covert that a man will marry a ho and raise a family, only to realize her true nature after she has divorced and taken half of his assets. The more ambitious the ho, the greater her scheme, and the more successful she will become. I respect hos, not sluts. Sluts give it up for free based purely on sexual attraction. Sex is great, but why not get something more meaningful out of the deal?

Dumb Girls: Have sex because the guy is cute or has nice things.

Ladies: Have sex because the guy has shown her value and earned her trust.

Hos: Have sex for services, material goods, or status.

Take a minute and think about which one you are. Sorry, not all of you are ladies. You don't have to tell me, but be honest with yourself. Most females were the dumb girl when they were young and then graduated to being a lady or a ho. Being intelligent doesn't put you in the lady category either. Universities are crammed with dumb girls with high GPAs who sleep with damn near any guy they think is cute and shows them attention. This is why college parties are so outrageous, dumb girls create high slut ratios. It's that *Animal House* freedom paired with the YOLO (you only live once) mentality. Hormones are raging, and people make bad decisions based on physical attraction. These college girls aren't dumb; they're just victims of poor judgment. Experience with asshole men will cure any young lady of being the dumb girl...hopefully. Sometimes, no matter the heartbreak or STD, certain women still let their vaginas control them the same way men are led by their dicks. Those women rarely graduate from the dumb girl stage and will always be *"Looking for Mr. Goodbar."* If you're over 22 and still give up free pussy, you shouldn't make ho jokes. You're worse than a ho because you're free.

Classy ladies shake their heads at dumb girls who slut around, but they absolutely hate hos because men love them. You know why women say things like, "I'm dressing like a ho tonight?" Hos have the most fun in life. They throw on the tightest outfit they can find; walk stank, and make your man ignore what you're saying just to sneak a peek. If you are not around to control your boyfriend's thirst, hos are equipped with the tools to take him from you or get in his pockets for the money he was going to spend on you. Many men want to be gangsters, but they don't have the heart to shoot a gun. Many women want to be hos, but they don't have the heart to be judged. This girl once asked, "Can we get a day without hos?" Do you know how boring that day would be? Hos are the reason men get fresh to death with the latest fashion. Hos are the reason men buy nice cars. Without hos, every dude in the hood would walk around with no haircut and rocking pajama pants. Millionaires on Wall Street wouldn't bother buying hair plugs or Lamborghinis. What would rappers write about if they didn't have hos to impress? No straight man gives a fuck about a Louis Vuitton belt. They're not wearing Gucci scarves to compete with other men. They wear it for the hos. Men want to be the biggest and brightest because hos are attracted to all that glitters. Ladies like nice things, but they're not going to fuck any man off the strength of his watch. A ho, on the other hand, will drain his nut sack if he's wearing that Franck Muller properly. We live in a world where a teenage boy can give a ho in his class a ride to the mall, and she'll fuck him for continued use of his services as a cab. Think about what that does to a man's ego at a young age and going forward. Those young men raised in ho heavy environments like the inner city or the small town, become obsessed with acquiring things that impress hos and could care less about being gentlemen that can win over respectable women.

Ladies aren't going to have sex for a ride to the mall. The most you get is a hug because they aren't for sale. Ladies don't want to be on the payroll; they want a partnership. This makes them independent, not submissive, and few men know how to properly interact with a woman who can stand on her own two feet. Ladies ask real questions: *Where do you work? Do you have any kids? Where do you see this going?* They take their time to make sure there are no red flags by interrogating suitors. Hos don't ask questions, and they don't care if he's out of work, selling drugs, or living off another woman, as long as he has gas in that Lexus and money to feed her. Fast women are more attractive to most men because they're the epitome of sex without stress. I call this Ass Appeal over Class Appeal. Even after a ho plays a man, he will still take his chances with more hos rather than put in the work it takes to impress a real lady with standards. Hos are exciting, daring, forward, and willing to reciprocate if you give her what she wants—that behavior appeals to the male ego and libido. Those women who fall into the lady category may feel that's unfair that grown men will still chase after the hollow experience of a fast ho, but sadly, it's just how immature men operate regardless of age.

FROM HO TO HOUSEWIFE

There's a debate in black culture: *Can you turn a ho into a housewife?* Most say "no." I strongly disagree and think this myth has been promoted in order to make non-hos feel better. This claim that while the ho may attract more men, the non-ho will get the ring first is bullshit. Being morally responsible with your vagina does not guarantee that you will win before a ho. That's the Sunday school crap that you're told to keep you from going to the dark side. Do you realize that your mother, aunt, or godmother was probably a ho in her day? Many females are currently in relationships and their men have no idea that they used to ho. By ho, I mean she has done something sexual in order to get something in return. Maybe you don't talk about it or you blame it on liquor, but you did it. You may be retired from the trade and living as a suburban mom, but those past acts still make you a ho. Don't judge another female for doing "Ho Shit" when you once fucked a man who wasn't your boyfriend because he took you to see a Tyler Perry movie.

One of my best friends, let's call her Rachel so I won't get yelled at, was at a party and this guy was trying to get with her the entire night. Rachel wasn't feeling him, so she ignored. Finally, he did what any thirsty man would do: he put his money where his mouth was. He propositioned Rachel with, "I'll give you $500 if you suck my dick." Rachel went to bathroom, put the money in her purse, sucked his dick for literally ten seconds, got up, and walked out. "He said suck it, he didn't say how long" was her response. She will never tell the man she's going to marry that story. Her future children will never know about any of the times she's fucked for money, handbags, or heels. The only person at that family cookout who will know that Rachel used to be a ho before she was a housewife will be me.

I firmly believe that seven out of ten girls are hos or have been hos in the past. Don't be upset, you know which percent you fall into, keep it real. There are many subcategories of hos. Just as Bubba Gump broke down shrimp, hos too can come in many forms. Pay My Rent Ho, Too Much To Drink Ho, Summer Time Ho, In Another City Ho, My Man Made Me Mad Ho, Groupie Ho, or the professional *I need money up front* Ho. Whatever category you are in, make sure you're not a Dumb Ho or a Discount Ho. Dumb Hos are the ones you know about, Smart hos move in silence. No one should ever know what man you're fucking or what you're getting out of him. The average guy isn't balling, so he relies on Discount Hos to make him feel like a stud. Discount Hos are girls who fuck for Red Lobster biscuits and a pack of Yaki hair. When I was in the mall observing the hos that traveled to Los Angeles for the NBA All-Star Weekend[4], I could take one look and tell what level of ho she was. Fellas were hollering at hos that were out of their price range, and it was comical to see their egos shattered one after another. I looked at these fake ballers in their skinny jeans and cheap watches with disdain. Did these pretenders seriously think a girl that looks that good, with a body that banging, came all the way to LA to go back to a one bedroom in Hawthorne and smoke weed? I didn't see one bad chick stop at the cry of "Ay what's ya name." Those men were used to Discount and Dumb Hos, not Smart Hos. The Smart Ho doesn't get pulled; she sizes you up then pulls you. Those are the hos I openly adore.

Let the record state that I have never been caught up with a ho, not that I'm ho proof, I'm just ho aware. The majority of women I

---

[4] NBA All-Star Weekend is held in a different host city each year. Due to the abundance of athletes who travel for the festivities, it's become the ho Mecca.

have become close friends with fall into the ho category and have been honest with me about what games they play. Knowing how my ho friends operate makes it easy for me to spot signs when a girl is hoing. You flew out to All-Star Weekend and you don't like Basketball, you're a ho. Let's not disrespect the Smart Hos by categorizing them with the sluts and Discount Hos that were also out in those streets competing. A Discount ho will return to her hometown and brag, "Girl, I shut down LA, I ain't even pay to get in the club!" Bitch please. You didn't shut anything down but your immune system when you fucked that dude raw because he said he was Lupe Fiasco's road manager. Smart Hos don't do that. A Smart Ho will go back to her hometown and to her boyfriend, kiss him passionately, tell him how much she missed him, and how wack LA was. She doesn't need to brag to local girls about the Diddy party she got in for free, the player from the Clippers who took her shopping, or the fool who paid for her hotel room and didn't even get a hand job. Smart Hos know a man's game and they know how to thrive within it. As they get older, they realize it's time to shut down the trips to Atlanta, and find a person that can provide for their services for years to come. Think of it like that Playboy Playmate who moved out of Hugh Hefner's mansion, and then got married to that football player. Like all smart hos, she realized it was time to invest long term.

Ask your mother how many weekend trips to Miami she took before you were born. Ask your Grandmother if she ever had to give the neighbor a little treat in order to make sure her children had groceries for the week. No, don't ask that because I don't think anyone would really want to know. The point I want to drive in is that hos don't fade into the darkness once they hit age 40. What happened to the hos from the 2001 All-Star Weekend? Where are the girls from the 2 Live Crew videos from the early 90's? I bet the majority are all mothers and wives now. You can't turn a ho into a housewife, yet it happens every day. Look at your family tree, before you make such an ignorant assumption that hos simply vanish. For those who are honest enough to admit that they have this mentality and are living that lifestyle, don't get down on yourself. Being a female who has done ho things isn't a death sentence. If you want a real relationship, not a convenience built around a bank account, you can stop at any time and evolve. If you're smart enough to use your body to get tricked on, why can't you be smart enough to use your mind to get lasting love? Your self-esteem may have been built on the attention that men gave you and the things they brought for you, but it is not tied to that. Your past won't define you unless you bring it into your future. Regardless of your reputation, there is always time left for a clean slate. Hos stay winning, but those victories are small battles, only a woman who can evolve past that shallow existence will be able to win the larger war.

5

The Basics of Being Basic

Two terms you'll hear throughout this book are "ratchet" and "basic." Ratchet is a term of endearment first given to hood rat girls raised in the ghetto, but has grown to encompass any woman of any race who displays low class, unrefined, and generally trashy behavior. From the trailer parks, to the suburbs, all the way to those spoiled trust fund brats on *Girls Gone Wild*, who can't wait to show off their fallopian tubes for attention, we are living in a ratchet world. Ratchets are as lowbrow as you can get, yet like hos, countless women secretly covet what they have. See, ratchets represent a carefree attitude, a primal behavior that says, "I'm not wearing panties, I'm drinking out of the bottle, and I'm going to give this guy a hand job on the dance floor, all because I feel like it." As crass as it seems, that's the kind of freedom that most people are afraid to exhibit. Everyone likes to unwind on the weekends, but every day is a weekend for a ratchet. This isn't a case of being supremely confident; it's usually a desperate cry for attention.

Ratchets have a chip on their shoulder, and the only way they know how to get it off is to show off like an eight year old at a family cookout. *Look at me I'm special*! They are the first to start dancing, they are the loudest laughers, and they wear outfits that are more trashy than stunning. All of this is to draw attention because in their backward world, eyeballs good or bad, equal accolades. When you hear people stereotype black women as loud and defensive, it's not a representation of the average African American girl. The image perpetrated on reality shows and bus stops across the hood are those of the ratchet. These savages are goons in lace-fronts, Hillbillies with eyeliner, and usually have an attitude bigger than the "G" on her fake Gucci bag. Ratchets are quick to fight, curse someone out, or tell you, "Ain't nobody got time for that!"

People like to laugh at these women. YouTube and VH1 have created an entirely new outlet for these girls to act like fools. However, when it comes to relationships, ratchets are the main women who become Bottom Bitches, single mothers, and claim, men ain't shit. To a ratchet, she is always in the right, the victim of some deceitful man, or a target conspired against by some jealous woman. If you attempt to reason with this type of personality and tell her that maybe she should date different types of men or hang around friends that are more positive, she will snap and put the blame back on the outside party. Often times, the ratchet response to my BGAE posts that call certain women out on bad behavior includes, "You should be telling men this stuff! They the ones out here cheating and lying!" Ratchets aren't able to see past their own perfect existence and realize that they aren't victims. They choose to give their numbers out to the same guys they refer to as no good because subconsciously the bad boys are the ones that make them moist. I've come across women who actively seek out the Waka Flocka[5] types because it's a look they find attractive, but fail to demand that he have anything other than dreads and a nice smile before they get involved. These women then cry foul when he turns out to be just another hoodlum. It's a tragically ironic circle of self-pity. Ratchets say they want a respectable man, but only respond to the traits of those guys who are just as unrefined as they are.

---

[5] Waka Flocka Flame is a popular southern hip-hop artist known for his hype sound as well as his dreadlock and tattooed look.

While there are many women who outgrow their ratchet beginnings, even more stay in the struggle. Classy Candice considers herself non-ratchet because she has a master's degree, hasn't eaten a McNugget since 2007, and enunciates her words perfectly. Nevertheless, when it comes to choosing men, she still has those fast food tastes. I'm often contacted by career women who are depressed due to their chosen men being unemployed and running the streets. Your parents didn't send you to school just so you could graduate and run back to the losers who will never make it out of the struggle. Are powerful men that intimidating or are you just that turned on by the thought of a man who has more inches on his dreads than points on his ACT exam? You should not cry about the lack of good men when you consistently pass up gainfully employed gentlemen for guys you think you can whip into shape. No matter how high you climb in life, having a ratchet desire for wolfish men will always keep you in the same dating pool as welfare queens and trailer trash.

RATCHET WHIP APPEAL

So if these women are so loud, obnoxious, and confrontational, why would any man ever want to entertain them? The rapper Juicy J famously said, "You say no to ratchet pussy, Juicy J can't." This line became a badge of honor for the hood rats of America, and disgusted the more classy women who not only have to compete with hos, but also have to compete with weave snatching girls with attitudes who take pride in their trashiness. Men do love ratchets...to a certain extent. You can sit there with your expensive Indian hair, Saks Fifth wardrobe, college education, and think you're a catch, but you are intimidating to the average man. You look fancy and talk intelligently. Men can't be themselves around you for fear of being judged. Ratchets, for all their faults, are great women to be with while a man's trying to figure out life. Easy to talk to, silly, and stress free, a ratchet girlfriend is the relationship equivalent of not declaring a major your first few years of college. Men of a certain maturity do not have time to invest in project "Fancy Bitch"; they want low maintenance with little responsibility. Call it "being afraid of real women" or whatever, but there is truth to that. Ratchets, in their Baby Phat accessories, Apple Bottom skirt, and Chinese Laundry heels, may look tacky to other females. However, men don't care where she bought that small ass skirt or if it doesn't match her shoes, they care how she looks in it. Designer clothing looks the same as Flea Market clothing when it's on the bedroom floor. Three hundred dollar hair weave looks the same as $19.99 hair weave in the dark. Ratchets are fun in the bedroom and out, and that wild streak attracts men that women who are more elegant would die to have.

Before you go patting yourself on the back for being Ratchet Supreme, there is a price to pay. Ratchet girls are perfect for good times, but as a man grows and matures, his want for the girl that drops it on the floor with no panties begins to dissipate and that need to have a girl he can take to business dinners and raise kids with grows. Being too ratchet can hinder your chance of a man throwing a ring on it. Before you dismiss this behavior as something you've seen but don't participate in, think again. The first sign of being ratchet is proclaiming with an attitude and eye-roll that you are not ratchet. The first step in not being ratchet is looking at your life without bias and having the honesty to admit that you do need to tone it down.

BASICA ALBA PLEASE STAND UP

The other term I mentioned was "basic." Basic women, or "Basicas" as I've named them, are similar to hipsters: those people who go out of their way to show how different they are for the sake of being different. In a more hip-hop world, it's not about organic lattes and thrift shop fedoras. It's about projecting an image of luxury when you're just as broke as the next bitch. A basic person's confidence doesn't come from who they think they are, but from who they pretend to be. Basic Bitches are the weakest women in the world. They mask their inferiority with brand names. Blame their shortcomings on others. Hate on things they don't have and put too much stock into what others think of them. Men love to exploit basic women because their shallowness makes them extremely easy to manipulate. He ordered a bottle of champagne, fed her sushi, and those basic panties dropped before she had a chance to ask what his last name was. So what's the difference between a Basic Bitch and a Ho? Hos smash for keys to a Mercedes; Basicas smash just so they can Instagram from inside his Mercedes. It's style over substance. The appearance of winning means everything to this kind of woman. Basic Bitches don't end up with great men. They end up with men who also love to bathe in basicness: the goon who thinks matching neck tattoos is love, the NFL rookie who wants to make her his fifth baby mama, even the get rich quick hustler who spends $40 a week on lottery tickets and promises her he is going to give her a house on the hill. Great men see basic girls as pussy, easy to game, and even easier to get rid of. Basic men see basic girls as the perfect wifey because no matter how flawed he is, she's not going to do better.

To be basic is to be conformist, materialistic, and unambitious to the point of parody. You watch TV to see how you should wear your hair. You wear clothes you hear everyone talking about with no regard for if it looks hot on you or not. You think you are swagged out, but your whole style is borrowed. Hair like Keri Hilson, shades like Angela Simmons, repeating the same slang as Evelyn Lozada. When will the emulation stop and the originality begin? It's cool to take what someone else did, but you have to add to it and make it your own. Let the bum bitches laugh at you. It's better to be called weird than be called a biter.

CARRIE BRADSHAW ON A BUDGET

Let's say that you are making $9.75 an hour with a closet full of authentic Louboutin heels and Gucci bags. You're living like a *Sex and the City* girl on the budget of Kevin from *The Wonder Years*. What's the point? Besides looking good for a night in a dark club, what do you get from that? You're not on a reality TV show. You don't go anywhere but to the club and to work. Instead of saving that money by buying flier shit that is half the price, you want to stunt like you've made it. Basic Bitches love to shut down the mall and shit on every girl in the club. Let's face facts. Spending $800 on clothing is not shutting down the mall. The mall owner will not run out, shake your hand, and say, "Damn! We have to close early today because you brought a Louis wallet." Dear Basica Alba, you are an idiot. You are not shitting on other women with your red bottoms because the guys you're trying to impress are going to pull the phattest ass or prettiest face, not the girl who looks like she stepped on a tampon.

Basic Bitches floss on people who aren't worth flossing on. They pack into the Hyundai, windows down so the neighborhood goons can see the Dior shades. They circle the block until after *The Maury Show* goes off to make sure all the neighboring ratchets can witness them step out of the car with department store bags. Then they switch into their mama's house with red bottoms on their feet as if Tyra Banks just gave them a runway challenge. This is all a cry for attention from people who don't care and don't matter. A Basica thinks it matters. She will tell you that she shut the block down, and guys were breaking their necks to look at her "sexy ass." Men break their necks for anything with tits. Even Ruth the 54-year-old mail lady with the misshapen ass gets looks. You're dealing with testosterone driven men; don't be flattered by their stares. In the end, you spent money, put on theatrics, and succeeded in impressing no one of importance. "Them hos were hating, girl." Who hated on you in particular? That ratchet across the way wears the same outfit twice a week, and you both fuck with the same low class men. Are you really spending money to keep up with her? Your life's goal is to stunt on a girl with a drawstring ponytail who wears Reeboks! At the end of the day, if you spend money on designer goods and end up sleeping with the same man as Reebok girl—you lost. Fashion is great, if you look good, you feel good, but stop trying to keep up with the Kardashians when you work part-time. If you want men to notice you, strive to be original.

FALSE IDOLS

Teacher: What do you want to be when you grow up?

Little Girl: I want to be Amber Rose.

Teacher: Who is this Amber Rose and what does she do?

Little Girl: …she um, I think she models…or something.

TV and film are huge influences globally, that could be the reason most people grow up wanting to be like someone else, but hold your heroes up to a standard. As people mature, idols usually change from superheroes or princesses to business icons or political leaders. Basicas never look beyond basic role models. These women don't want a dynasty or aspire to build an empire; they want all that glitters. They Kim Kardashian and think her blueprint was 'sex sells'. Using that misinformation, they try to emulate her. Basic women don't understand the role Kris Jenner and Ryan Seacrest played in making Kim into a brand long after those initial 15 minutes of sex tape fame were up. In their small minds, a tight dress matched with a nice booty means they too can run the world if they date the right rapper or ball player.

There are plenty of powerful women that young women can look up to and use as a blueprint. Oprah battled hardship and used education as a way to a billion dollars! Stop being hypnotized by the overnight luster of sexpot celebrity and be inspired by people who are making real money and leaving a real impact on the world. Do you know why Beyoncé's "Run The World (Girls)" flopped, yet a song about a man putting a ring on a woman's finger was a smash hit? Basic women would rather feel empowered by a man making her his possession than believing that women can do anything on their own. If it were called, "We Phat Ta Death (Girls)," that shit would have crushed the charts. Basic Bitches support basic concepts and aspire to be the next baldhead chick that gets knocked up by a rapper. You don't have to give into that.

YOU MIGHT BE BASIC IF...

A girl I was seeing in high school once told me, "I usually mess with grown men who drive Ac's." This meant that I, a teenager who caught the light rail and didn't drive an Acura, should have been honored to sample a vagina of that magnitude. Basic Bitches begin their ascent to Planet Basic at a young age. In the same way drug dealers impress young goons, the girls who hop out of the cars of ballers inspire Baby Basicas. Baby Basicas are taught that getting the attention of a guy with a car that had power windows and leather seats was proof that she had arrived at boss bitch status. Fucking for car rides to school didn't make you special then and fucking for car rides back to your shitty apartment doesn't make you special now. Do you know who has boss bitch status? That nerd girl who wrote your *Great Gatsby* book report, kept her virginity until college, went on to start her own business, and now owns multiple luxury cars. Ask yourself where your self-esteem comes from? Does it come from within, does it come from luxury clothes that few people have, or does it come from male attention? Penis does not make you popular, and the amount of men that lust after you does not make you better. Comparing how many guys asked for your number at the club, while it boosts your ego, shouldn't be the end goal. How many quality men asked for your number? How many of those guys actually offered to buy you a drink?

This isn't contained to romance, Basica Baller will be quick to take to Instagram and flood people with her selfies[6] full of caked on makeup or pictures of trips to "exotic" places, (which are usually commutes to basic locales that don't require much effort) all in an effort to prove something to those who don't care. It's great to travel and take vacations, but these women aren't sharing experiences, they're promoting exaggeration. Every trip to Atlantic City is hashtag: TeamFancy. Every concert she's in the nosebleeds of comes complete with a selfie of her with the

---

[6] Selfies are self-portraits usually taken with a smartphone.

caption, "Doing it big. #GetOnMyLevel!" This attention whoring is not done with malice toward anyone in particular; it's the only way she can feel good about her life, which points to a serious lack of self-esteem. The result of getting basic attention is an addiction to it, and in today's world of social media it's easy to fake the funk. At the same time it creates more competition because anyone with half a brain, proper lighting, and access to a push up bra can grandstand. When a guy showers attention on another woman instead of her, Basicas get defensive and clown on the guy for being thirsty or ironically call the other girl out for being basic. Basicas love to throw shade on people who are doing it big. "I'm not trying to hate but—" is the rallying cry of Basic Bitches. Saying you're not hating then proceeding to hate—really? Basica sees a guy she used to talk to riding clean in a new car, "I'm not trying to hate, but his mother put that car in her name because his credit ain't good." A boy tries to talk to you instead of your basic friend, so now she has to make you feel less special, "I'm not trying to hate, but he gets the number of every girl he meets."

People are entitled to opinions, but Basicas always have something to say, yet they don't say anything substantial. If you do not care, or if something is below you, then why speak on it? You hate Nicki Minaj...okay. No, you can't leave it at that, you have to run down the worst lines on her album. Why did you care enough to remember the verse if you are not a fan? You don't like Androids because you are Team iPhone...if your monkey ass doesn't own stock in Apple, you're not team anything, you're a consumer. It's cool to like what you have, but do not slander what others have with lame excuses like, "I don't mean to hate, but that Samsung battery dies too fast for me." Thank you Basica for taking time out of your busy schedule to tell everyone how they should feel about everything you don't like.

THE BASIC CYCLE

Basicism is not stumbled upon, it is taught in the Dojo's of Basicdom at a very early age. In some hood homes, it isn't uncommon to hear, "If you're going to run around with these little boys, you better make sure they're balling." Oh Basic Mom, you have done a wonderful job in teaching your daughter that a man in a Lexus is like hitting the mega millions. It's perfectly fine for parents to live vicariously through their children, but not when that life you want to live is superficial. Basic parents tend to have limited education and low ambition, so instead of saying, "You can be a rocket scientist and discover alternative means to fuel cars," Basic Mom says, "Go to school for nursing, it doesn't take that long and they start you out with good pay." There is nothing wrong with being a nurse if caring for people is in your heart, but why not become a cardiologist or a cancer specialist and use your brain to save even more people? Instead of saying reach for the stars, Basic mom is telling her daughter to be realistic. Picking an occupation you know you're capable of doing and one that gets you out of your mother's house as quickly as possible is the mindset of kids raised by Basicas. If you teach that line of thinking at an early age, that poor girl cannot help but fall victim.

Being taught to get by in life instead of exceling at life is the reason why there has been a resurgence of Basicnomics. Basic girls do not drink ambition because they have been raised to hate the taste of it. Have you ever wondered why a bright young girl would drop out of school when she doesn't have any kids or bills? It's her bloodline. "School is so boring; I don't even want to be a dentist anymore. My aunt works down at the courthouse and can get me a job." This cycle repeats itself each year. Some of you reading this come from homes that teach some of these things. You can't help how your family is, but you can strive to break that cycle. The next time you go out to the club, you're going to feel a need to look at another female on the dance floor next to you and refer to her as a Basic Bitch. Before you pass judgment on her, look at yourself. If you are in the same room as women you deem basic, trying to attract the same basic men and wearing the same basic luxury brands for esteem, what does that make you? The fact that you are breathing the same air with that level of primitive being is proof that your life took a wrong turn, and you, Miss "bad bitch," may be the most basic of them all.

6

Just a Friend

One of the more relentless questions I get has to do with male friends. *How can I tell if he thinks of me as more than a friend? We've been platonic for so long, how can I make him see me as more than his little sister? Can we go back to being just friends after sex?* I will address each one of these, but let me preface this by saying that it is one thing to be lifelong friends and then start to have feelings when you mature, that's natural. However, it is totally unacceptable for a grown woman to know she has a crush on a guy, suppress it, and try to pass her feelings off as sisterly because she doesn't have the courage to say, "I like you, and not in the help pick out my nail polish type of way." It is so much easier for a shy girl to exchange numbers under the pretense of "let's talk about schoolwork or gossip about my friend I think you like," rather than tell him that she wants his number because she thinks he looks good. By coming off as a buddy, she doesn't have to worry about the rejection of him saying he has a girlfriend or telling her he's not looking for a relationship. The fake platonic route is a no pressure situation that allows that girl to Trojan horse her way into his life. The stress comes into play when you two become close, and you have to admit that you want to take it to the next level. Now here comes the pain of "Does he think I'm pretty? Why hasn't he made a move? Have I told him something in confidence that turned him off?" It becomes an endless guessing game and a direct result of initially bullshitting about why you wanted to be friends.

You know damn well that you weren't looking for a new little brother in the first place. You were attracted to him, and now you are paying the price for being phony. Now, after months of hearing him talk about other women who you don't think are right for him, you want to scream because you can't take being overlooked—welcome to the female friend zone. If you're sick of being the homegirl or sister every time you meet a new guy, then you have to start being honest with yourself from the start. Why would you treat the man that gives you butterflies the same way you treat the ugly dude you gave your number to when drunk? "I don't want him to think I like him, so I'll play it cool." What kindergartener taught you how to pick up men? If you want him to look at you with the same lust in his eyes that he has for other women, you have to open his eyes to the fact that you're more than a cool friend. Clue him in that you have boobs, a functioning vagina, and most importantly that you want him.

YOU'RE NOT UGLY

It's been my experience that if a guy doesn't find a girl attractive he's not going to spend time with her, platonic or otherwise, unless he's getting something out of the deal. A man may give a hug and kiss on the cheek to the ugly chick that's super nice to him. He may drop a few text messages on the ugly chick that's letting him copy homework or loaning money. However, if it's just a platonic relationship, no man is going to risk taking an ugly girl out in public for fear someone may think he's hitting that. To be the female friend who he hangs out with in public means that he thinks you're cute. It sounds shallow, but men don't want others to mistake an unattractive friend for a girlfriend; it can ruin a reputation. If I refer to you as my little sister, but we are not related, you have to look good because you raise my stock. Other females judge a guy by how fly the girl he's next to is, and when a man is single, it's easy to attract one bad chick by being with another bad chick. Women are competitive when it comes to clothes and men, and an interested woman will notice a guy quicker if he is with a pretty companion. That jealous part of her may even make him out to be cuter than he is because he's with that other female. Therefore, even as a platonic pal, it is in a man's best interest for you to be girlfriend pretty!

Ask yourself if you are the girl he wants on his arm in public playing the role of friend to up his stock or if you are the hidden friend he doesn't want to be seen with in public. If you're in a situation where you and your platonic male friend are only hanging out indoors, he probably thinks you're not girlfriend pretty. Don't get depressed; just abort your Trojan horse mission because he's likely to let you down easy with a "I don't think of you like that" line based on looks. If he doesn't mind having you by his side wherever he goes, take that as a sign that you've passed his beauty test and be confident going forward.

YOU'RE NOT ONE OF THE GUYS

Don't guys want a girl who can talk about sports, who won't trip when they look at another girl's butt, and will hit the strip club with them? Negative! What you're describing is another man. A man doesn't want to be in a relationship with a person similar to himself unless he's gay, and even then, there needs to be some difference. Guys say dumb shit like that for the same reason little kids tell their parents, "I'm only eating ice cream for dinner when I grow up" — it sounds good in theory. In reality, having you be one of the guys will not fulfill his needs. It's awesome if you are into the same things he is, it gives the two of you something to talk about initially, but if every time you hang out you want to talk about Young Jeezy's latest song or Kobe's stats, you are going to make him look at you like a dude. You're not sending "take this vagina" signs; you're sending "I don't even have a vagina" signs.

I knew this girl in college who would always come up to me and talk about pro wrestling. I became friends with her because it was cool that someone with breasts would care about that stuff. Not once did she ever flirt or say anything remotely sexual, so I didn't cross that line. Years later, she scolded me in a Facebook chat about how I never tried to take her out. In her mind, she was flirting. In my mind, she was just one of my boys. If you want to take it to the next level, you can't leave it in the hands of a guy because men are blind as hell! By being faux platonic you're shooting yourself in the foot. I'm not saying pop your titty out and throw it in his mouth, but you can't be stealthy if you want a guy who sees you as just a friend to get the hint. That girl could have easily gone from Triple H to Triple X over the course of a phone call just by saying one dirty joke, but she went the shy route and regretted it later. Find a way to connect with him, show him that you two have a lot in common, but don't go so far down the guy road that he forgets that he's talking to a sexy female.

DON'T LIE TO YOUR GIRLS

Your girlfriend asks you what's up with you and Korey and you say, "That's the homie." Who are you fooling? You can always confide in a true friend, and you should let her know the truth that you want more. The reason many women don't let the cat out of the bag is that they are embarrassed that they allowed themselves to get in the friend zone in the first place. The friend zone is supposed to be for unattractive girls, and if you let your friends know that you are afraid of being rejected, it shows your insecurity. That's what friends are for, to breathe confidence when you need it. Here's what happens when you don't speak up and share your dilemma. Your female bff will start to crush on your crush. Realize that women don't interact with that many guys in close quarters. Once your girlfriend begins to see your so called platonic friend on a regular basis because you all hang out, it will lead to her forming feelings based on him being the closest guy around. Now she begins asking about him, and you will be so defensive that you start to make up reasons why she shouldn't try to date him because you are secretly jealous.

The alternative to this is to be a good friend and go along with your bff's plan to date the man you secretly like, while hoping it doesn't work out. The result is your bff ends up fucking the secret love of your life, and now it's awkward for you. He's wondering why you're not acting as cool as you were before and she's wondering why you want to change the subject every time she brings his name up. He was never your homie/brother, he was always the guy you wanted to be your man. If you had communicated how you felt, you could have avoided being hurt. Confide in your girls so they can help you figure out where you went wrong instead of pursuing him. Female friends make great interpreters during times when you're unsure of his feelings. That trick you learned in middle school of telling your friend to pass a note or drop a hint still works. Send her in secret to see him so she can interrogate with the classic, "...so what's up with you and my girl? Don't worry I won't tell her." It sounds juvenile, but given that you refuse to speak for yourself, this may be the only way to address the elephant in the room. Some relationships need an outside boost, and this is a foolproof way to lay the cards on the table without actually being at the table.

SEPARATE THE REAL FROM THE FAKE

How many male friends should a girl have? As many as she wants. Don't let anyone tell you that keeping male companions around is not dignified. If you feel more comfortable hanging with boys than you do girls then that's your right, but learn to separate the guys who you are truly platonic with from the guys you want to get to know on another level. If you meet a guy and invite him to hang out, he's going to be excited if he thinks you like him romantically. If he shows up and every guy in the dorm or work is flanking you, he's going to think you're hoing. I say again, keep your romantic male friends away from your platonic friends! Your intentions are innocent but remember people talk and slander. Those other guys are platonic in your mind but do you truly know their ulterior motives? They either think of you as their little sister or ass they want to tap once they get you drunk enough. These seemingly innocent friends may hate on the new guy to protect their spot.

It isn't just the males; other women who are jealous of the attention men give you will add fuel to the fire as well. When a hater chick who doesn't like you sees that all of these guys love to be around you, she's not going to think, "She's just a cool broad who guys are comfortable with." That hater chick is going to think, "She's sucking a lot of dick!" Next thing you know rumors spread that you hooked up with five out of the eight men that you call friends. One of them may even lie on his dick. He may not come out and say he had sex with you, but for the sake of his ego, he will give the rumor life. Now you have a reputation based on jealousy and lies. This is how the girl who hangs with nothing but boys becomes the girl no one wants to date. You can't change the perception, nor should you care, but don't expose your potential romantic interest to that by lumping him in with a bunch of boys because he doesn't know you well enough to trust you. In his mind, you could be smashing all the homies.

You think you had a good night at karaoke with your new potential boo, and then the next morning he's calling you "buddy" because he's heard the rumors and doesn't want to be the one who wifed the slut. You can't stop people from spreading lies; the solution is to keep your circles separate. If you have a group of boys who you clown with and party with, keep them on that side of your life. If you have a guy who you want to pursue a romantic relationship with, keep him away from that casual part of your life. Men need attention and assurance that they are special. Make it clear to your potential boo that you have male friends and that some may like you, but you see them as strictly platonic. Drill it into his head that he is the one you want to chill with one on one, and not a part of the homie clan. Clarify, ladies; it's a simple step that will save you from months of confusion.

TOO MUCH INFORMATION

There is such a thing as over sharing. When you are friends with a guy you like, why would you tell him the same intimate details you would tell your sister? Men don't listen that much, but their ears hit record as soon as sex is mentioned. If you tell him about cheating on your boyfriend, fucking on the first date, or getting an STD, that all goes on your permanent record. A year down the line when you two finally get the balls to start talking dirty to each other, he still hasn't forgotten about the back-up singer you cheated on your boyfriend with after the Jamie Foxx concert. Even if you two take it to the level of having sex, he may not want to commit to you because of things you probably forgot you told him. Men are extremely paranoid, they are consumed by this fear that they will mistakenly fall in love with a ho or slut and be made to look a fool. This leads a man to seek out those girls whose history is foreign to him. That way, he can Christopher Columbus her and pretend no one has discovered her vagina before he arrived. If you let all of the skeletons out of the closet, he may not be able to handle that. Even though he knows you are a good person, those two times you confessed to him about letting out your inner slut will make it hard for him to trust you. You want to be open and honest and share everything with a guy who seems like the perfect friend, but the things you told him as his platonic friend may not be things he wants to know about his girlfriend. Be selective; friends do judge.

SEDUCE & DESTROY

The main reason guys see you as just the friend is the lack of sexual attraction. You haven't sparked that side of him that makes him want to rip your clothes off, bend you over, and shift those kidneys. Instead, you've sparked the side of him that wants to play smack your ass, talk about TV shows, and get advice on which one of your girlfriends he has the best chance to smash. This isn't the movies. You can't just throw on a tight dress, do your hair differently, and suddenly he wants to jump your bones. You have to make him aware that it's okay to think of you sexually, and once a man thinks of you sexually, he's free to think of you romantically. All of the conversations you've had as his buddy, from what went wrong with his last relationship, what he's looking for, to his insecurities, can all be used as ammo if you have the balls to get off the sidelines and go to war for him.

How do you tell your friend you're ready for more? Don't confess randomly, "I want to be with you." Coming out of left field and asking for a commitment is an easy way to get shot down. I received an email where a woman failed because she waited until she was drunk, then confessed to her friend that she wanted to marry him. Her so-called best male friend stopped being a friend all together because it overwhelmed him. Do not go zero to sixty, learn to shift gears smoothly! Be calculating and get creative when expressing your feelings. Remember this is your friend, you should already know if he's in a good mood or bad and if he's being serious or silly. Wait for the right opening in the conversation, and when those moments present themselves, be aggressive. He has to see you as sex not sister, so forget writing a love letter, or giving him a promise ring, go for the sexual side. This does not mean have sex; it means bring out the fact that you two have sexual tension as well as an emotional connection. It is damn near impossible to defend against a woman who knows how to seduce. Once your friend sees you in that new light, even if he only half thought of you in that way, it will turn him to the possibility that Miss Perfect has been right beneath his nose the entire time. The excuse you're reaching for is, "I have no idea how to seduce. I'm too shy." Every woman knows how to seduce!

Say little things like, "You wouldn't know what to do with this" or "You're lucky we're just friends, I'd have you sprung!" Those innuendos challenge his manhood and spark his curiosity. Find ways to bring up your body, such as telling him casually on the phone that you just got out of the shower, or that you're wearing a new pair of underwear that makes your butt look phat. If a man is repulsed, he won't take the bait, but if he's at least 40% into you, he'll jump at your newfound kinkiness. As a man who had a female best friend for most of his life, I can say with confidence that there is always a line males are afraid to cross due to respect. However, if my bestie had seduced me first, the thought of fake incest wouldn't have stopped me from going there. If your guy friend doesn't fire back with his own flirting then you know how he feels. Any man that changes the subject after you hint that you're "wet for some reason," is not into you.

If he thinks of you that way, saying flirty things while talking late at night on the phone will open the door to something else.

4

He will flirt back and start to say things friends don't say to each other. I guarantee you that in less than a month after stepping up the flirting he will be the one that's screaming inside because he's starting to see you as more than his female friend. Don't worry about him thinking of you as purely sexual and not as relationship material. Remember, you're already in his life as a friend, which means you have that foundation of respect needed to be in a committed relationship. This step merely adds another dimension: lust. I don't care if he has a girlfriend, isn't the type to commit, or whatever bullshit excuse you keep telling yourself as to why you shouldn't go for it. Either you go for him now or end up the jealous best friend to a guy you never wanted to be friends with in the first place. A woman who acts gets the wedding ring; a woman who waits gets the wedding invitation.

THE FRIEND WITH BENEFITS

What happens after I have sex my friend? Rewind that, fast ass. Like any man, your friend should have to earn sex first. To figure that you already know him, and give in to your horniness is a mistake. You two were either true platonic friends whose feelings grew or fake platonic friends who for some reason couldn't confess those initial romantic feelings. Either way, even after the flirting and seducing, he has to put in the work to get to know you romantically. Sex, even with a good friend, changes nothing! The switch you want to hit isn't "let's fuck, friend." To really see if this can work, you need to hit the "let's date, friend," switch. Why should you date a man with whom you're already friends? M box women into categories and him to see you as WIFEY mater has to rethink the way he treats you, he has to learn how to con and appreciate you in a light that

If you just give your friend the you want something serious, he w to test those waters because you women are shaking their heads, " should know I don't just do that with anyone!" It doesn't matter, you're in the buddy box and didn't give the romantic relationship time to evolve into something more. The problem is that women assume that sex equals romantic feelings and girl friend will turn into girlfriend. Wrong! Don't set yourself up for failure. This route may seem more proactive than beating around the bush and telling him you like him, but giving up the bush, and then pretending that you're still happy being friends, is worse.

Six months later, and you two aren't anything serious or exclusive, just people who talk and fuck. Do you tell him the only reason you had sex was because you wanted to try a relationship? Do you force him to be with you by threatening to cut off the coochie supply? Do you bury your emotions and pretend you're okay being friends with benefits? I've found that many women are afraid to speak up, so they choose the latter. Let's pretend you play it the coward way and keep your mouth closed, suppress those emotions, and continue to be friends with benefits. He's still living his life, probably talking to other women, and being accessible only when he feels like it. Do you really think you can continue to talk to him every day, fuck him every weekend, and not go crazy? This man is your friend, you can tell him about what he's doing wrong in life, share secrets, laugh, and cry together, but why can't you face your fear of rejection and tell him that you want to give you two a shot? That fear of rejection can't be stronger than your love of being sane. Once you give into that fear and simply wait for something to change, you will go crazy! You resent him for not upgrading you to girlfriend, you resent yourself for being weak, and your entire attitude is negative because your life sucks. Trust me, I've talked to nearly a hundred women in this situation, and it's a trap that only gets tighter the ︙er you wait on him. The moment you find yourself unhappy ︙FWB situation, you have to say fuck that bff past, recognize ︙version of him is not the same as the romantic version, ︙'s best for your life moving forward—end it.

THE OTHER FRIEND TRAP

There is another type of woman who hustles the same way, but isn't a traditional platonic friend. I call them "Fromancers." Fromancers are women who agree to a purely sexual relationship to keep a man in their lives whom they secretly want a romantic relationship with, all under the cover of being "just friends." Fromancers refer to a man as "my friend," but it's code for a guy who she likes, sleeps with (in the case of virgin Fromancers it's oral sex), but isn't exclusive. Fromancers start as low stress dream girls for men because they play it cool and even promise not to get insecure or jealous—as if they can control that. For example, a Fromancer meets a guy at a baby shower, they talk for a month, and while there is a mutual attraction, she doesn't want to pressure this new romantic interest by referring to him as her boyfriend or potential boyfriend. In an effort to mask her true feelings as well as keep him from feeling smothered, this man is labeled "my friend." This is not a true friendship like the bff examples I spoke of earlier. These two are as good as strangers, and she most likely can't call him when she needs a favor or communicate with him the same way she can a platonic friend.

These women are so afraid to ruin the potential of an actual boyfriend that they overcompensates and shoot themselves in the foot by giving sexual benefits with no strings attached. So many women are afraid to say what they honestly want, leading them to settle for an objectifying role that doesn't make the man feel chained down or pressured to commit. "Oh, that's my friend," has taken on an entirely new meaning because women, unlike men, don't know how to lay claim. A man who likes a woman on more than a basic level doesn't call her his "friend" and settles for sharing her with the world. He takes actions to makes her his girlfriend. Maybe you don't want to jump in a relationship and neither does he, but if you like him in a romantic way, let it be known. Do not hide behind the friend label or wait for him to decide that you two should be more than that.

Ask yourself, "Am I a Fromancer?" Have you ever been in a label-less relationship where you became upset with the man for not giving you the official title, but continued to give him exactly what he wanted? It's not a man's fault for taking your "thanks for showing up" gift bag pussy; it's your bad for succumbing to fear and giving away too much for too little. Why do women torture themselves with this false title of friend when they want him as a man? One excuse this girl gave me was that once it passes a certain period, a friend with benefits situation should end, and relationship discussions should start. In other words, she believes friendship pussy should be promoted to girlfriend pussy for its hard work. You have the right to renegotiate the friend arrangement, but a man who's had his fill without having to work for it will not want to promote you. The thing to remember is that while a man can learn to love his friend with benefits for what she provides, he rarely falls in love with her. Similar to a Bottom Bitch, you become a comfortable convenience.

If you want a man to look at you differently, drop the friend/sister role and seduce him in the ways listed, but take your time to rebuild that bond as lovers before jumping into bed. If you like him but are confused as to how he feels about you in that respect, get the hint by the way he treats you in public or around other men, and never be afraid to test the waters by flirting. Can you go back to being friends if the relationship attempt doesn't feel right or there are no sparks in the sex department? Of course you can, but people rarely do. I wager the true reason you two were friends for so long wasn't because it was an emotional connection, it was due to an unsaid sexual attraction. If you give it a shot and there is no chemistry, you two most likely won't be as close because it was never a true platonic friendship to begin with. It is what it is, and losing a buddy is the risk you have to take for love. Ultimately, you have to keep it real with yourself. The word friendship has been misused more than Penn State showers, but you don't have to throw the word around just because everyone else abuses it. Be self-aware when making new "friends" and pursue accordingly if you are interested. You may be rejected, it may not work out, but it's better to go after the man you want than to secretly lust after the friend you don't need.

7

Sex Goddess or Sex Novice

You have to please your man to keep your man. That line has been regurgitated more times than Gerber baby food. Women are expected to be sexual goddesses in order to keep their men happy while men are free to be wack in bed with no fear of their lady stepping out for superior dick. We live in a society where a woman is supposed to be content with a man running up in her with a semi-hard penis while screaming, "Whose is it," for the two minutes he lasts. *Be happy you have a good man! Don't be greedy and demand sexual competence as well!* That's the June Cleaver[7] motto. On the other hand, no matter how good of a woman you are to him, if you don't sex your man the right way, you risk him creeping for a better vagina. Welcome to the double standard of sex.

Women who brag, "She couldn't fuck him like I could, that's why he keeps running back," are often right. Men will creep if they think another girl has a better skillset than the one they're with currently. The key thing to remember about the allure of new pussy is that men don't cheat because the other woman is prettier, they cheat due to the curiosity that maybe her sex may be better

[7] June Cleaver is the archetypal domestic as portrayed in *Leave It to Beaver*. Her 1950's housewife behavior is usually regarded by traditionalist as how women should behave.

than the sex they have at home. No man will ever tell a girl he's in a relationship with that her coochie isn't the best. Your boyfriend will keep your boring sex to himself, wait until the next train to new pussyville arrives, and then jump on board like a hobo in the night. Women, unsatisfied or under-satisfied have those thoughts as well, and they may creep off with new dick if their man isn't handling their business. However, love means more to most women than good sex; therefore, women who creep for sex alone aren't as common. Most females would rather deal with sexual shortcomings than find an exit because it's the love that completes her, not the orgasm.

Penis sizes vary in length and width, the man who controls it can either work it like a *True Blood* vamp or will just lay in it like Grandpa Joe. When it comes to vagina, what really makes it more appealing? The woman attached to it. All vaginas are created the same for the most part. I've vacationed in more than I can honestly remember and never have I thought, "Wow this must be that new space age coochie!" If a woman has bad sex it isn't because her physical vagina is wack, it's because the person attached to the vagina is wack. You may not know where you fall because no man has been honest, but there is a way to get to the next level regardless of how good or bad you currently are in bed. There was an episode of the *Chappelle Show*, where Dave Chappelle told Ron Jeremy, "Ron, I got my stroke from you." That's real talk. Little boys watch porn to get their stroke down because growing up they hear older guys warn, "You better tear that pussy up." That's a lot of pressure, especially when you don't even understand what "tear that pussy up" entails.

Little girls don't go through that anxiety because most of them think all they do is lie there. A woman can lay flat on the bed with her legs up yawning and still be told that she was the best he's ever had. It's the truth because at that moment of ejaculation, she is the best. It's only later, when a guy runs up in a vagina with superior skills that he realizes how wack Angela with the big breasts really was. I blame it on society. Young ladies grow up learning how to braid hair and match outfits; they never become obsessed with whether or not they can ride a penis properly. 14-year-old girls don't sneak off and study Nyomi Banxxx's technique—they're expected to learn on the job. There is a generation of women out here sleepwalking through sexual intercourse and as unimportant as it may seem, it is a huge factor when a man considers you a long-term relationship or a fling.

ALL COOCHIE ISN'T GOOD

How many women know how to fuck? Not make love, not have sex, but fuck his brains out and imprint his mind for life? There are women who have sex down to a science and know how to make any dick get hard, stay hard, and get hard again minutes after the first round. Then there are these shy as a butterfly chicks that fuck as passionately as they fill out job applications. Some of you reading this may deny being bad in bed and hide behind, "I never had any complaints, my boyfriends have always finished." Open your eyes; no man will complain to the woman he's having sex with if he wants to continue to have sex. Furthermore, any continuous friction against a penis will make a man cum; it's not an indication that you did anything right.

> **The Accidental Nut**: Shows up and takes her clothes off. He puts it in, then eventually cums. Not because she's good, but because it's a wet, semi-tight, hole.
>
> **The Pro Pussy**: Shows up, rips her clothes off, and puts it in herself. Now he's apologizing for cumming too fast.

Every girl thinks she has Pro Pussy, but most have been misled. In college, I spent a semester smashing this Accidental Nut. She was boring and I had to think about different girls in order to cum. Nevertheless, I told her that she was good. Why would I lie? I wanted to inspire confidence so I could keep having sex with her. Bad sex is better than no sex on a Saturday night. You don't need a man's assurance to know what category you fall in, just analyze your performance. The result will always be him ejaculating; unlike a woman, a man can orgasm easily. Therefore, you have to analyze how you brought him to climax. It isn't the nut that men cherish it's the overall experience. Regardless if he cums fast or takes a while, he's going to judge the steps that got him there. Next time you have sex think about a few things. Did you match his stroke like a good dance partner, or were you off rhythm like a contestant on *Dancing with the Stars*? Did you tease him with foreplay or did you lay there and let him ram it in without any build up? Most importantly, are you having a good time or are you dialing it in with a limp "oh baby yes," while waiting for him to get off you. If you're not excited about sex, then it's going to show. If you're nervous during the boot knocking or not feeling it, he's going to notice. He will still get his nut off, but it's only a matter of time before he starts to wonder if your ratchet homegirl has a better coochie than you do.

Here's where men and women differ. A woman can have a functional loving relationship and never complain about not climaxing whereas a man will lie, cheat, and trick to get a better nut. Weak Dick Davon can pull the good girl and keep her happy because women don't view his wack sex as a deal breaker. Raise your hand if you've been in a relationship with a guy who had a substandard stroke? Did you roll with the punches or did you find a way to sabotage the relationship and leave him? I bet 9 out of 10 of you stayed with Weak Dick Davon. The majority of women don't see bad sex as a reason to break up. True to their nature, they believe they can look on the bright side. As long as he treats you right, you can defend his lack of effort with, "Sex isn't everything. At least I have a good man." Most women are not sexually shallow, so the subject of sexual inadequacy only comes up AFTER they break up (hence the girl outside of the club screaming at her ex "that's why your dick is little"). Men aren't that selfless; bad sex is a deal breaker, and some will sabotage a solid relationship if her sex isn't on the level he expects. I had a love affair with one of the sexiest girls I've ever known, but her sex game was like a Marlins game—people were playing but the stands were empty. After months of trying to deal, I moved on to a Spartan who knew how to contract pussy muscles and inspire projectile semen. That girl never knew sex was the reason I stopped seeing her.

There's a ratchet anthem called "Yankin" by the rapper Lady, a girl-power song about an amazing vagina. *Can't even lie, fuck better when I'm drankin, ride dick like a pro/throw the pussy like I'm famous.* Why does she have to be drunk to fuck like a champ? Grown women who are open enough to be intimate should not be shy. You're giving him the ultimate gift, your body. There is no reason to close your eyes or be silent. Don't be scared to tell him to hit it harder and direct him to spots that feel good to you. Look down as the dick goes in and out, you know it turns you on. My amazing sister Adara once said, "I don't put in work at the gym so I can fuck with the lights off." Keep the lights on, be vocal, and don't frown your face at semen. It's cum, not acid; don't run from it, be filthy. Sex is inherently nasty, that's what makes it fun! In twenty years, you will be married and free to have boring sex, but while you're still on the market, be a sexual legend.

FREAK IN THE SHEETS

I don't want to live in a world where 60% of the women have Corpse Bride Coochie. Hump hump moan hump hump—it's over. That's sex without a pulse. You aren't a corpse you're a sexual goddess: now prove it. When you're beginning a relationship, it's tough to step your pussy game up. A woman doesn't want a new man to think she's a ho, so she holds back. Unless he falls in because you have the Grand Canyon for a vagina, a man will not resent how nasty you get once the lights go out. Men judge your personality by the conversations you two have during the daytime, come night there is no more judgment. Sex is a fantasy world where everyone is free to become their alter ego. Don't pull out all of your tricks the first time; ease him into fetish acts and role-playing as the months go on. At the same time, don't curve your aggression and dirty talk. Sex is 90% mental, don't be a hole, be a brain. If you want to hook him, appeal to his male ego by using reverse psychology. When you start sucking on your breasts after two weeks of only squeezing them, your lover is going to think that he's turning you out. In reality, you've been sucking your own tit and squirting since you were in 11th grade, but allow him to think he is the first to invoke these actions. It makes him feel as if he's conquering you. No man is going to run away from a woman who makes him feel like a king.

The rapper Drake once said, "I just want to see what that pussy's like so one time is fine with me." The majority of men feel that way; they want to see if you are unique or simply serviceable like the last girl. That's the allure of new pussy. Don't get consumed with looking like a ho. He knows you're not a virgin if you're fucking him after three dates, so stop acting like a rookie in the sack in order to prevent judgment. So many females have sent emails asking me to explain why men don't return calls after the first time they have sex. Of course it was the sex. Even if a man doesn't like you as a person or think you're not attractive enough to be his girlfriend, great sex will make him want a rematch. Great sex won't make him stay with you, but it may buy one more month, and in that time, you could win him over with what you do outside of the bedroom.

KEEPING THE FIRE GOING

For those women already in relationships, you and your man will easily hit a wall if you take sex for granted. Sex after a year in will never feel as exciting as the first few months. Your personality may have compensated for your expired vagina, but don't rest on your laurels, it's time to unleash the dragons like a true Khaleesi[8]. Sex can feel better than ever if you two are comfortable enough to P90X your freak muscles, meaning take it to the next level by constantly changing things up. Sex toys and pornography are cool, but there is an even better way to keep the hormones jumping—be spontaneous. He thinks he knows you, but you can get much nastier. Give him head in the car. Grab him in public.

---

[8] Khaleesi is the royal title given to Daenerys Targaryen, the mother of dragons from the fantasy book series *A Song of Ice and Fire* aka *Game of Thrones*.

Cook naked. Switch up the routine without warning! Sex shouldn't just happen at night and in the dark. Make sure to save the really nasty things for special occasions so you don't reach a point where you can't top your last session, but be sure you both are into whatever it is you want to try out, so it isn't awkward afterwards. Don't let Kanye West pressure you into getting him a big booty ho for his birthday. Most relationships rarely recover from threesomes, so if you want to bring a third party in, be sure you're both secure enough that you won't dwell on it afterwards. If you are down with the ménage, find a stranger, don't bring your friends, or even associates into the bedroom. I've yet to hear a story that didn't end with, "They started seeing each other without me." If you want the adventure of another woman, you can tease this safely with a trip to the strip club. Let him see you get a lap dance and feel up a woman. When you two go back home, he's sure to be fired up. No matter how you decide to spice things up, keep it entertaining and unpredictable.

Here's some homework for every woman still unsure of her pussy power. The next time you have sex I want you to test yourself to make sure you're not the Accidental Nut. I want you to be nasty, aggressive, and creative. Do everything in your power to make him cum with the fury of an AK-47. That pussy should be so good that after he cums he's content with lying in a pool of nasty wetness with the condom still on. This guy should not even want to wash your scent off his fingers! You have to be Michelle Pfeiffer in *Dangerous Minds*—you came in, changed his life for the better, and even after you're gone, he'll never forget you. That's the real definition of "Yanking."

8

But, I'm A Virgin

Virgins are like cops, I respect them, but I always feared coming across one. For me personally it boiled down to not wanting the hassle of putting in work when the light at the end of the tunnel was...well there was no light, you would have to be the first one to break through. For my virgins out there let me take you through how a male sees virginity from the moment of his sexual awakening. Teenagers will wait for their girlfriends to say they're ready for that next step because most of these boys are still virgins themselves, and take what they can get. Unless a young dude meets an older girl like a freaky babysitter or a young ho in the making, the only way he can lose his virginity is by playing by the high school rules: get a girlfriend, be nice to her, and hope that she deems him worthy.

Think about that, high school is the only social institution that guilt's boys and girls into having a relationship before sex. Those females who sleep around or have a new boyfriend every few months are labeled fast or slutty by the Regina George[9] crew. For young girls, high school politics mean a lot, so most are conscious about perception and require boyfriends. While there are always Senior boys and varsity athletes that create The Groupie Effect

---

[9] Regina George is awesomely bitchie Queen Bee from the movie *Mean Girls*.

71

and cut the line, as well as pockets of young freaks that don't mind dropping it on the cafeteria floor and making it nasty, most young women play by the rules of: get a boyfriend and then see what happens. During this period, most girls lose their virginity not because they are irresponsible, but because they feel loved by the boy with whom they are going steady. If your parents and teachers tell you that you should wait for sex until you find a person that loves you, even at 16 you will feel that it's the right time because you've had the same boyfriend since freshmen year, and you two are in love as far as you can tell. These standards make guys actually put in work, and in most cases these boys catch real feelings for the girls whose virginities they take.

That's the structure of high school. By the time a man makes it to college or the post high school working world, the majority of women he will meet will have gone through that experience of having sex with their high school sweethearts and will not see sex as a big deal. What happens is that the sex schedule accelerates. In the so-called "real world," men meet women who don't require relationships to give it up, women who consider talking the same as a commitment and give it up, and even women who are sexually liberated and just as horny as guys are, so they make him give it up. For the first time in a boy's life, sex becomes relatively easy to attain. On the flipside, there is still a large number of women ages 18-22, who didn't lose it to a high school sweetheart. The moment a woman like this admits that she still has her V-card, most boys run for cover because they do not want to go through that waiting period again. Males are always aware of their options, there are so many other females giving it up for less, and being young often goes hand in hand with being impatient. This leaves the virgin girl in a predicament where she's told that it's good that she's still "pure," but the actions of those males she's interested in show her that it's actually a huge turnoff.

VIRGINS ASSEMBLE

There are a number of reasons women choose to hold onto their virginity, but the results will be the same—dating will be hell and men will fear you. We live in a world where sex isn't treasured it's expected. Men of the past few generations don't have the patience or sensitivity to understand why any mature woman wouldn't just let him stick it in and get it over with. Regardless of how noble or decent your decision may seem, most men will greet your virginity with clenched teeth and the thought of, "What's the problem? It's only sex." A frequent question I get comes from women in college or the recently graduated. They want to date, they want a boyfriend, they want to build something real, but every time they confess their virginity, men run as if they just got the results of a paternity test. As a virgin, you can date successfully and find love, but it will test your patience. You will find several Mr. Wrongs who claim they don't mind waiting before you find that Mr. Right who will wait, but you can't let that discourage you. Worth waiting depends on being worth dating, and worth dating depends on being impressive. Virgins don't have to compete harder with girls who are fucking; they need to shine a light on how extraordinary they are outside of the bedroom. I've talked to a few virgins who play up the victim card and throw a pity party because guys zone out after a few weeks. I'm going to get in your face with fingers pointed and tell you that your virginity has about 30% to do with why you can't get a man to hang around. The other 70% has nothing to do with sex, and everything do with you not taking the steps to make yourself stand out as a woman worth waiting for.

DON'T BROADCAST YOUR VIRGINITY

There are some extremely awkward virgins out there who are so self-conscious about their virginity that they feel a need to broadcast it to dudes shortly after they meet. I'm not sure if this is a tactic used to scare impatient guys away or something they feel defines them and needs to be announced. Sex is the elephant in the room for a reason; it's difficult to talk about around strangers. A woman who has slept with twenty guys doesn't meet a new guy that night and say, "By the way, I'm fucking." She keeps her sexual activity to herself until she's comfortable enough to talk about personal things, and so should virgins. Maybe logic tells you that it's best to get it out there ASAP, this way he doesn't find out later and run off. This scare tactic will backfire more times than not. It is always better to let a man expose his true personality under normal circumstances. Telling him you are a virgin won't cause him to run immediately, an uninterested guy will still play it off until he finds an opportunity to escape. This means he will waste an additional month or so stringing you along trying to pretend he doesn't care because he doesn't want to look like he was just after the pussy.

Men go into the introductory stage assuming you're having sex, but hoping you're not having too much sex. When getting to know a man, pay close attention to how much information he digs for and what kind he's after. Gentlemen will keep it respectful and ask about your life; a guy after sex won't ask you anything deeper than how many siblings you have. Instead, he will have a million questions about ex-boyfriends and the last time you had sex. A man like that is in a rush, he doesn't want to waste his time with a prude, so he's unsubtly trying to figure out if you're down to smash sooner or later. Never reveal your virginity during this interrogation. If he's just after sex, you don't need to announce that you are a virgin in order to expose his mentality his conversation will tell all. Once you know what he's hitting for, you can now take matters into your own hands and decline his calls and follow up dates; all of this without having to put your business in the streets. Additionally, even if a man is being respectful, don't feel a need to overshare your sexual status. You don't want him to treat you as if you have a disease; yet, by making it all about your virginity the first week or so after meeting him, that's how he will treat you. Being a virgin isn't like having a kid, don't be forthcoming on the first or even second date. Wait until the third date or a month after being friends to open up about that. This may seem like a long wait, but this is a perfect amount of time to form a bond, and for him to earn that information. After a month of getting to know and like you, a man won't label you as the virgin girl with whom he hopes to have sex. Now, he actually knows you as a human being as opposed to that label. You're Lisa the Leo who hates frozen yogurt, but loves Kendrick Lamar. You are a person, not a sexual status, and that makes him less likely to run off once you shoot him down and prove that you are indeed a virgin.

Once you finally tell him your status and get the reasons out of the way, it will be a shock; be honest but don't give him an out. Virgins should never say, "I understand if you don't want to keep talking to me." What the fuck is wrong with you? You haven't had your cherry popped—that's not the same as being HIV positive. No need to make excuses for him not wanting you. By giving him an immediate out, you put pressure on him to stay. Of course he's going to say, "No, I'm not worried about that," whether he means it or not because you set him up to look like an asshole if he takes that bait. Even if he wanted to run, he'll hang around and fake it until he figures out an excuse that won't seem as if it's about your virginity (but it will be). It's better to play it off as if your virginity is not that big of a deal. Make him comfortable and let him know that you aren't looking at him as a potential deflowerer who has the responsibility to stick around. Show him that he's still just a guy you like who may become your boyfriend if he plays his cards right—nothing's changed.

Do not be self-defeating and assume a man wants nothing to do with you if he's not getting sex. Thinking that if you tell him he'll run off, will turn thought into reality. Not because you're right, but because you're sabotaging yourself. You see a guy you think is cute looking at you, but you turn away because in your mind, "A guy like that won't want a virgin." You go on a date with a guy who's wonderful, but then you start to ignore his phone calls or get too busy because in your mind, "A guy like this won't want a virgin." Stop doubting yourself. Are you not a sexy chick? Do you not have a bomb ass personality? Act like a prize and you'll be pursued as if you're a prize. All those women out there, do you think the only reason they have boyfriends is because they fucked to get them? There are plenty of females who take sex seriously and make men wait several months because they want to be sure before ending their vow of celibacy. Even though they are not virgins, the result is the same: A man will always wait for something that's worth it if the reasoning is sane!

BLOWJOBS & COCK TEASING

I had a bad experience with a virgin who continuously cock teased me. She would say perverted things on the phone, talk about all the stuff she wanted to do to me, and then would hide behind her virginity when I tried to have sex. It was probably fun for her, but for a young dude with a ferocious libido, it was torture. Men who have come away scorned by virgins often warn others not to get involved. There is no winning with a horny woman who's sworn off sex, but is cool with using a man as masturbation material. Women get horny, it's normal, and virgin women are often nastier than average. The term "Virgin Whore" describes seemingly pure women who do everything except let you penetrate. If you're going to be a virgin, be a virgin; don't create loopholes to get yourself off, knowing that the guy will be left hanging. You're creating bad karma for yourself, so when a man dangles a relationship, then doesn't go through with it, you'll know how it feels to get your emotions toyed with.

When you tell a man you're not ready for sex, then twenty minutes later you're giving him a blowjob like it's his birthday — you're sending the wrong message. No matter if he's inside your vagina or inside your mouth, it's sex. If you're going to be sucking him off after each date you might as well be having sex with him; you're getting the same result. Hand jobs to finish him off after a steamy make out session may send him home relaxed, but it will still make him resent you. Some virgins I talked to spoke of giving head to keep their boyfriends happy. If a blowjob doesn't go against your morals, fine, but think about this: If you are saving your vagina for the right man, shouldn't you save your mouth as well? You meet Mr. Right and he's the first to penetrate, but the ninth to drop a load in your mouth…doesn't make much sense, does it? Sex is sex, don't be hypocritical and cherry pick what you will and won't do, you come off as a confused little girl who really wants to live that life, but refuses to out of some misplaced dedication to some invisible rulebook.

HAVE A GOOD REASON

If you expect your understanding friend to stick around, then you have to have a valid reason as to why he's six months in and only getting hand jobs. Honestly, religion is the only legitimate reason to abstain from sex. No man wants to debate religion because it can potentially offend a woman and ruin, not only a shot at sex, but at being friends. If you tell him that you're not going to do it because of your god, he has no ammo to shoot that down. I had a friend who was Egyptian and a devout Muslim. She was gorgeous and had the kind of charisma that pulled men in and made them want her, me included. Her boyfriend decided to convert, and they were engaged. He thought this would allow him to cut the line and have sex before the wedding. Wrong. She didn't come that far just to cheat her beliefs. She was raised to wait until the wedding night, and that's what she was going to do. They soon broke up, but it's an important lesson. Being religious gives you a vow that no player can bypass, but never underestimate the lengths men will go in order to test your faith.

Waiting until marriage just because, isn't a reason I've ever come across as to why a woman keeps her V-card. The top reason seems to be waiting until someone earns it. The conundrum is this: During high school, girls are afraid to have sex because of pain and reputation. The idea that it will hurt is scary no matter how many times the older girls say you won't feel anything. There is also the fear that the guy who takes your virginity will run his mouth to the school or dog you out after he cums. Many young girls would rather not deal with that stress at that age, so they wait until they feel like the risk would be worth it. These women have high standards, mix that with paranoia, and no one short of Jesus Christ could get those panties off.

By the time that kind of female reaches college, she feels a need to be even more meticulous because being a virgin now makes her special. You haven't had sex, but most of the girls at college have, so that makes you rare. You may think, "Why would anyone floss their virginity?" Human beings will floss anything that separates them from the pack. For men, it's how many girls they have slept with. For women, it's how many guys they haven't slept with that makes them seem like a catch. Girls who are sexually active don't generally like virgins because some have elitist attitudes that they're better because they didn't bust it open for Juan in the 10th grade. If a girl survives her first year in college without "getting it over with," she becomes even stricter. Now only King Arthur can pull the sword out of the stone. This is a case of the myth growing and the hype of "Mr. Right" becoming unrealistic. Hopeless romantics want the Hollywood version of love where a perfect man falls for them like Jack fell for Rose after a few days on the Titanic. In real life, meeting that special person doesn't come complete with orchestral music to signal that he is indeed the one. These women ruin potential relationships by holding on, not to their virginity, but to the thought that no man is worthy to be there first.

TRUST YOURSELF

Lisa the Leo's boyfriend of almost a year is putting in work. However, Lisa is still waiting for the right one, because she thinks God will make that person glow bright purple to prove he's worthy. There will never be a definite sign that any guy is the right one, it's an educated leap of faith. Lisa is conflicted, her mind keeps telling her to wait, but her body wants her boo on that sexual level. Despite her pussy leaking like a BP oil spill every time they make out, she refuses to give in. Lisa's body is stressed and mentally she's exhausted because it takes a lot of effort to fight what comes naturally, especially when you're in love. For Lisa's boyfriend, her denial is an insult. He knows he's the right man and has proven that. The real problem is that Lisa has been a virgin for so long, that losing it will feel like losing an arm. That title of virgin is something she's used to and probably makes her feel special. Being a virgin does not make you special—you are what makes you special, and you will continue to be special, broken hymen or not.

There will never be the perfect time or a perfect guy who glows signaling he is the one. You will have sex, and it will probably be with a guy who doesn't end up marrying you. The guy may turn into a jerk or may continue to be a gentleman. No matter how he responds in the aftermath, you have to be able to hold your head high knowing you made the best decision given the knowledge you gathered before you agreed to have sex. You didn't come this far to be a one night stand, but don't wait so long where no human can measure up to your standards. Demand a relationship, wait until you're in love, flaws and all, and hopefully then you will feel like the time is right.

9

Online Dating Girl

Dating websites—the final frontier for those fed up with the selection of people they meet in their everyday lives. Work too much? No time for love? Just log in from the comfort of your home and eHarmony that shit. Tired of the thirsty guys at the club and bars? There's a mobile app for Match.com. Looking to fuck another girl's man, then AshleyMadison is for you. Dating websites are last resorts for older people with baggage. For those under 35, I think it's a lazy and counterproductive way to find a mate. "But my friend found love online and got married." Guess what? People have gotten married off Myspace, Blackplanet, *World of Warcraft* chat rooms, and any other electronic communication site you can think of. Any stat about those who "made it," you have to take with a grain of salt. If you put 200 lonely people in the same chat room, at least 10 of them are going to end up having sex or taking it further.

Before you throw away your money on a dating site, answer one question, Are you being lazy or do you have a valid excuse for why you can't get out and socialize? Women who are self-conscious about their weight or looks use these sites as a crutch. Shy women see it as a safe way to meet men without the threat of rejection. Divorcees think the keyboard protects them from being hurt again. All of these women have esteem issues. They know they're great ladies with engaging personalities, but they don't think they have that x-factor that would make a man walk up and ask their names in real life. By taking the interaction virtual, those women even the playing field. Men online aren't privy to the flaws, they look at your best photo and read your best attributes. When you begin talking with an online guy he's free to focus on the real you, not the physical appearance or emotional baggage of a past relationship.

What happens when he finally meets you in person and you're not as airbrushed as that picture you hid behind for months? What happens when he finds out that your ex is still in your life and has a short fuse? What happens when you realize he overlooked the part where it said, "Has children"? Making him fall in love with you via messages or phone calls isn't hard. He's falling for the idea of you, not the flesh and blood reality. You still need to seal the deal face to face, and this is where most online relationships crumble. There are great women online because they are sick of looking and sick of the games. The same can't be said for men on these sites. If that man is as great as his profile makes him out to be, why is he paying a website to match him up? The hard truth is that there is a new generation of men who use these sites to hunt for insecure women they can charm out of sex, money, or both.

The inherent problem with these sites is that men don't take it as seriously as women do; most sign up to picture surf. I don't care if you like to hike and bicycle; add a full body picture so I can make a decision. She's 5"6', no kids, doesn't smoke, about average body, drinks socially, spiritual not religious...okay, but are you fucking? That should be the first question you answer because that's what most men who pay for these sites care about. I surfed a dating website for research and the first thing I thought was, "Why didn't I sign up for this when I was single?" Not because I needed help, but because it's so much easier than the crapshoot of approaching strangers. For a serial dater, online dating is like shooting ratchets in a Forever 21. Post a pic, write an intriguing bio, and "wink" at a dozen pretty girls. At least two will respond, and you're off to a new world of sex. This is easier than normal life because it accelerates sex for men. Before you two meet for the first time you're going to talk each other's ears off, become fast friends, and because of this superficial bond, the first date will usually be a guaranteed sex date if it goes well. Although the tables are turned and you have the upper hand on a dating site, you are still competing with other women. A man who's spending $20 a month on this experiment is not going to talk to one girl at a time. He's going get his money's worth by arranging to meet up with you and at least one other girl. Only after the meeting will he decide which one of you ladies, if any, sticks around after that sex date.

On the other hand, there are men who are online looking for real love. Older men who are widowed or divorced are not really in social circles, which makes this is a great way to meet pretty young things. Guys who tend to be a little heavy or extremely shy can become Superman on these sites and show what great personalities they have. However, when you look at the hot women on these sites, they are very specific. Ironically, they want more than personality from a guy that loves dogs and hiking. They want Channing fucking Tatum! She wants a man her age or a little younger, not fifteen years older; there goes Grandpa Widower. She wants a guy who's athletic; there goes the wealthy engineer who happens to tip the scales a bit. These ladies are more likely to settle offline than online because online even marginally attractive women get inboxed with dozens of messages as soon as they sign up. Unlike the happy hour bar, these women have a vast selection and can afford to discriminate. As a result, those men looking for authentic love end up lying to get close to them because they know they are online competing with men that are more attractive. Hotassmess.net is what this online dating world should be called. Still think it's your only shot? Let's look at some of the common reasons women sign up to be sure that you fall into the needy, and not the lazy category.

IT DOES THE WORK FOR YOU

We do in depth research so that your first date is like your fifth date. What do they actually mean by "research"? Seeing what city he grew up in and whether he's a dog person or cat person is not research. The entire point of dating is to form a bond; you're discovering them one conversation at a time. Getting a laundry list of semi-personal facts doesn't tell you anything real. You can't measure chemistry by comparing questionnaires. She could be a Conservative Baptist and he could be a Liberal Atheist, but when you get together, it could be the greatest love of all time. Dating is not checking off, no smokers, 80-100k a year, and no one with kids. That's not real life. To go into a first date already knowing the main points of a person's life is like reading the script before seeing a movie—you have to pretend to be excited at each turn. This can turn out to be boring, and those things that come out naturally and lead to funny little stories that give insight are missed. Then there is the honesty factor that comes with such a scripted meeting. Men know what girls are looking for, so they embellish when answering those online questions. Guys don't self-deprecate on a dating site, they make themselves look like gods. He's a perfect man who loves everything and plays every sport, has read every book, and seen every movie. The first date becomes less about getting to know him, and more about figuring out what was bullshit and what was real.

I DON'T HAVE TIME

I'm so busy with work. I can't meet anyone with this schedule. You're not that damn busy. In the time you took to fill out that questionnaire, you could have been dressed, out the door, and meeting your friends for drinks. You're not busy you're lazy. You want to shop for boyfriends like you shop for shoes, four browser tabs open, deciding which will look best this summer. "Girl, I think I'll go for light skin and husky this season, that may be my fit." If you're too busy to find a man, you're too busy to keep a man. What happens when you're dating? Does your work schedule become lighter? You didn't have time to go out to the bar, but now you have time to go out to dinner? Even when dating exclusively online the amount of woman-hours spent inboxing and chatting back and forth will start to fill up your day, what happens then? Once it becomes semi-serious, there are certain things you have to sacrifice and there will be time you have to put in to make it work. Meeting someone is the easiest part of the relationship because it's the least time consuming. Stop treating your heart like an Amazon wish list. Close those browser tabs and get your lazy ass up and out.

I'M SICK OF THE SAME CROWD

Wack city, wack club, wack DJs, wack men! Are they really that bad, or are you bitter and closed-minded? You don't live under Jim Crow law; you can go anywhere you want to. You are in that club because you chose to go to that club. Music's not going to make men want to approach you. The DJ spinning your favorite song isn't going to make you cut loose and be less shy around guys you like. Stop blaming the surroundings you choose, and start analyzing the choices you make. I can go to Yelp, search your city, and find ten places you never stepped foot in. However, you don't want to go to those establishments because you're intimidated. "It's a white crowd," "They charge too much for drinks," or the classic "I don't like their music." Didn't you say you wanted a different crowd? Do you really want to listen to French Montana songs or is this just another excuse because you're afraid to fail?

So where do you go after you drive past the new place that your friends think is corny? You run back to the same hole in the wall clubs, with the same ratchet friends, complaining about the same broke men. The next day you're on a dating site trying to find a new crowd, but when you type in the radius, the race, the interests, and so on…the guys that pop up are the same as the ones who were at the club. You don't want a new crowd. You want attention from the crowd you're used to, but don't know how to get it! If three guys from that same hole in the wall had asked for your number it wouldn't have been "this is wack" you would have smiled and said, "It was fun tonight." Social events are as fun as you make them. If you want a man, you can pick one out in real life the same as you can pick one out from a list of profile pictures, all it takes is a confident tap on the shoulder as opposed to a click on the mouse.

FACEBOOK & TWITTER BOOS

I'm not going to pay to be matched up, but what about boys on social networks. I seem to connect with some of them and wouldn't mind seeing where it goes. When it comes to Facebook, there's this pattern where most of the people you become romantically interested in are guys from the past who you may have overlooked. I've had nearly all of my best friends from high school call me with news that they finally hit such and such who we all used to crush on. To connect with a former co-worker or classmate is great, you have a shared past in common and plenty time to renew a relationship with each other. The problem becomes one of convenience. Are you settling for these Facebook men because you're in a slump and they happen to be the only eligible guys hitting you up? Be honest, how much of it is genuine interest in him and how much of it is a need for some form of male romantic attention? If you were getting interest offline, would you still give Ben from the old job your number? Loneliness can make whores of us all, but it shouldn't lead you into a "something to do" relationship. At the same time, if you're willing to be proactive and actually do most of the rekindling offline as opposed to inboxing, this avenue can be just as fruitful as bumping into someone you used to know at a coffee shop and getting their number. The key is not to chain yourself to the computer, but to bring it into real life early and often.

Twitter is slightly different in that it's a group of relative strangers who you interact with randomly. I have a homie from the Midwest who I met on Twitter, and he let me in on his world of DM[10] pimping. He had smashed dozens of women since he joined Twitter, using it much like those men who sign up on

---

[10] Direct Message is a form of private messaging on Twitter that allows you to communicate without it being publicly displayed on the timeline.

dating sites use it—profile picture search and destroy. I've followed women on Twitter and thought, "If I wasn't married, I'd hit," based on how they look. Comparatively, only five or six of those women have ever made me think, "If I wasn't married, I'd date," based on the quality of the things they wrote. Point being, it's primarily an image driven device for men to pussy scout superficially, with a slim chance of a man actually relationship hunting based on a connection. The problem again isn't with the men; it's with the female intention. If a woman wants to use Twitter to have fun and maybe hook up casually with eye candy, it's a godsend. If you are a woman looking for love, you will be in a position of once again weeding through the bullshit, deciphering what part of his bio is legit, and then hoping you didn't reel in a Catfish[11] or player.

Long distance relationships built off the internet be it on Facebook, Twitter, or dating sites, are usually an exercise in planning when to meet up for sex. Talk for months as if this is legit, finally meet up, have sex, and then you go back to your hometown and wait. That online man will either say, "This could work," and make it official or he will suddenly stop hitting you up as frequently, leaving you to get the hint. In short, heartbreak can still happen. There is no electronic short cut for finding a good man. It's time to get back to living your life more proactively. You don't need to hide behind a keyboard to have confidence. Connect to reality and leave OKcupid to the lazy girls that make excuses. Stop putting your life on display for a bunch of thirsty internet nerds and predators. Spartan up and showcase your assets in the real world the same way great women from the past did before the invention of the modem. Put your freak'em dress on, take a few shots of something non-fruity, and get out there ready to meet people the old fashion way—offline.

---

[11] Catfish or Catfishing is the act of pretending to be someone else on the internet, either by stealing pictures or falsifying a lifestyle.

10

10

Becoming a Spartan

en are taught to be strong, tough, and never to take shit
from anyone. "Nice guys finish last," is embedded in
their brains. Therefore, when it's time for a man to go
for what he wants, he goes for it. The most successful men in this
country don't give a fuck. Bill Gates screwed over Steve Jobs
when creating Windows. Steve Jobs screwed over his best friend
just to make a few more dollars from Atari. Mark Zuckerberg
fucked over a few classmates en route to 50 billion. Are these men
defined by those steps or vilified because of them? These men are
praised! Morally ambiguous acts are ignored because history only
remembers the end results. Ruthless aggression and self-
preservation are not evil things. Men stab each other in the back
and then shake hands over drinks; it's the business of life. Why
aren't females taught these things? Instead of putting themselves
first, women are told to be considerate and selfless. From birth,
they have been beat in the head with this notion of "That's not
right, that's not lady like, sisterhood rah rah rah!" Fuck that. Your
mother may have told you to wait your turn like a good girl, but
I'm saying cut in front of that other bitch. Club Success is about to
hit capacity, and you don't want to be the odd woman out.

Romantic comedies, cartoons, even the material they teach in
school, it's all sexist bullshit meant to keep girls in the kitchen.
Look at history and see how they labeled Cleopatra as a whore,
called Joan of Arc a crazy lesbian, and painted Elizabeth I as a

frigid cunt. Who do they parade as modern American Royalty? The Kennedys. You should aspire to be a first lady whose job was to overlook adultery and sit there and wave in that nice, soon to be blood splattered, pink dress. Where are the real women? Those who refuse to play by the rules and want more out of life than what a man allows her to have? I created a category for such women and labeled them Spartans. Much like the Greek warriors who fought against all odds, these women refuse to surrender and bow before the status quo. Men either flee from Spartans or marry them. Either he is threatened by her strength or smitten by it; there is no in-between. Being a Spartan is not about being masculine. It's about embracing the full power of being a woman and realizing that men worship what's between your legs and weaker women are infatuated by your control of it. Every female has the tools to regain this power and deprogram herself, but few have the confidence to be aggressive and self-serving. If you're tired of playing your position as the sex object, catering to others, and doing what society tells you is "lady like," then read on.

Spartans: The strongest women on the planet.
They follow no woman. They obey no man.
They aren't offended they offend.
They don't wait they take.
They are the Alpha Females.

The first step in becoming a Spartan is to erase the fear and inferiority complexes that have kept you in check your entire life. The defensive attitude that you think protects you from getting hurt is poisonous. The pride you take in having or doing basic things is a thin mask that will never hold up. The bullshit roles you play to keep friends liking you and strangers from judging you do nothing except keep you subservient to trends and loyal to users. Do not hold on to those lies you tell yourself to keep your head high. Do not gloss over these words and deny that you have complexes. All the anxiety, worry, and indecision you have inside of you, no matter how deep you have buried them will continue to keep your self-esteem stagnant and your confidence largely false. Before going to the next section, I want you to go deep inside and unearth all of those feelings that you hate to think about, confront them, and then let them go. I don't care what happened to you in your past, let go of those feelings of anger due to bias, discrimination, and any unfairness. I don't care how you look; skinny, fat, short, or tall, close your eyes and let go of those feelings of unattractiveness that keep you self-conscious. I don't care what your perceived social status is, no matter if you wait tables or ring up customers, let go of those nagging feelings that you are somehow inferior to the wealthy. You are a woman; you can withstand immeasurable amounts of pain, show truly unconditional love, and give birth to life. You. Are. The. Shit!

Men kill, wage wars, lie, steal, pay, beg, and betray each other for women. Are you really going to believe the bullshit that you are soft, replaceable, or just a sexual release? You are the most powerful of all human beings! It's time to embrace this fact and shake off the habit and traditions that men have saddled you with in order to keep you obedient and unsure of your place in this world. Take some time to truly appreciate how important you are in regards to the role you play in this universe. Spend a moment basking in how potentially great you could be once you had the self-esteem and confidence to really not give a fuck. What do you have to fear from a man rejecting you, a woman not liking you, or a group of people judging you? Life is Sparta, a world tailor made for the strongest women to succeed and ingeniously designed to keep the weakest women in their place. Decide which side you want to be on, and then continue reading.

SPARTAN LAW #1
HE'S ONLY HER MAN BECAUSE YOU ALLOW IT

A good man is hard to find when you search within limited borders. If you find a man who has everything you're looking for in a mate, and the only thing standing in the way is another female—fuck her. It's survival of the fittest, and like Leonidas in *300*, you have to be willing to kick the next bitch in the chest and watch her fall into a pit if she's standing between you and victory. If the girl he's with isn't strong enough to keep a hold on him, then that's her fault. I'm not talking about adultery; I'm talking about boyfriend/girlfriend relationships. Those titles are only as strong as a person makes them, and if her man wants to stray then obviously he wasn't in love. You can't technically steal someone that goes willingly. You can't wreck a home that a man was only using as a temporary layover. Everyone has free will, which means you're not guilty of taking her man; she's guilty of not doing enough to make him stay. When you meet Mr. Right and it's revealed that he has a chick, don't shy away from that, embrace it. The last thing you want to be is a side ho. Side hos are complacent; they play their part and wait on the man to finish with his old girl. Spartans don't wait they take. Ask about his girlfriend; make him feel comfortable talking about her. Evaluate how he treats his girlfriend, internalize how he talks about her, and pinpoint their true problems. After you gather enough intel, you will be able to see clearly if he's a scumbag just looking to cheat on his girl, or if he's a good man who's searching for something genuine. Once you decide that you want him, erase his girlfriend from his life.

The first step is to make him give this peasant girl a two-week's notice. This isn't a person who works at Burger King trying to get a job at the Post Office; he's not allowed to keep his old job while applying for his new one. If he's serious about getting with you, she has to go. A man will not want to leave his sure thing for a girl who he hasn't even sampled yet. That's his problem. If he wants to continue the sexting, dates, and eventually get sex down the line, then he has to make that hard decision to end his current relationship. Give him a deadline. Not only does he have to break it off with his wifey, he MUST tell her the reason why. This may sound unnecessarily cruel, but men will fuck their ex-girlfriends until those exes close their legs and move on. If you make him tell this peasant, "It's over because I met someone else," that's devastating. Unless she's the dumbest girl on the planet, she will take huge offense to not being good enough, and never give him the ass again. This deathblow must be landed! You made him look like a jerk but at the same time you made it damn near impossible for him to two-time you with his old girl.

Women constantly ask me "how can I get him to leave her?" You hook him, and then take away his narcotic. The hooking I'm talking about is not a dip in your vagina! By having sex, you give up your power. Hook him with your personality and the tease of sex. Make him love your personality by being more fun and engaging than his girlfriend, then when he's enamored with you, cut him off. Men want what they can't have more than they want something they are used to having. Tell him that you want to be with him, and then let him give you an excuse about how his girl needs him and how he doesn't want to be mean by breaking her heart. That's the game he's feeding you in order to have both of you. In reality, he is not tied to her permanently; it's a choice. Stop calling him after hooking him with two months of bomb personality and the tease of what you would do sexually if he were yours, and then see how fast he drops that peasant. It's all about desire, and when you represent something new that he wants and can't have, you hold all the cards.

Her pussy is a Honda; your pussy is a Maserati. Just the thought of driving it will make him give her up if their bond is weak. You have to sell yourself as if your vagina could cure cancer. Lust is a powerful weapon, and for a man who's having sex on a regular basis, your seduction has to be on point. Nevertheless, don't be like those cliché women who fuck with married men and say dumb things like, "He said he would leave her for me." Of course he did, he was trying to get in your pants. No matter how heavy the teasing gets, remember this one simple rule: <u>Do not have sex with him until he's your man</u>. You're scouting for a relationship, not dick, so keep the physical activity limited. This simple rule is often neglected and women run back to me with, "I screwed up and slept with him. Can I still make it work?" Have discipline! You're dealing with a man who is getting sex, so you not giving it up will not make or break him. You have to sell him on the fact that not only can you make him bust in less than sixty seconds, but you can also keep him interested in your conversation. The brain is more attractive than the vagina. For him to say, "She never understood me like you do," is checkmate.

Don't be afraid to go after any man that sparks your interest. Women meet guys with girlfriends all the time, and let's be honest ladies, they are often two times as appealing as the single men you run into. You chitchat at the market with them, spend hours at boring parties laughing with them, one is probably @'ing you on Twitter right now. Taken men are all around you, and usually they are the main ones saying everything you want to hear. So how do you come on to him without seeming like a ho? Men will think, "She's flirting with me and knows I have a chick, so she only wants sex." Let him gas himself up, Spartans don't care about false perception. You know that you're not a ho and that you won't fuck him until you get what you want first. Let him think; you'll show.

If you are unsure if this taken man is into you, put out feelers. Test the water by hitting him hard with sexual innuendos. Saying things like, "Your girlfriend better watch out for me," will drive him crazy. Make sure you have a way to get his number, email, or any way you can continue to talk one on one. Asking for a number is hard for novices, so if you're in training I suggest going for his Facebook or email. Social network requests are innocent and casual enough to where you shouldn't fear rejection. Once you are in contact with him, go hard. If you see him post something randomly online, inbox him something sassy to spark his attention and lay the seeds that you may be into him. If it's late at night, inbox him teasing that his girl must not be around if he's bored online. Unleash your sex appeal and thirst trap him! I don't care if you're not that kind of girl, you have to act like it because the odds are stacked against you. Pretend as if you're playing a role as the villain, then give it all you have like you're Heath Ledger in *The Dark Knight*. A few days of flirting aggressively, being witty and talking dirty will reveal if he likes you or not. He may love his girl and keep it innocent, but I doubt it.

The next step is talking on the phone and meeting up to talk face to face. You will have to let him be sneaky for the first two weeks or so as he gets to know you. It's okay to let him creep off and call you because no man is going to leave a girl for someone he's only talked to a few times. Give him time to get to know you. This way both of you can see if it's worth pursuing. Remember, like any new guy in your life, you will over-like him at first. Take your time to get to know his story; don't just go after him based on looks and chemistry. Once you are sure he's right for you and want to take it to the next level, give him the ultimatum that it's either you or her. You already know their bond is weak off the strength that he's calling you on his lunch break instead of her. Once you win him over mentally, having him break that poor peasant girl's heart is the easy part. It's a hostile takeover, and there will be victims, but in the end, if you have a chance to own Netflix why would you continue to work at Blockbuster Video?

The entire notion of taking another girl's man is controversial because some women don't think it's right. Right is a direction, so who cares what anyone else thinks. This is real life, there are no boundaries, and the only rule is "Don't go after your friend's man!" Other than that, boyfriends of associates, co-workers, strangers, former classmates—those men are all fair game. Those girls aren't your actual friends, so why should they dictate whom you date? If you want someone, go after him! Do you think men respect the fact that you have a boyfriend? Guys see a taken girl as the ultimate challenge. There is no reason women can't use this same method when on the hunt for love. You're not going to go to hell or get seven years of bad luck. The worst that could happen is that a younger, sexier version of you pulls this same trick and takes your man when you start slacking. You are better than his girlfriend! Your heart pumps cheetah blood built from Athena DNA. There is no man who you can't take! That's what you have to believe in order for this to work. If some baggy-eyed girl who looks like she's been crying for the past two months shows up at your job calling you a home wrecker, I want you to look her dry coochie having, weak personality possessing, non-Spartan ass dead in the eye and say, "You're welcome. Because if it wasn't me, it would have been someone else."

SPARTAN LAW #2
SHE'S NOT A BFF SHE'S A SIDEKICK

There can only be two Spartans per group of friends. One will be the leader; the other is equally as powerful but lets the other take the lead...for now. The rest of those girls are followers. Being a follower isn't a terrible thing, Batman needs a Robin, Beyoncé needs a Kelly, and imagine how dysfunctional a crew of girls would be if there wasn't one to settle down the clucking and take charge when trying to decide where to go on a Saturday night. Most women play their position and never realize the balance of power is not in their favor. On each season of *The Bad Girls Club*, someone always makes the comment, "You don't belong in the house you're not a bad girl." Why would they put all boss chicks in one house? Those producers cast two alpha females and then surround them with weaker women who are easy to manipulate—that's brilliant TV. You attack with pawns because Queens are too valuable. In real life, it's the same way. Go to any club and you see Spartan #1, maybe Spartan #2, and the rest of those girls are pawns. Spartans will have their girlfriends on their clit harder than they will have a boy on their clit. She texts you all day, she wants to hang every weekend, and she complains when you're chilling with a new girl. She's not gay, she's been Spartan whipped. You are everything she wants to be but can't, so she has to settle for being your best friend in the world.

Girls pimp other girls. It's nothing new, but people never talk about this. There are women who can command car rides, never repay payday loans, borrow handbags for life, and even prostitute their weaker girlfriends to their male friends with a snap of a finger. As friends, you look out for each other, but there's a thin line between being supportive and being exploited. I remember wanting to take my platonic female friend's best friend out on a date, so I asked her about it first. My homegirl told me, "Don't waste your money taking her out. I'll tell her to fuck you." This girl was supposed to be her close friend; they were together five days out of the week, but at the turn of a dime, she feed her to the wolves. Personally, I love alpha females who are so charismatic that other girls sell their souls for the right to be in their inner circle. Some may think it's fake, but those girls are being true to their nature. The wolf is clearly a wolf. You're the thirsty ass who dressed her up like a sheep then cried victim when she brought the claws out like, "Duh, Spartan!" What's fake is to follow behind someone who's clearly using you because you want their approval. You're chasing behind an alpha and idolizing her because she's in control. You can't fault her for knowing how to use the power you covet.

There will always be Queen Bees and Worker Bees, but this isn't a caste system. You can rise the ranks and become one of those Spartan Queens. I want every woman reading this to evaluate the relationship she has with her circle of friends and determine where she falls. Are you the first phone call when shit goes down, or are you the one they conference in? Do you get invites to all of the hangouts or are you hit with the bullshit "Girl, I didn't think it would be your crowd." Of course, 10 out of 10 women are going to claim she's a boss or say some politically correct bullshit like, "We're all equals," but those odds don't add up. You don't have to admit it to me, or anyone else, so long as you know where you stand. If you're near the bottom it's time to rise and be on equal footing with that Queen or do what Kim Kardashian did with Paris Hilton, and separate from the hive in order to find your own Worker Bees to rule over. You may never rise up and become the Queen of Sparta, but you should strive to at least be the Duchess.

SPARTAN LAW #3
BITCH WITH A CAPITAL "B"

I read that the word "bitch" went through resurgence during the 80's because more and more women were becoming players in the corporate world. Bitch was meant to insult a woman who was domineering. Men in pants didn't like a woman in a skirt walking into the boardroom and being authoritative so the word "bitch" became fashionable again. Rap music has overused it, but I still see that term as being positive. If a man can be overbearing in order to get the job done, he's seen as a tough leader who's respected and feared by his peers. When a woman does the same thing, she's a bitch who's hated. Who cares? If I were a woman, I would legally change my name to Bitch because I would be just as assertive as the big boys. People are going to talk about you behind your back regardless if you're a sweetheart or a hard case. Are you going to make the guys at work cookies and let them smack your ass or are you going to embrace that role like a true Spartan and command respect? They may call you a bitch, but I guarantee they won't say it to your face because they fear you too much. I bet Oprah's a super bitch. For everyone who loves her, those who do business with her have to fear the power she wields. Empires are not built on hugs and smiles; they are built on fear. Fear lasts longer than love.

In the professional world, a woman doesn't have to sacrifice her gentle nature and act macho. It's better to mask your fangs with a smile. However, there are sacrifices that must be made in your personal life. Being Selfish = Being Successful. Love is not a stop sign; it isn't even a yield sign. Spartans don't choose dick over self. You have dreams and aspirations. Why should you sacrifice that because the man you love is on a different path? Men ask women to move across the country, pawn engagement rings, and do anything that's needed for the good of the team. If you want to go to grad school or take an internship, will he be there to support you in the same manner? It doesn't matter what his answer would be because you shouldn't arrange your life around a man. Love doesn't abandon love, but love will wait. If you have

98

moves you have to make to better your life, don't let some weak man guilt you about not being loyal, and don't let him hold you back. This is your life Spartan. Your destiny does not end with you getting a ring and popping out kids. Stop thinking about what others want; you have as much right to your goals as he does, and you always come first.

There's a book called *Why Men Love Bitches,* and while I have yet to read it, I think its success has a lot to do with the title. The idea that men pass up the typical sweet and submissive woman in order to be with the raging bitch is prominent in this society. Any time a woman can get a behind the scenes look at why she fails where other women have succeeded it sparks interest. Your inability to tame a man has nothing to do with not being a bitch in the jerk sense of the word. Strong men respect other men who compete as hard as they do, and take advantage of weak men who follow the leader or half ass their way through life. That same mindset also draws a strong alpha male to an alpha female. A woman who refuses to back down, is decisive about the things she wants, and speaks her mind freely will gain his respect. This idea that only a wimp or mama's boy would let a woman take the lead is propaganda. Being a bitch has nothing to do with being "mean" and everything to do with having a level of confidence that leads to authority. President Obama doesn't have a dainty first lady like JFK had; he has a strong woman who admittedly will argue her point of view when she feels Barack is wrong or being aloof. Men love being in control, but there are times when they are just winging it, and in that instant, it is crucial that a man has a friend, lover, and confidant who he trusts to take the lead. Those are the bitches men love.

SPARTAN LAW #4
ACT LIKE A LADY, THINK LIKE A HO

Where can you find all the good, successful, educated men? They're right there waiting for you to talk to them, but you don't like making the first move, so you let them come and go. Hos don't have that problem. Hos know that a closed mouth won't get fed, so they make it their business to keep their mouths open. If a ho sees a man who looks like he may be doing it big, she's going to go over and introduce herself. She can be the baddest chick in the lounge or the ugliest, either way she's not playing the wallflower game. Hos are aggressive and have no problem with walking over and making small talk because the mission is bigger than the possible rejection. Waiting for a sign doesn't exist in her world because every man is an opportunity to win. That kind of mentality may be fucked up when it comes to using people, but when you're a Spartan looking for love and not a come up, that mentality will erase the concept of failure and change your life.

When most men reach a level of success, they no longer feel the need to put themselves out there like a thirsty guy would. Mr. CEO isn't going to walk across the room and ask out a woman who could reject him. So what does he do? He waits for an obvious sign, an associate to introduce him, or simply moves on to the next woman who's showing clear interest because his ego can't risk rejection. You and a ho are both sitting by the bar, you have the same type of outfit on, and you're even cuter than she is. However, she's going to get Mr. CEO first because the fear of failure hasn't glued her to that seat. She's waits for an opening then springs out of her chair, ready to chat him up. You can sit, roll your eyes, and call her extra, but the reality is that you chose to let opportunity pass you by; she took it. You are both in need, yet you would rather downplay it for the sake of bullshit pride. Can you honestly say you don't want a well-dressed, handsome man with a career? If you don't want that, then why the hell are you out mingling in the first place? A ho is after a trick, a slut is after a dick, and a Spartan is after a partnership.

The old way of thinking was, "If a man is interested, he will make it known." Yeah, and the old way before that used to be the man with the strongest body odor in the cave would attract the most fertile females from the tribe. Evolution has changed the way men and women interact, and while there will always be guys who will approach you first, you can't box yourself into that waiting method for the sake of an outdated tradition.

Spartan up, go for what you want, and don't let insecurity convince you that you aren't his type or that you need to wait until after you loosen up with several drinks. The longer you wait, the more your nerves will intensify. Walk over and introduce yourself, flirt the way a ho would, but leave him wanting more. Work your charm, even pay for his drink once you finish talking, and then switch away. Not only will he call you that same night under the pretense that he wanted to make sure the number worked, he will call you every night afterwards because you just rocked his world. Making a bold first impression by doing that which few women are willing to do, will give you a head start to a man's heart. No matter how handsome or how powerful the man is, he's putty in your hands because you exude power and all men want power.

SPARTAN #5
CAN'T TAME A SPARTAN

Let's review your road to victory. You found the man you wanted, destroyed all obstacles in your way, and made him yours. Now your focus shifts from getting a man to keeping a man. Some say men like submissive women and women like to be dominated. Those are half-truths. Men love being in control, and getting their way makes them feel like kings. When the world at large pulls a man down to reality, having a woman at his disposal gives him a feeling of superiority. Men do like a woman to submit, but not without a fight. What keeps a relationship interesting is the battle of wills, and Spartans are no pushovers. Women like strength, a powerful man that gives them a sense of safety. From the husky linebacker with the petite girlfriend who cuddles up to him like a teddy bear, to the runway model who falls for the D-boy because his aggressive personality radiates dominance, the common denominator is power. Still, there has to be a balance. If you relinquish your power and give him complete control, the excitement ends. It is fine to let him take charge, but that is something that has to be earned by showing you he's just as strong as you are. In practical terms, arguments shouldn't be shouting matches but more like debates where you challenge him to prove that his way of doing something is better than yours and vice versa. That *Lion King*, Simba wrestling with Nala mindset is where the sexual, mental, and emotional chemistry becomes combustible, and it's during these debates for control that you will know that a Queen has found a strong and worthy King.

Meeting the man of your dreams can lull you into a sense of comfort; the more you love him and let him lead the way, the more dependent you become. The more dependent you become, the more you will believe you need him. Once you believe that he's irreplaceable, you become open to exploitation. Wonder Woman can take off her bracelets to make love, but she's still Wonder Woman. You don't have to be hard and tough 24/7. If your character is that of true strength, you don't need the armor of detached emotions. It is okay for Spartans to let down that guard and give into that feminine desire for a strong partner, but she will never let that man run her! Every relationship is different, and part of getting to know each other is understanding when to give in, when to stand firm, and when to compromise. Let a man be a man, but make it known that you are his woman, not his daughter and if you feel you're not getting that level of respect, remind him early and often. Money is another way men enslave women. The biggest mistake any woman can make is to become financially dependent. I hate reading emails about, "I can't leave him because he controls the money" or "I have no money to leave him." You came into the relationship with your own purse, and you have to keep it filled no matter how much money he has. Men get into the habit of buying gifts, paying for things, and then throw it in your face when you step out of line. Even strong women like to be treated like princesses, but don't get too comfortable. If he puts gas in your car or pays the light bill, it can easily flip into every argument ending with, "Don't I look out for you?" What does paying a bill have to do with staying out all night, or not returning a phone call? By deflecting the real issue and making it about how good of a man he is, it guarantees that he comes out smelling like roses. Independence doesn't stop once you form a partnership. There is a level of self-sufficiency that a

Spartan must maintain, even if it's done in secret. Never allow your livelihood to be tied to someone outside of yourself.

Can Spartans be dick-whipped? Of course, but they dare not let it show. Spartans battle good sex with good sex. If he's putting in work and making you cum, don't get dicknotized; coochitize him back. All women strive to keep their man content; Spartans piss on content and strive to keep her man constantly hard. Porn stars are actors. Not because they fake orgasms, but because they're acting out a male fantasy. They're telling him how big his dick is, how she's a dirty slut, where she wants his cum, etc... They are paid to be dominated because men want to beat off to submissive women. Think of yourself as his exclusive porn star every time you climb into that bed. You can be brilliantly filthy without demeaning yourself. Watch *Titanic*; Rose wasn't getting fucked in that car she was fucking Jack. You are not his pussy, he is your dick; know the difference. Don't lay on your back and get fucked, fuck back. Don't let him eat you out, you sit on that face and grind. Don't accept that he's tired, grab his penis, and get it hard by any means necessary! Too many women go to sleep without orgasms because their men are selfish. This is Sparta, not cumming is unsatisfactory, and you should not roll over and go to sleep without objecting—"You owe me one!"

Not all women have what it takes to be Spartans, and that's okay. If you aren't strong enough to be a Wonder Woman, take bits and pieces of these laws in order to become a better woman. Self-confidence, decisiveness, and having authority are key. If you take anything away from the Spartan code and apply it to your life, it should be those. This lifestyle is not about being mean, selfish, and bitchy. Being a Spartan is about reclaiming your role in this world. No longer will you allow your professional life to suffer because you fear some invisible hand is holding you back. No longer will you be the worker bee in your group of friends because you want to play nice. No longer will you shy away from a man because you don't know what to say to him. You are a Spartan, this world and everything in it is yours for the taking.

PART TWO:
MISTAKES WOMEN MAKE

"Success does not consist in never making mistakes
but in never making the same one a second time."
— George Bernard Shaw

11

Dating
VS.
Coming Over to Chill

There was a social media debate about $200 dates, and if that amount of money was too much to spend on a girl. The consensus I gathered from the men who weighed in was, "If I pay that much I better be fuckin that night!" That outrage not only speaks to the lack of value modern day men place on females, it proves there are entirely too many women spoiling men with cheap pussy. I'm not professing that you place a monetary value on your vagina, but there should be an investment on his part to prove that he is serious about you before he gets it. Time and energy are the biggest investment a man can make to show that his intentions are true, and his interest is real. If he puts in the time to come see you and focuses his energy on getting to know you, then that shows that he is committed to something. It could be getting sex, or it could be getting a girlfriend, it doesn't really matter initially, as long as he's showing that you have value. If a man values a woman, he respects her. Only from that respect can an authentic relationship grow.

One of the biggest complaints I hear is that there is no courting anymore. Everything would be perfect if the person you most liked made an effort to do all of the romantic things guys are supposed to do when trying to impress a woman. Why would any guy waste that energy when women cave in and give them whatever they ask for without even bothering to negotiate? Men figured out a long time ago that a woman who is thirsty for any kind of love is worse than a man who's thirsty for sex. No matter how loud you complain about not going out, never spending real time, or feeling unappreciated, if you like him enough, you will continue to talk to this kind of man. This guy is seemingly your only or best option, which leads to you being the one who sacrifices to make him happy. The fear that standing your ground will push him away is what keeps you from checking him.

The man isn't enamored with you in that same fashion, which means there is no fear. If he pushes you away, oh well…he was most likely going with the flow until he met a better woman anyway. Even if you complain about not being taken out, it will fall on deaf ears because he knows it's all bark and no bite. There are two types of men when it comes to not taking a female out. One is lazy, spoiled, and thinks you're bluffing. This type of man will duck a date with you until you put your foot down and prove that he is not your only option. The second is cocky, entitled, and doesn't value you at all. When it comes to this last type of man it's not about the amount of money he has to spend; it's about you being expendable. Therefore, if he has to choose a high priced meal or the threat of you saying, "Don't call me unless you're taking me out," he'll keep his money in his pocket and find some other woman who enjoys McRib more than Prime rib because you're nothing special.

WHY DATES MATTER

Let me break this down with a ho example, because hos always know their value. There is a Savvy Ho in this corner; she's cute, knows how to accentuate her positives, and bait men. In the other corner, there is a Classy Lady. She thinks she's classy because she has morals and doesn't care what a man has, only if he's nice to her. The Classy Lady meets a man, starts to talk to him daily on the phone, and after a week this feels real because the guy talks a good game. Classy Lady wants to see her new boo, and keeps asking when they're going to go on a date. The guy is too busy to go out to dinner and a movie, but tells her that she can come over any time after work. At first, she thinks maybe she shouldn't go over his house this early in a relationship; she's classy...but they talk every day and it feels as if she's known him forever. Classy Lady gives in to his offer to come over and chill, but promises herself that she's going to stay classy and not do anything sexual with him. Maybe she has sex with him, maybe she doesn't, but 9 out of 10 times, the battle is over. Once a guy knows you're a Come Over And Chill girl, he's going to have you coming over all the time until you have sex with him.

Once your "friend" gets his fill of that cheap vagina that he didn't have to work for, he'll get busy again and neglect you. This is the part where a woman will cry the victim, but she allowed herself to be played. You spent weeks if not months going over to his place, you talked about bullshit, accidentally met members of his family, and ignorantly believed he liked you for you. Remember, all of this he did from the comfort of his own home, around his schedule, on his terms. He wasn't dating you; he was penciling you in when he felt like it. Of course he's going to take you for granted. You have no value and slaved yourself for his affection! You can think you're different and that he's different, but go through the motions of being a come over and chill girl, and you will see for yourself that it hurts your long-term relationship goals.

Hang out in his bedroom, fuck like rabbits, have pillow talk about the future you two only have in theory...and repeat. After two or three months of coming over to chill your vagina will expire, your attitude will become more clingy and serious because you're falling for him, and the guy will begin to distance himself. His vanishing act will begin small; your "friend" will make an excuse as to why you can't come over this week. The next week he may have sex with you one last time, but he's weaning himself off, so it'll be quick and not include the usual hanging out and light conversation. A few weeks after that, the only communication from him will be in the form of brief text messages. A month later, you're going crazy, asking everyone's advice, and considering popping up on him to ask what you did wrong. I will tell you what you did wrong. You gave this man everything without once making him work for it. The Classy Lady just got played because she didn't value herself.

The Savvy Ho, on the other hand, isn't thirsty for love and will never be played in this form. The Savvy Ho is more concerned with getting into his pockets rather than getting a boyfriend. Savvy Ho meets the same guy as Classy Lady, but she's not going to come over and chill with him, she's going to tell him (hos always tell, never ask) to meet her at some swanky restaurant. She's going to eat and drink, play with his dick in the car, then leave while he's hard. The guy's turned on and full of confidence. She touched his dick on the first date, so in his "I'm a pimp" mind, he's confident that he can have sex with her the next time they go out. What happened was a classic case of misdirection. That entire first date was the ho using sex as bait to stroke his male ego and get this idiot open. The next date Mr. Fake Pimp will try to get her to chill at the crib because that's his environment. However, the Savvy Ho avoids the basic bitch house date and continues to get him out in public where she can spend his money and do her trick research to see if homeboy is cashing out or in the struggle financially. If he doesn't mind spending big on dates, it tells her he has money. She will keep seeing him, fuck his brains out after she gets a pair of shoes or a bag, and see what else she can get with her Pussy MasterCard.

The catch is that this Savvy Ho is secretly doing the same thing with one or two other potential sponsors, auditioning these men until she hits the jackpot. This is a far cry from how the Classy Lady operates; she focuses on one man at a time, blindly investing everything into a "friend" who she barely knows. Due to having other prospects, Savvy Ho isn't emotionally tied down to this man. If he's a broke dude who takes her on cheap dates or keeps offering to make her a home cooked meal, she will cut her losses, stop answering his calls, and move on to the next guy that is winning. This act ends up bruising the trick's ego because he thought he had her open after that first date, when in fact, he was the one on the hook. Hos are the reason men fear $200 dates and run the opposite direction when a girl asks, "Can you get my hair done?" because they probably were hustled or know a few dudes who were exploited by hos. I'm not saying follow that lifestyle; fucking for goods is an empty existence. Be a Spartan, which includes acting like a lady while thinking like a ho. A ho is smart enough to date multiple men in order to give herself the best trick options. You should date multiple men in order to give yourself the best romance options. A ho knows her value. It may be a ratchet Juicy Couture bag, or it may be a condo on South Beach; either way, she gets something. A lady of class has to know her worth too. Not the worth of her pussy, but the worth of her heart. It starts with getting a man to date you instead of taking you back to chill at his place.

THE COME OVER AND CHILL GIRL

If you see a commercial for Olive Garden and tweet, "I wish someone would take me out to eat," yet you have a "friend," you're losing. The guy friend you've been fucking on and off for months should be taking you out to eat, not the strangers on your timeline. If a man hasn't treated you to the movies since *Taken 1* came out, you're losing. Liam Nesson's found time to do ten movies and a sequel since then, and you couldn't find one guy who liked you enough to pay 3D non-matinee prices? Why are you settling for date night at a bum's crib that consists of hard dick, reheated Chipotle, and a bootleg Kevin Hart DVD? It blows my mind how a woman will get caught up with a user, let him put all kinds of mileage on her vagina, and she never even sees the inside of his car during the daytime. Stop losing!

You don't necessarily need extravagant date nights, but he needs to invest time and energy. He's investing time to talk a good game and get you open enough to come over, but where's the energy? The hardest part of relationships for lazy men isn't talking on the phone and playing the "I really like you" game. It's leaving his comfort zone to take you somewhere. A man doesn't want to be bothered with finding something to wear, gassing the car up, and thinking of somewhere to take you. It's not about his money; he doesn't want to exert that energy on you because he doesn't value you. He would rather spend most of the night doing shit he actually wants to do, then fit you in late at night when he's bored because you allow that behavior.

Some trailblazer had a genius idea years ago. He came up with the concept of "come over and chill" which is Latin for "You're not worth the effort, so come over, sit on the edge of my bed, watch Netflix, and drink this Peach Ciroc until you're tipsy enough to let me finger you." It's delivery pussy for the lazy man. Instead of spending money and leaving his comfort zone, he lures you over and puts the pressure of home field advantage on you, knowing that eventually you will give in. It doesn't sound like a great plan, but it works...over and over again. Right now, some girl is lonely and in like with a guy she met a week ago. All he has to do is make a strong case as to why coming over will be better than going out, and he's on his way to easy ass. A lonely woman thinks it's better to sit on the edge of a new guy's bed and get molested than it is to sit on the edge of her own bed and Facebook stalk her ex-boyfriend. Just because going over to chill is something to do, doesn't mean it's something you should do! Ask to go on a date. Better yet, steal a little bit of confidence from the hos and demand a date. Stop being happy just to have a man who likes you! Not only is he supposed to like you, he is supposed to court you. Your charisma should be so fucking electrifying that any guy who is privileged enough to go out on a date with you should be going out to buy new clothes, getting his car waxed, and scouring Yelp for the most romantic places he could take you on a first date. Quality women are earned, not given away for free. Don't let him take you for granted as if you're just another bitch. You are the Queen of Sparta, owner of a 24-karat vagina that these peasants aren't even worthy to smell. Show confidence and you will always be treated like quality!

You are a lady, not a ho, which means it's not about getting anything out of him except time and energy. He doesn't have to drop a lot of money on the date to show that he values you, it's the effort he's putting in, not the star rating on the restaurant that's most important. Don't buy into the excuse that, "We can get to know each other better if we're alone." No shit, but shouldn't he earn that right to be alone with you in the first place? Furthermore, don't accept his excuses about being busy. If he wants a woman of your stature, then he'll sacrifice time to make it happen. Stop letting these ordinary men tell you how busy they are. Mark Zuckerberg is busy, Barack Obama is busy, but they still find time to take their women on dates. He has time to come pick you up, take you back to his crib, and spend two hours trying to fuck, then he has time to take you out on a real date. Demand respect, know your value, and stop going over to chill.

THE ONLY OPTION IS NOT THE BEST OPTION

This woman wrote me an email trying to figure out a way to tell her "friend" that she wanted to go out and do things. They hadn't gone on an official date since the first week they started talking. At the heart of the problem was the fear that if she were too pushy he would cut her off. Welcome to the wonderful world of, "A shitty option is better than no option." If a woman hasn't had a guy approach her in months, she begins to think something is wrong with her. When a guy who is her type finally comes around, she falls hard. He may not take you anywhere, and you may be bored and frustrated 80% of the time, but it's better to be talking to this lame than to be out in the club hoping someone comes over and asks your name. Wrong!

Women always have options. You like him, he's witty, and he's handsome. That's three stars. On the other hand, all he wants to do is smoke and chill. He claims not to want a relationship, yet you're always over his crib giving it up like your body is his exclusively. To top it all off, he only makes time to do things he wants to do. That's three strikes. Do the pros outweigh the cons? Do you like this man because he treats you good, or do you like him because he's the only guy around to treat you at all?

I understand that it can be hard for some women to find an attractive guy who has the nerve to ask them out, but that is no excuse for handcuffing yourself to the first man that asks for your number. Don't sell yourself cheap because you like his complexion and think he's funny. You can find someone more hilarious and twice as handsome if you Spartan up. Don't take up for his laziness by claiming you're a homebody that prefers to chill anyway. You know damn well you would jump at a chance to do something exciting if he offered it up. Even homebodies like to get out to Six Flags occasionally. If the dog from *Lady and the Tramp* had his bitch eating Italian, a grown ass man can afford to take you out of the neighborhood. If you start a relationship by making it easy for him, then he will always treat you like a cheap date. Why should he change when being lazy and not doing shit for you has gotten him this far? Don't wait until you're at your breaking point to leave him alone. The moment you feel like he's not putting time and energy into making your friendship grow into something more, rectify it or move on. Being by yourself is always a better option than being devalued.

I remember being cursed out by a girl I was seeing, and it really opened my eyes to how females wait until the very end to voice their concerns. This girl, let's call her Gia, had been distant the last time she came over to chill with me. We ended up not having sex due to her attitude, which seriously pissed me off because she lived pretty far for me to be transporting her for company alone. Gia called when I got home and asked why I didn't take her out anymore, complained that I don't make her feel pretty, and said she was sick of crying every time I dropped her off. It blew my mind at first, but I had to be honest with myself and let the truth in. I didn't want to take her anywhere; all I wanted was to hit it when I was bored. In the words of the poet Onika Maraj, "If she ain't trying to get it, then she get dropped off." We had fun, she was pretty as all hell, but something was missing that I couldn't put my finger on. She wasn't girlfriend material in my eyes, so it was dick and DirecTV for her.

As much as I liked Gia, I didn't value her at all. Instead of being a man, and telling her after the first few weeks it wasn't going anywhere, I continued to gas her head up and use her for what I wanted. Not once did I think about what Gia wanted until I was confronted on the phone that night. Here was a girl that looked like the chicks MC's rap about, sweet and polite as she can be, and I was being a jerk, holding her back from being with a man who would have worshipped the ground she walked on. I'm glad she stood up for herself and put her foot down because she helped me become a better person. After her, I never treated a woman like that again. A man will take advantage of you for as long as you will let him because it doesn't feel like he's doing anything wrong by having you come over and chill. When beginning any new relationship no matter how serious it is or isn't, know your worth, and demand to be more than a Come Over And Chill Girl.

12

Loser Lover

I have my own place, nice car, and no kids. Men should want me, but why don't they? There is a misconception that because a woman is independent and doing well that a man would choose her over a broke chick who lives at home with her mother and has two bastard children. Here is the reality check: Bum bitches stay winning because the average man could care less about a woman's net worth. Common sense would dictate that all men should strive to have a relationship with a woman with ambition and a career, but that's rarely the case. Guys don't want to have sex with the girl with the green eyes because she has a Benz; they want to have sex with her because of how she looks. I call this the Cinderella Effect. In the story of *Cinderella*, the Prince passed up all of these wealthy and classy women for one who spent all day scrubbing floors for her stepmother. Those jealous women were quick to point out that his object of lust was just some dirty ratchet chick who only got clean for the evening, but in the end the Prince didn't even see that as a negative! Men don't care where you come from; they are more concerned with how sexy you looked when you walked into that room. Men hunt for trophies, not financial equality, which means Cinderella wins because she looks the best.

So why can a man fall in love with a loser and live happily ever after but a woman can't? Women need more than a pretty face to be truly happy. There remains an old school need for a male provider, one who does what a man is supposed to in terms of bread winning. Even independent women who wear the pants and pay the bulk of the bills expect their man to be able to stand on his own feet. I've heard so many stories from women who have been with guys for years, and their main complaint isn't cheating, it's that their men aren't doing anything with their lives career wise. If a guy fucks you and never calls, you learn and become a wiser person. If a man pops in and out of your life using you, eventually you will smarten up and stop being his timeshare. However, to be crazy in love with a guy who is content with being at the bottom financially is a situation that will play on your maternal need to help him, sucker you into his excuse that it's the world against him, and brainwash you into accepting that it's your job as his girlfriend to be Captain Save-A-Bro. He's not a bad man, just one without a future, and trying to hang in there and be supportive will eventually pull you down to his level. Your boyfriend will tell you that he loves you, he will marry you, and he will give you kids, but he will also stay at the same pay level, waste money on dumb shit, and blame others for his lack of success until the day he dies. To love a man with no ambition or drive is like having an adult kid who refuses to move out of the basement. Is that seriously the person with whom you want to spend the rest of your life?

Let's forget all the superfluous rules like, "He has to be yay tall and without kids," and get to the most significant question every woman in the world should ask before they agree to go on a date: Is he gainfully employed? The #1 way to prevent falling in love with a loser is to recognize what kind of person he is before you become involved romantically. If he's not going to school, (I'm talking full time; not taking one class at community to keep his mother off his back) then he should have a J.O.B. *No Romance Without Finance* should be tattooed above your vagina, so you never forget this simple yet effective rule. I don't care how cute you think he is or what excuse he gives you as to why he's not working, a grown man who relies on favors, handouts, or old lawsuit money to live isn't going anywhere in life. How are you going to explain to your friends that you can't go on that cruise because your boyfriend is almost out of the money he won in a car accident 14 years ago? Girls talk about, "I do this for my man, I do that for my man, I'm a good woman," but what the fuck is your man doing for you besides half eating your coochie and taking you to McDonalds once a week?

It's not about how much money he is making right now, it's about him working toward making more in the near future. If he has potential as a boyfriend, that should mean he has potential to be a husband. You can't raise a family on the money from a nonexistent rap career or invention idea that he has no idea how to invent. There is always a job available, but most dudes think they are too good to flip burgers or stock shelves. The people who are too good for those jobs are called "college educated," and if he was too lazy to get a higher education or learn a trade, then he can't complain about entry-level positions. *The economy is bad...* is the most bullshit excuse in the world. How can he complain about the economy when he has on new Jordan's and preorders PS3 games? The economy can't be that bad if his ass is giving money to Nike and Sony. If you let a man think it's okay to be lazy and feed into his conspiracy theory that the Republicans, Illuminati, and haters are holding him back from filling out applications, then you're just as dumb as he is. Women need to start telling these clowns like my wife told me a long time ago, "I cost!"

A FOOL & HIS MONEY

You can tell a lot about a guy by the way he manages his money. Some idiots actually think Rick Ross[12] is a financial advisor, and will splurge the little money they have on black gold chains, foam posit sneakers, and top shelf liquor. One of my boys hit me up, and told me that a mutual friend of ours was going to use his tax return money to buy a summer home. This fool doesn't even own

---

[12] Also known as, The Boss, Rick Ross is a Miami rapper known for vivid lyrics boasting of luxurious lifestyles and wealth.

a year-round home! Losers will brainwash themselves into thinking they deserve to buy the same shit men of means buy because they want to live the life MC's rap about. If you have a boyfriend that you know is only making a certain amount of money, don't go Ray Charles and pretend you don't see him blowing his money on stupid things. *I don't want to seem like I'm counting his money.* Count that shit! Obviously, he needs help budgeting; so help your man.

Last week he was borrowing money from you to get an oil change…come pay day this idiot is buying ounces of Kush, every flavor of Ciroc, and a fitted hat to match those pair of kicks he doesn't even wear. Something isn't right mentally. If you've taken on that role as his girl, then you need to stop holding him down in ways that encourage his irresponsibility. Instead of saving him when he's in too deep, teach him how to swim so he doesn't have to constantly beg you for salvation. Point out the obvious lack of saving going on. If he tries to take you out to a fancy dinner and you know damn well AT&T has been calling for that iPhone data money, tell him to spend it on his bills. A man has pride, and he will want to share the wealth with the woman he loves to prove that he is a provider. However, if you know he is living paycheck-to-paycheck, skip Ruth's Chris and make him put it in the bank.

BUSINESS IDEA, NO BUSINESS PLAN

Everyone and their mother has an idea for a business that can make them rich—that's a good thing. Most of those people don't know the first thing about making their idea a reality—that's a bad thing. There is a lemonade stand mindset that guys have that makes them constantly tryout these asinine hustles. A little kid wants to earn money, but doesn't feel like waking up early to deliver newspapers, so he starts a lemonade stand. That's genius and progressive at age seven. However, a grown man can't just open up a lemonade stand in front of his crib, a legitimate business needs a plan, financing, marketing, etc... If your boyfriend comes to you with some idea for a line of women's jeans because he saw how much money Nelly made off Apple Bottoms, don't jump for joy. First, think about where he's going to get the money to produce these jeans, think about where he will sell them, and finally ask yourself, "What the hell does he know about women's fashion?" If your boo doesn't know the difference between LLC and INC., odds are he's not about to become the next Russell Simmons. This doesn't mean you have to shoot his dream down, it's proof that you need to help him become more business minded. Help educate him on what it will take to make his business work and don't back down when he yells, "I know what I'm doing, girl!" Ego will make him think he is just as smart as these people on TV getting rich quick, but those people didn't get rich quick, it took years that weren't publicized.

As his woman, be the logical one and steer him to make decisions that are practical. Be careful when investing your own money or the money of your friends into your boo's venture. Everyone knows someone who was caught up in one of those pyramid schemes. Selling Acai Berry juice or timeshares to a dozen friends in hopes of becoming a millionaire isn't a terribly bright idea no matter how many company statistics your boyfriend tries to shove in your face. Even if the scheme sounds legit, you should still be strong enough to keep your man away from your friends and family. If he borrows money from your folks, he's not going to be the one they're going to call for a return on investment—you are. Above all, do not bankroll his business idea yourself. I know how women pretend to be broke but have nest eggs for rainy days. Your boyfriend wanting to open up a kiosk in the mall is not a rainy day, so do not dig deep in your purse, and help him to pay for the first three months' rent. It takes years of losses for most businesses to turn a profit—years! Don't give in, don't apologize; educate him, and then let him put in the work to make his dream come true. If he's on the right path, maybe cosign a business loan and take partnership, but even then make sure you are doing it because you believe in the business, not out of love.

EXCUSES DON'T PAY THE RENT

I used to try to play my mother when I was in elementary school. I would go in the bathroom and pretend to throw up so I wouldn't have to go to school. That worked maybe twice, and then she said, "You'll feel better when you get to school. Move your ass." Losers are like little kids, they make excuses as to why they can't do something because they know it gives them a pass. *My man is very hardworking, but he's going through a hard time emotionally and hasn't been working since his grandmother passed*. Bitch please, his grandma died a year ago, and when she was around he only called her to borrow money. These guys will give you all kinds of falsified diagnoses as to why they aren't as ambitious as they should be. Bi-polar, depression, the pizza burnt the roof of his mouth. The little kid in them makes them think they can bullshit their way to easy street. The astounding thing is there are a large number of women who accept it. "At least he's not cheating on me or running the street like Tanya's boyfriend, and he does go help his cousin move furniture on the weekend." Stop being content with the fact that your man is not cheating or gooning, and start expecting a lot more from a boyfriend than the ability to not be a criminal. Comparing your boyfriend to the worst-case scenario instead of comparing him to the average or even above average men in this country is such a basic bitch concept. Instead of pointing to some drug addict who treats his woman like shit and patting yourself on the back for not being in her shoes, how about you point to the guy who pulls up to a restaurant in his Bentley and opens the door for his wife. What's the difference between that woman and you? She wanted more.

Do you seriously want to marry a man who only works weekends and is paid under the table? Do you want to raise kids with someone who is going to teach his children that it's better to slip on a floor and get a settlement, than it is to climb the corporate ladder? Take your titty out of your boo's mouth, and tell him to have goals that don't involve getting signed to Def Jam! You're out there working two jobs, and he's sitting at home making an excuse as to why he can't find one—that dick must be magical for you not to see his illusion. Taking care of a man isn't romantic or sexy. Any woman with self-respect isn't going to let a grown ass man live off her, cry about life, then scream at her because things aren't going his way. You fell in love with him for his personality not his pockets, but that doesn't mean you can't demand growth. If you genuinely love him, push him to be the man you know he can be, but never allow him to drag you down by continuing to be the loser he's become accustomed to being.

13

Are You Being Played?

Since I started BGAE, I have received hundreds of emails from women not only seeking advice, but from those looking to share their unique experiences as well. This girl— let's call her Kay, met this guy—let's call him Jay. Jay was a polished and professional business owner, but despite his lavish lifestyle, she didn't get open off the wining and dining. She dated Jay for four months, and during that time, she fell for him hard. She thought enough time had passed that she could let down her guard and have sex with him…and then this happened:

> Last Thursday, we went to one of my favorite restaurants. I had a great time. I was feeling it. He knew it too, and knew when we got back to my place it was about to go down. (I mean I hadn't had sex in four months!) So he dropped me off at the door and "went to look for a parking spot." I came upstairs to my apartment and waited to buzz him back in. It took a little longer than usual but street parking is ridiculous here, so it didn't seem too suspect. Anyway, he rang the bell and I buzzed him in.
>
> Fast forward, we started fucking like rabbits. About 20 minutes in, he stops and says, "Babe you hear something at the door?" And I say "no. " But he stops to "go check it out" and comes back, says he didn't see anything, and we keeping going…

> When we were done, I got up to grab some water and I notice that ALL of my electronic shit is GONE: MacBook, iPad, iPhone, iMac, camera...The only thing left was the big ass TV mounted on my wall. I WAS ROBBED. I looked at my door, there was no forced entry but it was unlocked. So immediately I thought, his dumb ass came to check the door when we were fucking and forgot to lock the door, then some bold nigga took the opportunity to rob me.
>
> I called my best friend who stays across the hall to see if he saw anything. When I described the night, he was alarmed because when I told him about *** parking the car and coming up for us to have sex, he said it seemed strange because he saw *** coming into the building with two of his brothers. He thought I was having one of my usual house gatherings and that I invited all three of them over. So I'm guessing you've already came to the conclusion: yep, when that nigga stopped to "check out the sound heard at the door" he was really just unlocking the door for his brothers to come in to steal my shit while I was getting dicked down. Nigga was fucking me and stealing from me SIMULTANEOUSLY!!! The first time I fuck him, he robs me blind...

The crazy thing is that this guy isn't an anomaly, but the norm. Her story is extreme, but every day a relationship ends with a robbery. Kay had her iPad taken, but most women have their dignity, trust, and sometimes virginity taken by scum like Jay. Don't get me wrong, there are women that use and abuse men as well, but men can hold their hats on, "at least I had sex." No woman is going to look back on being suckered with a smile because no penis is worth feeling stupid. "Only dumb bitches get caught up" is boldface lie #6. Right now, there are thousands of intelligent women being set up by men who aren't half as smart as they are. How is this possible? Is it the sex, the looks, or maybe these guys are criminal masterminds? I'm convinced that 98% of these heartbreakers aren't Keyser Söze[13]; they're regular guys

---

[13] Keyser Söze is the brilliant antagonist from the film *The Usual Suspects*.

who have one critical attribute—The Bullshit Factor.

The Art of Bullshit isn't about how good your lie is it's about how convincingly you tell that lie. Female Hos sell sex. Male Hos sell dreams. If a man is in predator mode, he will approach a girl that he finds promising, size her up, get to know her, and then use that knowledge to exploit her main weakness. If the girl is broke, she will get open once the player tells her how well off he is financially. If the girl is an intellectual, she will get open once she sees that the player is extremely well read. If she's ratchet, she will probably bust it open once the player buys her a bottle of Moscato and talks in depth about *Love & Hip Hop Atlanta*. Not all men are fascinating, rich, and intelligent, so they have to fake it until they make it by exaggerating or flat out lying. "I'm Jim. I work at Macy's, and I share an apartment with my brother," isn't going to make any panties moist. Therefore, it becomes, "I'm James. I'm a buyer for a major retailer, and I'm staying with my brother while I shop for a new condo." This James looks a lot more promising than broke Jim. He's not making up a fantastic lie; he's merely stretching the truth like Gabby Sidibe in a pair of S/M boy shorts in order to get your phone number. Once he wiggles into your life, he then tests the waters to see exactly what you are looking for in a man. From here, he goes about creating a fantasy of himself that coincidentally fits all of your wants...wow. That right there is how players game you.

WHY MEN PLAY GAMES

Sex, money, and lodging are the top reasons a man will play a girl. Sex is obvious; all males are after that, even the nicest ones. Most women will tell you that they know when a man is merely after sex and that they are player proof. Ha! While you can put up your reality distortion field and try to convince yourself that you know the signs of a pussy hunter from those of a man who is genuinely interested in you, the average woman only knows the generic and basic signs of an amateur player. Veteran players have a much more complex bullshit factor than a thirsty dude has. Thirsties can't keep from saying something freaky, they constantly ask you to come over and chill, and trick on you as if you're a ho. Helen Keller could see through that kind of weak ass game. A veteran player who treats sex like a chess game and enjoys the hunt more than the actual penetration is willing to deal with waiting and rejection while he figures out the puzzle to your pussy. In the same fashion, a man who is after money or searching for lodging will also hang in there for the long run as well. These veteran players tend to confuse women by feeding into their limited understanding of "game." Most females believe that a man who sticks around has proven himself, but for players that's a false notion that they thrive on. By hanging around way past the fling stage, these players are making it seem as though there is something substantial between the two of you. In actuality they are doing what Jay did, lulling you into a sense of comfort so they can rob you blind.

Money isn't the root of all evil, not having it is. Therefore, bum men will *Don Juan Demarco* their way into a woman's heart if he suspects that she is naïve. Getting money from women isn't as easy as getting money from a man, and it takes a person fluent in bullshit to pull it off on a large scale. This usually begins when the player sells the girl on himself and all the big things he is doing, then slowly he asks for help, always promising to pay her back double what she gives him. The first few times a player will indeed pay your loan back. It's all game; he's building faith so he can get deeper into your pockets. You let him hold a hundred dollars; he gives you back the hundred and takes you out to dinner. You don't feel guilty about helping your man because he's looking out for you as well…at first. Next time it's "…oh shit my car is in the shop, can I hold five hundred?" Finally, the player is ready for the big hit. He calls in real trouble because he doesn't know how he's going to come up with three thousand dollars to get him out of a bind. Having already proven that he pays back his debt, you go to bat for this man. You don't have that kind of money, so you're calling family members, asking for a G a piece that you will pay back by the end of the month. Once you get the player that money, this bum realizes this is probably the highest amount he will be able to hustle from you, so it's time to escape and move on to the next woman. This type of loser is sneaky; he won't simply vanish. In order to avoid repayment, the player will create some fake argument in order to break up with you, and then disappear. Not only is your love life gone, so is that money, and your family is now talking shit behind your back about how you're a silly bitch. It doesn't feel like you were played because you two were together for months, but the writing was on the wall the first day he borrowed money. That man saw you as means to an end, never a true girlfriend.

Lodging is the hustle no one talks about, but it's become the most prevalent because it allows a player to get the sex and the money while a woman is putting a roof over his head. Remember when moving in with someone was a huge deal? Today, men are quick to default on their lease as soon as they pull a girl who has her own place. Moving in isn't out of love or a want to be with you 24-7; many times it is just convenient. It starts as temporary then he never leaves, but you don't mind because you get to play housewife without a ring. The key word is "play." Until you have a ring on your finger and he's paying an equal share of the bills, you're only living out the fantasy. There is a huge difference between moving in together and him moving in with you. I know several guys who live rent-free, play video games during the day, don't clean, and wait for play wifey to come home and cook. If you two are going to live together, it should be equal. This means splitting bills, chores, and not using the person you love as *The Help: Next Generation*.

Regardless of his true objective, be it sex, money, or a place to crash, once a player gets his fill or the victim begins to see past the bullshit, he makes up an excuse to end the relationship or flat out vanishes. The player learned what worked and what didn't, and now he's off to play the game again with a new girl. Meanwhile, you're left behind trying to figure out what went wrong with a guy you genuinely thought liked you. No matter how honest you think that person is, figure out what he wants from you! Take those rose-colored glasses off, get over the butterflies of having a boyfriend or friend who tells you that you're special, and ask hard questions when getting to know him. That girl Kay who was robbed, had her guard up from being hurt in her previous relationship. She was defensive and cynical, but Jay was patient and attentive, which eventually softened her up for the big hit. You can't defend against a player as you would defend against the run of the mill thirsty guy. Thirsty men are not trying to play you; they're trying to have sex, as soon as possible. Players are more suave than thirsties. They don't have a timetable because they're investing in something bigger than one nut.

He hasn't even pressured me for sex he's a good one! Let go of that outdated method of thinking and realize that men know you think that way. It's reverse psychology ladies, and it plays on your "shit don't stink" ego. A player gasses you up to think it's your personality or looks that attracted him, when in reality it's your money, sex, or lifestyle that he wants a piece of. Time does not bond you, communication does! You and another person can be trapped in a coal mine for five days, but if you are not willing to open up to that other person, they won't be calling after you're free to see how you're doing. The lack of communication has made you two as close as strangers. If you had poured your life story out to that other person while trapped, then they would have become invested and considered you like family after you escaped. Deep conversation is how you bond with someone! Players don't open up; they let you talk about your family, your job, your likes, and dislikes. They're researching you, not talking to you. Players will talk about themselves, but they won't go beneath the surface because the first rule of playing someone is don't get too close to your mark. Jay spent four months getting to know Kay, but Kay never truly knew who that guy was beyond the basics. Talking to someone and talking with someone are two different experiences, and communication is a two-way street in a legit relationship.

KNOW THY SELF

You think you're beyond being played because you're smart, you look good, and had older brothers that knew the game. Then why are you going through the pain of heartbreak? You have to know your weaknesses. When a player sizes up a girl, he looks for certain signs. Therefore, you have to know where you're vulnerable first before he capitalizes. Physical insecurity is often the first thing a player goes for because how you look often determines how you behave. I know a few heavyset women who had low self-esteem, and because of this, they allowed handsome men to come in, sweet-talk them, and get in their pockets. Being a healthy woman shouldn't make you desperate. These assholes are going for the stereotype, "fat girls will do anything for their men because they can't get anyone else." Don't play into that trap. If you have esteem issues, you have to face them in order to turn that negative into a positive. I will tackle the specifics of physical appearances in the coming chapters, but for now, agree to be honest with yourself and contemplate if your physical shortcomings are an issue that leave you open for exploitation.

For other women, their flaw could be loneliness. They have a Rapunzel complex where life has been hard, and they desperately want a prince to come save them from their current situation. Single Mom's, reformed hos, and girls on the rebound from a long-term relationship all fall into this category. A player will analyze you, see that life has beat you down, or that men have hurt you, and then throw on his Superman cape to fake save you with his grand promises. Every woman has an issue that could make her susceptible to being played. It's your job to seal those holes, and not jump for joy when a man seems as if he's the missing piece to your puzzle. No man can make you whole, if you're broken then that's a repair job that has be done from the inside out, never from the outside in. Check your thirst for love and affection at the door, know what aspects of your life you feel dissatisfied with, and be mindful of those things when getting to know men, if he's a player he will pick up on those weak vibes.

KNOW THY ENEMY

Your boyfriend had another girlfriend all this time. The love of your life suddenly changed his phone number and vanished. Your husband has another family complete with kids and a dog. This isn't created by the producers of *The Maury Show*; this is real life for many women. How do you stop yourself from being played in the first place? The easy and unrealistic answer is, "Don't trust men." No, that's how you find yourself bitter and in debt from therapy. Education is power. Treat any guy you date like an SAT Prep book and study that bastard as if your future depends on it because it does. You meet a guy; he talks a good game, cool. Now over the course of the next few weeks cross-examine his ass. Any reputable job checks the background references of their potential hires. Treat your vagina like it's the most sought after job on the market, and check that man's credentials. Men aren't going to want to give out personal details if they're trying to play you. They want to stay mysterious; that makes it easier to escape when the shit hits the fan. When you attempt to get close, players will make you feel guilty about interrogating them. Don't get caught up in that reverse psychology trick of, "Let's worry about us right now, not me back then." A girl that doesn't dig for information is a girl that's waiting to be fucked over.

There are only so many lies a man can tell before that shit collapses like a house of cards. A lie built on top of a lie isn't going to hold up for two or three months, keep asking him hard questions and eventually cracks will begin to form if he's not legit. "I knew something was funny about the things he was telling me," is a quote from a girl who told me that she was played. If your intuition is screaming that something is off, then why didn't you check his bullshit when your brain raised that red flag? Common sense is a better superpower than x-ray vision. Stop being blinded by good looks or fast talk, and start fingerprinting these clowns. Being nosey is annoying, but it's better to be annoying than to end up a sucker. Knowing his full name, where his mother lives, and his Facebook password doesn't make you his girl. Everything you think a man should do to prove himself to a girl he likes, he knows you're checking for and is three steps ahead of you. A player will do all the little things women put stock into just to appease, and you have to be mindful of that. A man that's really down for you goes the extra mile without you having to ask, he gives much more than he takes, and his life story is an open book. Listen to your brain, not your heart, and always question his motives. If you think you're being played by the man you're with, then chances are you've already been played.

14

Dating the Same Types

Why do I keep meeting broke men? All the men I attract turn out to be losers. Why do the good-looking ones always hurt you? Where can I go to meet a good man? Finding a man is akin to curing cancer for most women. Black women are especially frustrated, as the pool of educated, funny, humble, good looking, non-baby mama having, black men appears to be smaller than Ja Rule's fan base. There is an entire "Black Men Ain't Shit" movement where some black women, disappointed with the eligible bachelors, slander their own race. Ironically, this slander is followed by those same women continuing to date those same men...um, that's like me saying Taco Bell tastes like dog shit before pulling into the Taco Bell drive thru to place an order. The backlash against these women who complain and then stick with those no good men has turned black women into a caricature. There is this angry black woman stereotype of the hand on the hip, eye rolling, Taraji P. Henson from *Baby Boy*, woman who just can't win...nor wants to win. Black men look at these women as drama queens who just need to be dicked down, and then they'll shut up. These stereotypical black relationships are more tragic than funny because it isn't just Tasha Mack from *The Game* or Yvette from *Baby Boy* fantasy roles, real women act this way too, and there is no director around to yell, "Cut!"

Despite being mocked and parodied constantly, some women still live out that ratchet romance, but when the drama occurs, they place all the blame on the race of the man she was laid up with, not the choice she made to give that man her heart. All men have asshole qualities. To say, "black men ain't shit," tells me that you haven't dated anyone else. Women of other races refer to these guys universally as "jerks." Asian, Caucasian, Klingon, you name it; if you log onto Facebook you will see a woman broken up over a man who played her. Never will you see them proclaiming, "Chinese men ain't shit" or "Indian men ain't shit," all races have "ain't shit" representatives who suffer from the type of immaturity that makes them want to play women until they get what they want, and then dump their asses.

Is there something in male genes that makes all of them horrible and untrustworthy, or is this a result of women ramming their heads against the same brick wall by dating the same type over and over again? Surely if you can find one man who is not a dog, that disproves the statement, "All men are dogs." Hundreds of thousands of non-dogs live in this reality, so you have to accept that old belief as ignorance. Once you accept that old belief as ignorance, you now must take a survey of the type of men you keep falling for. Ask not only the reason you attract these unworthy men, ask why you are attracted to them as well. There is an old joke that goes like this: "Doctor, my arm hurts when I do this." The man raises his arm in a strange position. The Doctor replies, "Then don't do that." That sums up the advice most women who find themselves constantly heartbroken need to take. If you line up all the serious men you have dated, I bet the ones that hurt you all have major things in common. If history shows you that guys with those traits are no good for you, take the doctor's simple advice—don't fucking do that!

Every woman wants to find a good man, but what does that actually mean, describe a "good" man? Is he someone who doesn't commit murder or drown kittens or is this referring to someone who will say all the things you like to hear, do all the things you like to do, and look exactly the way you want him to look? One woman told me she wanted a man who's successful, not living paycheck to paycheck, and could afford to take vacations twice a year. That's understandable, but add on the traits you want externally because unless he's stepping out of a Bentley, how he looks is how you will decide if he's worth your time initially. Let's say that a Jewish girl wants an Italian stallion with a six-pack. She sees a guy who's acting *Jersey Shore* stereotypical at the bar, but his looks make her overlook his gross behavior. I'm willing to bet that if that juicehead asks for her number or attempts to make out, she's going to follow what her eyes like, not the list of "good man" qualities her heart desires. A black woman can claim to be non-ratchet in her desires for a quality professional man, yet appearance wise she's after a guy who looks like Chief Keef, but with 2 Chainz swagger. Unless you specifically date an entertainer or athlete, you are not going to find a professional African American male that walks around with neck tattoos, dreads, a Gucci belt, and has legal means of employment. It's time to stop putting the blame on the ignorant men you keep spreading your legs for, admit that you tend to go for style over substance, and take responsibility for associating with these dirt bags in the first place.

GET OUT OF THE HOOD

People tend to segregate themselves, creating a subconscious divide not much different from the pre-Civil Rights era. What starts as hanging with those you're comfortable with, ends with you only hanging around those that look and act similar to the way you look and act. Let's start with blacks, they tend to live in segregated pockets of the city, party within those same pockets, and date within those same pockets. While there are wealthy black communities, they don't come close to equaling the amount of hoods. While there are many distinguished events hosted and presented by African Americans, they don't come close to the amount of hip-hop nightclubs in any given city, nor do they radiate the same exciting vibe as what my Asian friend calls, "the black club." Being born into this pocket is no excuse for sticking to the script and staying in this pocket. Four straight relationships has yielded two drug dealers, one mama's boy, and a guy that thought *John Madden Football* was an occupation. If you're always meeting broke men, then you're in places broke men inhabit. I'm in Antarctica, why do I keep meeting penguins…it's such a mystery! You know damn well that when you see three liquor stores and two churches on the same block that you've entered Brokeville. Basic men do not travel more than ten miles from where they rest. If you live in the nice townhomes two miles from the projects and keep seeing a guy at McDonalds that you think is cute, chances are he's from those projects. If he's at the same local happy hour bar as the WIC ratchets rocking a Rolex, common sense should tell you that it's too good to be true. Take off your basic bifocals and stop thinking that because he has on Air Jordans and a pristine fitted hat that he drove down from his mansion to shop at the local EBT supermarket and happened to bump into you. He's from up the block just like you are.

Let's say you're a woman with a degree, a blooming career, and looking to save money to get out of the hood. You're going places, so why would you continue to date from the same pool of men as the project chicks? "Why can't I find a rich man?" Because rich men don't hang where you hang! If you fish in the sewer, you can't complain about not catching salmon; branch out and take your ass to a lake. That's not a call for you and your friends to scrape up $600 for a bottle in VIP, that's only going to attract fake ballers who did the same thing you and your friends did. The solution is to get out of those segregated pockets and explore the more diverse and cultured parts of your city where the professional men shoot pool or listen to jazz. I'm not saying you can't find a diamond in the hood, but it's always better to play the percentages. If you continue to shut out the rest of the city because you have an obsession with thugs, you only have yourself to blame when you end up living paycheck to paycheck, raising a child alone, or visiting him in prison—you chose that type of man.

This isn't just a smack on the head for blacks and Latinas. I've seen white women with the world going for them segregate themselves and do the same thing. It may not be the thuggish guy that makes their hearts flutter, but the lost puppy hipster type who looks like a dirty Adam Levine. Don't lie to yourself, the "bad boy" vibe turns you on, but how much longer can you waste precious time on pointless projects? I've had a few different white friends who were un-dateable on paper, spoiled, pill problem, Peter Pan complex...and ironically each one found some girl that wanted to save him. It's not a woman's job to save a man. Undisciplined white girls love the Jesse from *Breaking Bad* types just as much as undisciplined black girls love the Stevie J from *Love & Hip Hop* types. Women from various cultures have one thing in common, this notion of, "I can fix him." If you did fix him, he would cease being the type of guy you wanted in the first place. You're attracted to the mess, turned on by the attitude, and feel a sense of accomplishment as you try to transform him. You raise kids, not men! If you say you want change, make that change internally by letting go of the superficial lust you have for the "bad boy" or "swag king" types you're accustomed to dating. He turns you on—big deal! Discipline your pussy! Once you have learned to discipline your attraction for those personalities that have burnt you in the past, change externally by surrounding yourself with higher classes of men from other walks of life.

STOP BEING RACIST

The first Caucasian girl I dated as a teenager would only let me come over when her father wasn't home. She was down with the "swirl," but she knew her redneck father would flip out. Do not let your parents dictate whom you see. Most bigotries are passed down generation-to-generation and are a result of tradition, not personal experience. Be freethinking. Never accept that as an Indian woman, you can sleep with an Italian but can't bring him home. Don't be that Asian woman that dates a Jamaican man, but when her parents ask if she's seeing someone, she lies. There is no legitimate reason why races should not mix, none. Your parents lived in a different era, therefore respectfully give them your ass to kiss and broaden your 21st century shopping list. People are closed-minded and will continue to judge why you are with who you are with, but their judgment has no power! There are some black women who take this stance, "I'm black and it's in me to only want someone who looks like me." You can't help who you're attracted to, but are you saying that biologically your body screams for an African American male and an African American male only? There has yet to be scientific evidence that says races are genetically engineered to be more attracted to their own. It's the result of habit and social influence, not biological disposition. Indian men have dark complexions but don't get much sisterly love. Puerto Ricans are interchangeable with black men in NYC, yet they can be just as light as some Caucasians. So what's really going on? It's not complexion it's cultural—a forced boycott on other races due to the tunnel vision you grew up with. In the case of dating outside of your race, it isn't looks that hold a person back, it's personality, attitude, and how you can relate to their life. When breaking down blacks and whites, the personalities can often be so distinct that it seems as if they are talking a different language. One black woman told me the reason she did not date white guys was that she had nothing in common with them. How do you know that if you never talked to any of them on a deeper level than work chitchat?

Stop taking what you see on TV at face value. Not all black people like to listen to rap and twerk, not all Asians love robots and watch *Dragon Ball,* and not all white people love cheese and play beer pong. In this day & age, the cultural line isn't that gaping. 80's babies and 90's babies understand other races much more than people from the baby boom era. Today you can find a white guy that talks like T.I. and is up on all the black Twitter topics. You can also find a black guy who doesn't use "nigga" at the end of every sentence and would rather talk about skateboarding. Miley Cyrus is proof that you are now living in the melting pot. When going outside of your race, it is all about finding the common ground. He likes to hike and follow Dave Matthews on tour. You like to walk the mall and would rather buy a Prince CD than see him live in concert. Don't dwell on those little things! Just because this white guy never watched *Martin* doesn't mean you can't laugh with him. He may not understand the great weave debate, but is that really a deal breaker? Does he take you out, show you a good time, and treat you right? Those are important. Being able to reminisce about favorite Kool-Aid flavors is not that critical. To quote the timeless Lana Del Rey, "You were sorta punk rock, I grew up on hip hop, but you fit me better than my favorite sweater." Put your prejudice aside, and open up your dating pool.

WHAT DO YOU BRING TO THE TABLE?

Before you complain about the quality of men you meet, take inventory of the kind of woman you are. It's not a crime to aim for someone on a higher level than you, but damn, be realistic. If you want a man who makes six figures and is in excellent shape, but you're making under 40k a year and overweight, what's the appeal? Men don't mind dating down a class...or two, but those women still have to be appealing. Whatever your situation is, if you're not the Queen of England, you have to lay your ego to the side and seriously ask what makes you alluring. In your heart, you know that you are the best woman ever, but on paper, you may not come off as worth taking seriously. Good job, but it's not a career. Cute, but not drop dead gorgeous. Educated, but not Ivy League. Few people are firing on all cylinders, but that doesn't make you less extraordinary. It's the things you can't see or measure like trust, loyalty, and compassion that will make you an exceptional partner. However, the baller you're after can't look into your soul and see how perfect you are.

Any man just getting to know you can only go off how you present yourself. What about you during a meet and greet would make this successful and attractive man date you? A cute face and a pretty smile come a dime a dozen. What else do you bring to the table? This goes back to the Wifey or Pussy characterization. When a successful man is looking to settle down, he looks for a partner, not a dependent. Your intangibles have to become tangible in order to prove that you are as exceptional as you claim. The reason low rent men are always approaching you is because even at 60k a year and a little chubby, you're doing better than he is, and just like you, he wants something above his level. I knew a girl who worked part time at Wal-Mart, no plans to go to school, and was constantly ragging on men she met, "All I meet are these losers." You pull in $400 every two weeks and aren't looking to move up in the company or get a higher education. Who's the loser? Those men are after you because you are in their league!

Before you cry and complain that you deserve better, ask yourself if you've put yourself in a position to be better. Forget about what a man sees it's about what you see when you peer into that mirror. If you're stuck dating losers and attracted to mediocrity, it's possible that you see yourself on their level. If you regard yourself as average, then you will always attract average. You can pull just as many wealthy, honest, or good-looking men as the next woman, but you can't do that if you don't know what league you play in. Stop entertaining guys in the old average league and set your sights on men in the premier league. Why are you afraid to talk to these elite men in the suit and tie, but comfortable talking to basic boys in white tee's and sagging jeans? Professional men don't bite, and they will talk to if you have the courage to rise above your own self-consciousness. For a man of substance, there has to be something besides sex (which he probably gets often) that makes him want to come over and talk to you, date you, or be with you. Before you go expecting men to treat you like Ivanka Trump, get your life in order. If you want more out of the men that approach you, first demand more out of yourself. Investing in education leads to more money, working out leads to a healthy body, and dealing with your emotional baggage leads to a happier you. All of those things contribute to high self-esteem, and you will never reach your potential without a full tank of that.

WHERE DO SINGLE WOMEN GO?

After reading this chapter, you realize that you need to have an open mind when deciding which men get your number. You no longer pigeonhole yourself by only looking at the guys who dress like Tyga. You are prepared to travel outside of a five-mile radius for events. Finally, your life is in order and you are operating like a woman that's advancing in life and not some Basica who's stuck on the treadmill of a dead-end existence. Are you ready for the super-secret location of where the good men stay? The answer is…everywhere. There is no magical bar or lounge where all the handsome, single, moneymaking brothers assemble. Men want women, so they attend events where they think the quota of competition from other men is at its lowest and the availability of fine women is at its highest. This means good men are out at the regular places right alongside the bums. Winners are in the clubs, they are at the happy hours, but they're also stealthy. They're in the back row of the church every other month checking in. They're in the supermarket looking for frozen entrees because they don't have a woman to cook. They're standing next to you in line at the coffee shop. If you look around and see a man, he could be the one.

Stop looking for a fairy-tale place where you walk in and every handsome man makes eye contact and then fights to reach you first. That Disney Princess mindset is setting you up for failure. I don't care what your type is; you've been hoodwinked the past few relationships, therefore, your type is obviously not the right fucking type. I don't care if your girlfriends don't want to go out to new places, those bitches are back-up singers, and you're the Gladys Knight of this shit. Your girls aren't putting a ring on your finger, so if you have to venture out alone, do so. Spartans don't hunt in designated spots the world is their safari! It is not the places you go to, it's about the type of man that you have on your radar when you're there. Look past the standard you're accustomed to, and you'll be amazed at all the eligible men that you would have overlooked before in favor of Mr. Same Shit Different Tattoos.

15

The Ninety-Day Rule Is For Fools

S teve Harvey's ninety-day sex rule is the dumbest concept since prepaid legal. While this screening process may look good on paper, in reality it's a prolonged, outdated, and potentially torturous way of telling you things you should have figured out three weeks in. Waiting ninety days to have sex does not mean the man is worthy, good, or won't hurt your feelings. It means he is patient. Come day ninety-one you can still be just as unsure of his true motive as you were on day twenty-one. What this rule does more often than not, is drive away just as many decent guys as jerks. Even the most noble of men are hard pressed to wait that long. Remember this is the ADD generation; both men and women move fast when it comes to having sex. Given the fact that sex is so easy to attain, a man who's seen as a catch (i.e., attractive, wealthy, or talks as if he has sense) is less likely to wait.

Let's say you are crushing on Pretty Ricky with the trust fund because he's tall, dark, and owns his own business. Ricky has a shit load of options because other women are just as impressed with him as you are. However, these women are on a much more accelerated sex schedule than the Steve Harvey disciples. You want him to wait three months just because a book told you. He's going to wonder what the hell is wrong with you. It sounds like one of those diet fads that people go on because they can't discipline themselves from eating ice cream at 1am. This sex diet is telling a man that you have ventured so far down the slut or ho path that you need someone to put a child safety lock on your vagina. That's a slap in the face to any man, and it tells them that you can't use your own adult brain to figure out that he's not running game. This insult combined with other romantic options that don't feel a need to follow a rule will lead to Pretty Ricky walking out.

"If he didn't wait, that means he wasn't worth it," is not a proper way to separate the good from the bad. All men want sex—good, bad, and in-between. If you want to wait until you know him on a deeper level, that makes perfect sense, and any man with decency will respect that and happily play by those rules. However if you want to wait for a set time period, that makes a man think it's less about a connection and more about jumping through a hoop because you can't form your own opinion. Nice guys who don't want to be foul and have sex with their ex-girlfriends would rather end it than continue to frustrate themselves while you pretend to be a born again virgin. I had a girlfriend who was celibate and wanted to wait for sex. I liked her a lot, so I waited. Embarrassingly, we broke up due to something unrelated, and she had sex with another guy the next week. She confessed that she was vulnerable and added that she wanted to have sex with me during the first month of our relationship, but didn't want to give me the wrong idea. She denied herself so she wouldn't be judged, yet had a one night stand...this is the type of confusion that leads to mistakes when you deny yourself what the human body desires. She used sex as bait to keep me around, despite the fact that she had gotten to know me enough to want sex. Once she was free of the pressure of a relationship, she gave in to her urges with a person who didn't pose an emotional threat. Her hormones and emotions were out of whack due to sexual confusion of her own making.

Women will always have sex with whomever they want to regardless of the sanctions they place on their vagina. That's the truth, so let's stop trying to outsmart each other by coming up with meaningless rules that frustrate the body. <u>If you want to have sex, have sex</u>. If you want more than sex from him, then you should already be in a relationship before spreading your legs. If you can't get a relationship out of him, then don't fuck him! That's a rule that makes sense, not waiting a certain number of days. Ladies, you will never stop second-guessing when to have sex or not, but suspend your ninety-day rule and allow me give you some insight into how men actually think about fast sex, and then decide for yourselves.

> ### If You Give A Man Sex Too Early, He Won't Want To Commit.
>
> ### False!

A mature man doesn't care how long or short it took him to have sex if the woman is quality. This theory of once he hits it, he won't act right is asinine. Sex doesn't fry the male brain; it won't make a "good" man turn into Mr. Hyde. If he acts differently after sex, it's not a transformation—it's a revelation. That guy was always an asshole, now he's free to show it because he got what he wanted. Men filled with lust, passion, and sperm crush on women so hard that they can't tell what feelings are authentic and which are overblown due to the hormones. Once men have sex, and that lust, passion, and sperm are gone, they are free to act normal again. The sooner you have sex, the sooner you see the normal him. If he acts differently, you should thank your vaginal walls for unmasking him before it was too late. Go ahead and wait those ninety days. If he changes up on you on day ninety-seven, you're screwed because you probably love him at this point. If you gave him the coochie after the third date like you truly wanted to, you could have saved yourself time and tears. If a man is really down for you, having sex won't change his feelings negatively. If he just saw you as sex from the start, it will merely expose him for who he is—a pussy hunter. Stop counting days and start using your analytical skills to see through his bullshit factor. It doesn't matter how long you wait, he's still going to flee after the mission is complete if you don't actually get to know him.

Having Sex On The First Date Makes Men See You As A Slut.

False!

The first date is always too early to have sex because neither of you know each other well enough, it's pure horniness. However, it's not a death sentence. Things leading up to sex, and the way it went down tell guys more about your personality than the actual act. If you two have been talking for half a week, you agreed to a house date, and then started stroking his cock as soon as he whipped it out, that sends a sign that you're filthy and probably do this often. If it took more effort, but the result was still sex, that same guy may see you as a good girl who couldn't turn down a great man. All men have egos that will rationalize first night sex by saying, "I fucked because I'm that good, not because she's that easy." The day after the first date sex is what actually determines how he feels and where it's going to go.

Women throw the term one night stand around loosely to avoid being seen as easy. "It was nothing, just a one night stand," allows her to objectify that male, so that if he doesn't call the next day it feels like she was the user, not him. One night stands are usually the result of a wild night, not a date with someone you've been talking to for a week or more. A critical mistake is referring to him as a one night stand, when he's someone with whom you have been getting to know and forming a friendship. By calling him a one night stand, you mentally distance yourself from what could be the start of something positive and lessen how you actually feel about him. If that man gets a feeling that you think of it as a mistake or a sex toy, not the result of him being a great guy, it crushes his ego. Just like you threw the label of a one night stand on him to remain in control, he will throw the label of ho on you to cushion the blow of you hurting his feelings. If you have sex quicker than you feel you should, don't underplay it as something negative, own up to it as what it was: undeniable chemistry. By doing this, you won't feel like you got played and get defensive about what happened, and he won't feel like you regret it and get defensive about your response.

Most guys never call the next day because they are scared to death. A man will question why you had sex with him. If you had sex because you were just horny, not because he was impressive, then he risks falling in love with a nymphomaniac who he can't trust. If you had sex because you liked him okay, but it was more about being sexually frustrated than chemistry, then he's scared that calling you will make him seem like a lovesick simp. No man wants to come off pressed the next day, nor do they want to come off as a guy who is trying to wife a ho who just wanted dick. Ladies, tell the truth, most of you don't stop and think that men are just as nervous as you are after having sex, do you? I've been on the other end of that situation where I've waited for the girl to call. I picked up the phone ready to dial, then put it down because my paranoid male mind was screaming, "If she wanted you she would have called by now!" The woman was across town doing the same thing. In the end, the potential relationship never starts, not because he thought you were a slut, but because he didn't know you well enough before the sex to say, "She's not that kind of girl. Let me call her and see if we can hang tonight."

You don't know that he's a gentlemen or a jerk. You will assume which category he falls into based on if he calls you or not. He doesn't know if you're a lady or a man-eater. He will assume which category you fall into based on if you call him or not. If two people are stubborn, no one calls anyone, and feelings get hurt. If you like a person, it is okay to call after sex. Don't assume anything! Take it into your own hands, know where you stand, and save yourself the stress of guessing and worrying. Don't feed into the stereotype that sex on the first date is a deal breaker, and have the balls to reach out first if necessary. There are people who got played after first date sex, and there are also people who went on to have strong relationships after first date sex. First impressions aren't always the final impression.

If He Waits Three Months, That Means He Wants ME For ME.

False!

Three months isn't a long time, but when it comes to sex, it can feel like forever. Don't confuse being worth the wait with constantly being shot down. Even choirboys are going to test you at each turn to see if this weekend will be the one where you give in. The real reason men wait it out is the confidence that they can break any chick down regardless of how many times she says, "I'm not ready." When you go out with a veteran of the game, he's going to show his sensitive side. He's going to give gifts. He's going to make you his girl. You will even meet his family. All of this is so he can get brownie points, and all men know that getting brownie points accelerates sex. Even if you tell a man straight up, "I don't do anything until I'm three months in," he won't run away because his ego will counter with, "Yeah right, three months for those other guys means five weeks for a G like me." Every man on this planet thinks he is remarkable enough to make a girl have sex sooner than she planned. When you stick to your guns and don't give it up, he may respect you, and maybe by then he will have started to love you. However, making him wait too long can cause him to resent you for being a tease if he doesn't understand your reasoning.

Step into the shoes of your boo. He's been on his best behavior and passed all tests, and still you deem him unworthy. He tries his hardest, shows you how bad he wants you, and still he only gets a hand job. If sex was war, you would have just water boarded this dude for months because you want to torture him into revealing that his love is true. Withholding sex will not make him love you more! It offends him further. I can't stress how serious men view sex as the ultimate sign of attraction, especially in a relationship. Many women give it up when they aren't committed, so when a man is falling in love and doesn't get it from his girlfriend; he doesn't know how to take that. He thought he was special, you're showing him that he's just like the rest, and that doesn't sit well. Sure, waiting a month or two will make him respect you more than letting him hit the first week, but taking it to the level where you damage his ego can backfire. Ninety days are up, you have sex, and he tells you that it was so worth it while secretly plotting on getting his revenge. I could fill a trunk with the amount of, "Why is he acting funny?" emails I get from women who tortured their mates, then had to suffer through the backlash. One in particular was the epitome of what I'm writing. This girl made her boyfriend wait months because she had a bad reputation that she was trying to repair. Her guy stuck in there and then literally the next day after they had sex, he was on Facebook flirting with girls openly. Weeks had passed when she sent me the email, and he was still being disrespectful. She didn't want to leave him; she just wanted to understand why he changed all of a sudden. He resented her for using her vagina as bait, and immature men will always use immature tactics to make you pay. Don't make him wait for the sake of waiting; have a solid reason that you can clearly communicate to the man you like so you're on the same page when it comes to sex. It doesn't take three months to see if someone is real or fake if you ask the right questions and pay attention to details.

Only Have Sex With Exes So Your Numbers Won't Increase.

False!

There are females who love sex, but they don't want to seem like whores, so they recycle the same circle of people. You're ping ponging your pussy between four different ex-boyfriends because they don't count. Meanwhile, the new guy you meet who you really want to have sex with has to wait until the Mayan calendar restarts to get between your legs. Your exes aren't putting in any work; they aren't taking you out, or showing you attention. They are benefiting from just being available. Whose rules are you following now? Is there a handbook they give out in high school that says it's okay to be throwaway pussy for your ex-boyfriends and then act like a saint around the guys who genuinely care about you? At the pearly gates, Saint Peter will not flip through all the dicks you've taken and say, "Denied entry to heaven! You fucked one too many guys on earth. You should have just recycled Craig instead of giving Lamont new pussy." That's stupid. If you want to have sex, have sex with the person you want, not the guys you're familiar.

Sleep Around Like A Man, That Way You Won't Get Attached

False!

Who says men don't get attached? Males catch feelings just as hard as females do, that's a human trait. Remember, men are filled with that lust, passion, and sperm that clogs the brain. Only after he gets that out of his system can he truly open up. Females, on the other hand, think the next level has to come before they give it up. Men want to get to the sex so they can see if they actually like you. As a woman, you want to get to the relationship to see if he's worthy of your sex in the first place. That difference in opinion is where the problem lies, and the reason compatible people miss each other like trains in the night. When a woman talks of sleeping around like a man so she won't have feelings, it's idiotic. You can't just become a man; you're a woman for a reason. Females have superior sexual standards, this isn't by accident, it's a necessity, and it keeps the universe balanced. Women desire a mate, a provider, and a partner that is more than a physical release. To try to change that will cause more damage than good because your instincts will be confused, and your emotions will shift uncontrollably.

Go out and test this theory by sleeping with every guy you think is cute. I bet you will feel emptiness rather than emancipation. If you do prefer that way of life, I suggest you go to Vivid Video and get paid five thousand a scene to do it on camera. There are very few women that can turn their emotions down and sex drive up. For most, there is always that inherit balance. Those women who claim to be "like a boy" when it comes to sex are usually running from something rather than embracing sexual freedom. Some had an ex-boyfriend break their heart, so they go numb. Some have gone through physical transformations and are receiving male attention for the first time, so they go dick crazy. Other women have heard too many stories of how men are dogs, so they play this "men are meat" role to keep from being a statistic. Dating, sex, and dealing with untruthful men sucks! However, you can't shut down and try to play by a set of rules you don't truly understand. Satisfying your normal sexual urges and fulfilling that need to be in a meaningful relationship where sex isn't what he's sticking around for can be achieved. It's up to you to be patient when finding a man who will give you both.

Three date rule, ninety-day rule, or trading in your female desires for male ones, none of that is an exact science that will save you from being played. You're not like every other girl, which means have sex when you feel comfortable, don't rely on a gimmick to solve your uncertainty. Be it six days, or six months, you still have a 50/50 chance at love after the bed stops squeaking. Do your research, trust in your judgment, and fuck whom you deem worthy. If you're not a virgin, you've already made up your mind that you are ready, so don't deny yourself because the host of *Family Feud* told you to wait three months.

16

Assuming You Know What Men Think

I received an email from a high school teacher that was simple yet profound. She wrote of how she began a discussion in class asking how the boys felt about a multitude of things like marriage, virginity, and falling in love. Immediately, the females in the class began to answer and answer and answer...finally this schoolteacher told the girls to be quiet and let the boys chime in because no one can tell girls how a boy thinks better than an actual boy can. At that moment, the teacher had an epiphany. She had done the same thing in life that these teenage girls were doing in the classroom. She thought she knew everything about men, but in reality, she needed to "shut up and listen!" Not until I read that story did the fatal flaw of presumption really come into focus.

Every woman knows something about men but few truly understand them. Their knowledge of male behavior is taken from word of mouth, their limited dating experiences, siblings, and the media. Usually, these are generalized examples based on superficial observations. The problem comes when those generalizations transform into certainties in her brain. Now, instead of trying to figure out what kind of man the one standing in front of her is, she makes an assumption based on limited information like clothes, manner of speaking, or physical appearance. He's a pretty boy; that means he's a player. He's fat; that mean he's a trick. He's old; that means he's a sugar daddy. He has on Fila sneakers; that means he must be broke. He has on glasses and a gold watch; he's a professional. He keeps telling you how sexy you are; he wants to fuck. He tells you how smart you are; that means he sees you as something serious. Women profile men based on their clothing and looks the same way police profile men based on skin color and if their hoody is up or down. They also take basic actions and read too much into them as if all men say what they mean and mean what they say. This is a desperate attempt by those ignorant females to fit all men into a flow chart.

These assumptions spread like a virus, and suddenly she knows everything about men because one out of the four guys she's dated matched her stereotypical prediction. Next, this know-it-all woman will try to give advice to her girlfriends based on misinformation. *Girl, I told you to leave him alone! I knew he was trouble by the way he kept smiling...men who smile a lot have secrets.* It sounds like a joke, but it's serious. Once a presumptuous woman gets rolling she will have you believing that his zodiac sign is a reason you should break up, the fact that he calls his mother once a day is proof that you should marry him, and then blame her own single status on the fact that she keeps meeting guys who grew up as the only child. It's all b.u.l.l.s.h.i.t! However, in the mind of a rash woman, it's as factual as the Earth being round. If a know-it-all is proven wrong, it's only an exception to the rule, never proof that human beings are much more complex than ratchet horoscopes and birth placements. Only when these women are faced with an unexplainable heartbreak or meet a man who does not fit into any box, will they open their ears as this teacher did, and shut up.

Thinking back on the beginning of BlackGirlsAreEasy.com, I remember that a lot of early correspondence being started with, "I don't usually read relationship advice but..." They believed they knew what men were all about, how to tell good from bad, and capable of getting to the finish line of love on their own. Somewhere along that route, they lost their way, became confused, and found my website, which is one of many, but spoke the truth in a way that made the most sense. Women are prideful, and it takes true maturity to admit, "Maybe I don't have the opposite sex figured out." My advice connects with women who are open-minded, and infuriates those who prefer to fold their arms and claim to be omnipotent. Those who remain stubborn or who have not faced relationship roadblocks may read half an article then click back onto mediatakeout because they do not need my advice...yet. If you're reading this book, it is safe to say that you don't think you know everything but aspire to know more than you did before you picked this up. Nevertheless, there are still some fragments of misinformation lodged in your brain that need to be cleared. Here are some of the biggest misconceptions about men.

IF I ASK FOR HIS NUMBER, HE WILL THINK I'M A SLUT

I am so sick of the "he'll think I'm a slut" argument when it comes to getting a guy's number. All men want sex. The lust for a woman's body drives a male consciously, and subconsciously. It has been and will continue to be the nature of man. If you come over to a guy, flirt, and tell him to put your number in his phone, he will feel good about himself. That male ego is doing the money dance, and his brain is lit up like a Christmas tree screaming, "I'm going to fuuuucccck!" That is not a reflection of you; it's a reflection of male overconfidence. Men are used to working to get a girl's attention. The moment you come and give it unsolicited, his esteem will gas him like a zeppelin. This man is going to call you quicker than he would have called a girl who he had to approach, and he will be quicker to try to see you than he would some girl who gave him mixed signals. This is where you're thinking, "No shit, he thinks I'm loose!"

Men think all women are loose until proven otherwise. If you aren't going to suck his dick the first night, then you should not be worried about his perception. Women who fear looking desperate and hard up probably lack self-control. If you approach Mr. Super Sexy Dime, give him your digits, and he calls you the next night to go out, how will you react? You approached him because you liked him enough to risk rejection, will you like him enough after the date to assume the doggy style position on his couch? His thinking you're easy won't affect you unless you are EASY. If you are disciplined, then his attempts to have sex with you won't work. Let him whine, "…c'mon, stop being a tease. You came after me," then huff and puff because you're not giving it up. In the end, you don't owe him sex because you approached him first. This kind of man will either leave you alone because he doesn't like you in a girlfriend way or keep getting to know you because you showed him that you are attracted to him, but are still a lady with discipline that deserves respect. To sum it up: yes, men will be more excited if you approach them first, but it is not a turn off or a sign that you are a slut.

WE HAVE BEEN TALKING FOR A MONTH; THIS IS REAL

The feeling of hopelessness after a man suddenly vanishes on you is not tied to sex but to the potential of where the relationship was going, and the connection you thought you had. Women who read too much into what a man would just call, "kicking it" and take his affection, attention, and continued communication to mean that this is serious are as common as rhinestones on the nails of ratchets. Time alone does not bond two people. You have been talking every day for a month, but if a guy hasn't dropped his guard or taken extra steps to really get to know you past the point of hanging out and having sex, then it's just as serious as the first week. When men feel serious about a woman, they get serious and lock her down. One month, two months, or a year…If he's literally just chilling with you with no sense of urgency, then he thinks that your relationship is a good time, nothing more. Look at how he treats you, not how long he's been around you.

HE IS ALWAYS WITH HIS FRIENDS; I'M NOT GOOD ENOUGH

Women and men enjoy different activities; no matter how much you have in common and how much you love being around that person there will be times when a man has to be "the other him."

It's like how at your job you're more professional and reserved than when you're playing cards with your girlfriends on a Friday night. A man is not curtailing his attitude and behavior to that extent, but he cannot do the same shit around you that he does around his boys. You can learn to play *Call of Duty*, love the Lakers, and recite J. Cole lyrics line for line, but you will never be a male. Maybe he has another woman on the side, but the odds are that he runs off to his friends so he can maintain that balance.

When women aren't around, men can truly cut up. Say misogynistic things that they won't be judged over, fart, wrestle, clown, and talk the type of shit reserved for brothers. Fraternal groups have been around since the Stone Age because men have always needed to be around other men. Pause. If he's kicking it over some dude named Booman's house four out of seven days and only seeing you two, then you have an issue where he sees his friends as more entertaining than you are. However, if that time he chills over at Booman's house is even with the time he spends with you or only on specific nights when a game is on, get over your jealousy. I know you want him to be up under you, but let that man go be a man.

HE DOESN'T TAKE ME ANYWHERE; I'M UGLY

If you are constantly stuck in the house chilling and sexing with your man, it is because you allow it. If you are insecure about your appearance, being in the house just adds fuel to the fire. If you are worried that someone else thinks that you are ugly, that means you subconsciously think you are ugly. If you know that you are attractive, stop concerning yourself with the reasons why he's not taking you out and demand that he take you out. Do not ask to go on a date, tell him. There are men who lock a girl away ashamed because she doesn't look like a coke bottle and there are men who do the same thing because she does look like a coke bottle. Jealousy and shame both have the same result: a man wants to keep you away from other men. Most men fall in the middle. The middle being, he's just lazy and doesn't want to do anything that doesn't comfort him. Come Over And Chill mentalities don't stop once you're in a relationship. Why go out when he can order in? Why go to the movies when he has a collection of movies he has already paid for and likes? Why go out to impress you when the river of pussy is flowing endlessly under his roof? Give him a kick in the ass and tell him you expect to be taken out, or find someone else who will take you out. Nevertheless, if you have self-esteem problems about your looks you need to address them. Do not project it on a man who is just being lazy.

I'VE MET HIS MOTHER; THIS IS SERIOUS

You should be properly introduced to the family, but meeting the parents isn't as big a deal as it used to be. I get emails from women who met the mother, the cousins, the grandma, the heroin addicted uncle, and went to the Memorial Day cookout, yet they're still in relationship purgatory. There questions always point to, "I met so and so. That means he's thinking about making me his girl/marrying me." Men do not think that far ahead. I've accidentally introduced so many hos to my mother that she probably thought I was a pimp. Taking a girl you're talking to around family is convenience, not proof that this is some Edward and Bella love affair. You two are not betrothed because he invited you to a wedding. He probably wanted to earn brownie points or have a sure thing set up because eligible women at weddings are looking to get married. Do not let meeting his relatives and even becoming close to those people get you excited. You can call his mother every other day and go shopping with his sister on the weekends; congratulations, you've made new friends, but you're still not in the family! Until he says he wants to be serious and shows you that he wants to be serious, don't let going over to Grandma's house and hearing stories of, "He never brings girls around," gas you.

HE DIDN'T CALL AFTER THE ARGUMENT; HE DOESN'T CARE

Women change moods like Rihanna changes hair color. Men get exhausted chasing behind you after every blow up. It does not matter if he was wrong or if you were wrong, a man is born with the gift to put problems on the backburner. You're mad…you're going to be mad for a while, so he's going to go about his life, and then check in when he feels it's a better time. That could be the next day, or it could even be the next week. Either way, a man is going fishing mentally until he's prepared to deal with the situation. Do not take that to mean he does not care. Women get angry and want instant results. Instant! There are women who will yell for twenty minutes, tell a guy to leave, and then run out to his car to argue some more. She wants to cure her anger by getting an apology, understanding, or some act that shows that her man got her point of view.

The worst thing a man can say while being yelled at is, "Are you done?" A woman is never done until she feels like justice has been served. No matter if it's forgetting to take the trash out or looking at another girl's ass, she has to let it out. A man knows that there is nothing besides getting on his knees and slicing his wrists open that will cool an angry woman down. Therefore, he walks away and stays away until you calm down. It's a male's logical response to your emotional reaction. Eventually, he knows that if he wants to be with you he will have to talk it out, but he doesn't need to do it on your timetable of immediately. You don't have to respect that, but understand it.

HE KEEPS IN CONTACT WITH HIS EX; THEY'RE HAVING SEX

Everyone's ex situation is different. Me personally, I was cool with a few after we broke up, but we were not true friends to the point I needed them in my life. I kept their number in my phone because I knew that being amicable with them meant I could still get that "what are you up to this weekend" bored sex. Once a relationship gets serious, most men cut their exes off because their needs are being met by the new woman. However, since men do not like to hurt feelings intentionally or burn bridges, his version of cutting a girl off isn't deleting her number, it's to stop calling her. A woman who is with a man for three months and has the title will wonder why an ex's number is still in the phone. His excuse is, "I don't talk to her. Maybe to wish her a happy birthday..." That's half-true. He may not talk to her on a weekly or monthly basis, but what he can't say is that she's still in that phone because she's his backup.

If the current relationship ends, or his current girlfriend pisses him off, the ex is there to stroke his ego with that old school comfort conversation or if he's a cheater, comfort coochie. As long as you relationship stays solid, she won't be an outside threat. However, many females are dealing with guys who have exes who their man considers family. His ex can become like a sister, but the history never erases. So even though they are platonic for now, consider her a sister who doesn't mind incest. These type of exes are even more dangerous, because unlike the backup exes, he actually talks to her on a regular basis. If this "sister-ex" is a Spartan and decides out of the blue that she wants to go back to what she had, or doesn't like you for him, she'll take him with no problem because he's more loyal to her than a girl he's only been with for part of the year. To sum it up: no, a man isn't having sex with his ex if he keeps in contact, but he is keeping the door open in case you don't work out.

IF HE TALKS TO GIRLS ONLINE; HE IS PLANNING TO CHEAT

Facebook and jealousy are like Chad Ochocinco and head-butts; it will ruin everything. Nevertheless, paranoid people continue to mix e-life with real life. Men are social people, especially when it comes to the opposite sex. The more attractive that woman is the more he will want to interact with her because it's natural for a man to befriend women that he thinks of as attractive. This is similar to the way most guys have pretty females as platonic friends or play sisters. Even if he does not want her romantically, his shallowness still acts as a magnet to bring her into his life in another role. Talking casually with her isn't proof that he's sizing up this online girl and testing the waters to see if she's going to be his next girlfriend or mistress. All men flirt. Regardless of the level of relationship, a man will say little things to women out of habit. The level of flirting reflects a man's true intentions. If he doesn't respect what you have, he won't check himself. If he does respect your relationship, then he will keep the level of flirting light and playful. Liking a girl's picture or calling her "boo" online is not a reason to have a meltdown or even start an argument. If he likes every picture, tells her good morning every day, and has conversations about hanging out, then it's gone beyond natural flirtation—now you can say, "He ain't shit."

The average man interacts with several women online daily. These girls are likely pretty or have qualities that you don't have, which can make you insecure. He is not going to live in a cage because you feel threatened by another woman who he barely knows. He will get upset, and this girl will become a legitimate issue. Do not think that this show of emotion is because he likes her. It has nothing to do with her. It's because you're trying to control him. There will always be men who are looking for something better, and they will allow another woman into their hearts via a Wi-Fi connection. You cannot assume that every man is sex hunting online. If you go looking for drama, you will find drama. Hacking his password and stealing his phone shows a lack of trust on your part, and when men feel threatened, they get defensive and act out. Fear becomes reality, and by obsessing over that online girl, you will drive him to that online girl.

HE HASN'T SAID THE L-WORD; I'M BEING PLAYED

Men do not like saying, "I love you." It goes against every macho bone a man is taught to have. The only scenarios where a man gets a pass is when he's marrying you or when you're hurt. Men play around with the word to test the waters. Some will say, "I have love for you," "That's why I love you," "I'm loving you right now," and so on without saying it straight up. I'm an exception to that rule as I have never been afraid to say it, but someone like me was even worse because I would say it to girls who I had deep-like for, yet wasn't in love with. The point is, if he says it directly, hints at it with wordplay, or never brings it up, it doesn't matter. Your main concern is feeling loved. The feeling of someone loving you is distinct, and if you can't recognized that feeling and point to it in your life, you are in trouble.

There are hardcore German parents who never said the L-word, but their kids felt the love from the way they were treated. As long as your man is hitting that mark when it comes to giving you that genuine feeling of love through his actions, he can drop "ditto" on you like Patrick Swayze for the rest of your life. You want to hear the words because it's supposed to be a reflection of how he feels inside, but don't let that drive you crazy! Some women may feel a burning desire to scream it; other women feel like the hardest of men and rarely say it. Understand that neither way is right or wrong. *I love you* is not a magical spell that will make everything perfect. No problems will disappear, his feelings won't turn authentic, and no words will become truthful. Get out of the backwards habit of thinking a man saying, "I love you," is the same as loving you.

HE SAID I'M THE WIFEY TYPE; HE PLANS TO MARRY ME

I will be the first to admit that men lay compliments and praise on thick even when they don't have to. Males are very impulsive, and if you do not know how to read their level of hyperbole, you can set yourself up for heartbreak. Every highly contested overtime game is, "the greatest game ever," every new Jay-Z verse is, "probably the best since Blueprint," and every girl who makes him cum in under five minutes is, "the best I've ever had!" These men are not lying to themselves; it's the excitement of the moment that makes that experience feel like it really is the greatest. Every man is still a little kid inside, and they all remember what their best Christmas present was from when they were kids. However, you can't ask them when they're six years old, you have to ask them at seventeen because only then can they look back and compare.

The same thing goes for judging women. Every man has met a girl who he thought was unbelievably funny, sexy, and intelligent. He had to tell everyone about her, introduce her to the world, and pillow talk her ear off about how special she was. You're going to get gassed by his words and actions. You want desperately to feel like you're different from the rest of these women, and his words are sweet validation, but slow down. You have to keep a 'wait and see' attitude, or you are setting yourself up for disappointment. Most women tend to be a Super Nintendo. It was the best gift ever, then a few years later he got that PlayStation under the tree, and it not only replaced that SNES as the best Christmas gift, it stayed there. If a man says you are the type he could marry, it's a great compliment, but understand where it's coming from. Is the man who's saying this a person you've known for a while and has truly experienced the various sides of your personality, or is this coming from a guy who's known you for a short while and is infatuated by your newness?

Men who drop the L-bomb after sex or propose marriage with no ring after something great happens are caught up in the moment. Don't get sucked into male impulse and start picking out wedding dresses, updating Facebook statuses, and telling your girlfriends he's the one. You're falling for him because he's giving you the level of love you've been searching for, but you have to use common sense. So many women are confused when a man leaves her or starts to distance himself after the honeymoon period[14]. These women look back to the good times when he called her perfect and claimed that she was a blessing. To have someone reject you and start dating another woman after being told how you were his soul mate hurts, but don't be bitter, understand his thinking. Not every man is lying to you when he proclaims your greatness or tells you you're different. He is most likely caught up in the thrill, needs time to calm down, and truly get to know you before he can stand behind those words. Yes, you are special, but until he is down on bended knee, holding something he spent three paychecks on, then assume he's just talking out of his ass. If he truly thought you were the wifey type, you would be his wife.

---

[14] The Honeymoon period is the initial 3-4 months of getting to know a person where everyone is on their best behavior and full of lust, joy, and optimism.

PART THREE:
LEARNING TO CHOOSE, NOT SETTLE

"The minute you settle for less than you deserve,
you get even less than you settled for."
– Maureen Dowd

17

Fat, Ugly, Awkward...
So What

Y ou get what you believe you deserve in life. Every morning you wake up and judge how worthy you are of a promotion, of a man, of happiness. No matter what you project after you leave the house, it's what you honestly believe when you look in the mirror that will either hold you back or propel you forward. Are you pretty? Are you nicely shaped? Will others look at you and think the same? That security or insecurity may seem like an internal debate that has nothing to do with the face you put on for the public, but it absolutely determines the quality of man you attract. Beauty is subjective, but no matter how much you make the "it's only skin deep" argument, you cannot take away the fact that looking good makes you feel good. You're thinking, "I know I'm sexy, and I still can't meet anyone decent." I don't believe you.

To feel sexy is to be confident. To be confident is to be fearless. Being fearless results in going after anything you want and never shying away from the moment. Most of you feel good when looking in the mirror, but your confidence falters when it's time to shake hands with the man of your dreams. Beauty, confidence, and coolness are the traits of a woman who will always win. If you're falling short in the quality man department, it's not because you're a hamburger away from being *Precious*, flat chested, or you have your father's chin. It's because you have yet to master all three of those mandatory traits.

In your lifetime, you have seen a woman you didn't think was as pretty as you are, but she was cuddled up with the kind of guy you think you should be with instead. How is that possible if men are so concerned with looks? Even Stevie Wonder can see that you're gorgeous, yet you're still single. Men don't fall in love with a face or an ass. They fall in love with a soul. That electrifying charisma that extroverted women possess, that sexually charged swag that hos corner the market with, even the quiet mystique of a bohemian artist—that's the energy that sucks men in. A dick getting aroused is child's play: a skill that all females are capable of regardless of looks because sex is simple stimulation. Love, however, is a complex meshing of energy that has nothing to do with skin tone, nose length, waist size, or breast cups. Therefore, it's never about how good he thinks you look. It's about how magnetic you are when you appear on his radar.

There are women who approach me for advice, and the first thing they say in terms of physical description is, "I'm okay. I'm not Meagan Good or nothing." That's the first problem. By comparing yourself to a woman you see as superior, you're limiting who you can attract. When you go out and see a cute guy, you're going to shy away or awkwardly stumble through a conversation with him because you have a mental block that says, "Why would he want me when Meagan Good types exist?" The relationship, a real one anyway, is over before it started. Not because he thinks that you are beneath him, but because YOU FEEL that you are beneath him. Girls with low opinions always settle for less. I'm not talking look wise, I'm talking treatment. The pretty girl with low self-esteem can get married to a handsome football player with abusive tendencies, but she will never escape because a part of her feels she deserves that abuse. The 200-pound woman with the cute face can end up with a nice looking guy, but he's a bum who takes from her more than he gives. Again, she won't abandon that man because that level of treatment is all she believes she will ever find. Think back to any man who has ever treated you badly, and think where your esteem was right before you met him. Those men don't pop up from out of nowhere; you attract those lowlife men by having a low opinion of yourself. The prime example of feeling ugly = attracting ugly is Kelly Rowland from Destiny's Child. In her song "Dirty Laundry," Kelly finally dropped her guard and let the world in on how Beyoncé's fame took her to a negative place in her mind. While Kelly was fake smiling and congratulating Bey, internally she was beating herself up with thoughts that fans would never love her in that same manner. When it came time for love, whom do you think this negative, angry, and bitter Kelly attracted? She pulled in a man who reaffirmed what she was thinking, beat her down even more, and added fuel to a fire that she had built in the first place. Do not lie to yourself when it comes to how you truly feel when you look in that mirror! If you continue to bury your true feelings when it comes to looks and/or status, and try to mask the disappointment with some false sense of pride, the charade will not hold up.

I'm not going to bullshit you and say that I believe every woman is equally beautiful. I'm a man, and therefore I have a bias based on the women I grew up attracted to as determined by my culture and influence. That means that my eyes do not speak for every man. Guys are attracted to various women for various reasons that are most likely a result of the women they've seen in their lives, not some mythical default image of beauty. While my taste means the world to me, it should have no effect on the next person. Some of my readers go so far as to send me email attachments with pictures asking, "Give me your brutal honesty, am I pretty?" Me saying you're just okay looking, your co-worker saying you're more cute than sexy, a guy at the bar drunkenly calling you ugly, it's all baseless. Your self-confidence is all that matters, and if you believe you're beautiful and carry yourself as if you're the best looking girl in the room; you will attract the men you want. Ranks or comparisons are for men's magazines and frat boy arguments. To land a guy who you see as a perfect ten and who treats you like a perfect ten, makes you a perfect ten—that's the end of the "who looks better" discussion. You can't just start believing you're better looking than Ashanti and get your turn with Nelly overnight. It takes time to build your esteem, and more importantly, it takes discipline not to compare yourself to other women in the first place. Let's talk about some of the major reasons for lack of confidence: weight, looks, and nerves. If you're willing to open up and be honest while reading this section, you will wake up tomorrow thinking differently.

You Would Be Cute If You Lost Weight

America is a country where they put bacon on everything; therefore, "Paris Hilton skinny" is the exception. Still the media with its Hot 100 lists continue to cherry pick those women who are two missed meals away from being Karen Carpenter, and tell you that's ideal. Black and white America in particular share the biggest divide when it comes to weight. It's become almost stereotypical to assume all black men lust after big asses since Sir Mix-A-Lot dropped "Baby Got Back." On the other end of the spectrum, white men in general have been painted as thinking any woman over a size six is fat. Caucasian women like Christina Hendricks of *Mad Men* fame are made out to be special exceptions to the rule: the desirable fat chick. Black women like Beyoncé are touted as proof that you don't have to be anorexic to be sexy…as if King Bey weighs over 135 even during a bloated week. It's all media influence. It tears the average American woman down and rebuilds her, only to sell her more Hydroxycut pills and Slim Fast.

The difference between fat and phat, besides a "ph" instead of an "f," is opinion. Different strokes for different folks, and each man has a surprisingly wide spectrum for how large he would be okay with in terms of wifey. That doesn't mean go out and run your cholesterol through the roof like, "fuck it someone will want me, even after they cut off my diabetic foot." No one wants to look like the mother from *What's Eating Gilbert Grape,* and you need to live long enough to enjoy that dream guy, so being a healthy weight should always be the top priority. At the same time, don't let being twenty pounds heavier than you were in high school make you depressed. An old crush surfing through Facebook may think, "Damn, April let herself go!" You didn't let yourself go, you let yourself grow. The human body evolves over time due to a number of reasons, becoming more of a woman doesn't mean you are now less of a woman. If you are out of shape, go to the gym, cut out processed food, and live cleaner. You're not going to revert to a size 2 and a B cup, but you will lose the excess fat and fill out your new frame with the kind of curves that men consider grown and sexy. Stop chasing a number on the scale and start chasing the confidence to feel better than you felt when you were that high school weight. Fuck what body type men claim to want on social media; most of those nerds are grandstanding and would love to plunge head first in your plus size pool. Thick, phat, healthy, curvaceous—those are labels meant to empower you, but you don't need that shit either. Regardless of what they call you, the key is to feel beautiful when you look in the mirror. Do you turn yourself on? If the answer is no, then you have no business dating in the first place.

Let's say you're happy with your size, you would like to drop a few more pounds like most women, but you are content. Congratulations, you're on the right path to finding the man you deserve. The next step is harder than dieting and a bigger struggle than pulling those jeans up over all that ass. I'm referring to the art of talking to men. You walk into a bar, a guy looks back at you. Once your eyes lock with his, the moment of truth begins. Lack of confidence will cause your brain to scream, "He thinks I'm fat. He doesn't like bigger girls. This shirt doesn't really show off the weight I lost. I'm not his type!" All of those rapid-fire mental roadblocks pop up leading you to crash and burn before you even talk to him. Was that "damn I look good" glance you gave yourself before leaving the house total bullshit? No, you did look good, and you still look good. Females overthink how others perceive them because they're not sure how to perceive themselves. Don't let doubt kill your confidence and cause you to relapse into thinking you don't measure up. The confidence of "big and beautiful" will shrivel up when face-to-face with an actual man because you're only half a sex symbol! You talk confident around friends, but be able to say and believe that when you're standing in front of a guy.

I've met some bigger women with extroverted personalities; they have no filter and don't mind making conversation. These are usually the type of women that always pull the kind of man others would deem "above her." Alternatively, they are used as mouth pieces to hook their shy friends up with men. A girl like that hits the club, dances her big ass off with any and every guy who comes toward her, and suddenly she's not being laughed at, she's being pursued. Haters may frown and make up false reasons why men are talking to a girl like this, but it's not sex or money. It's the magnetism of her personality that made her popular despite her waist size! After it's all said and done, that confident big girl won't be back to the club for another few months, if at all, because she gets enough phone numbers to keep her interviewing potential boos for weeks to come.

Then there's the timid big girl aka Miss Thick, who only came out because her friends laid a guilt trip about how she's boring or forced her to play the role of designated driver. Those girls tend to be extremely introverted and reek of fear. Miss Thick leans against the wall, plays on her phone, and tries to disappear because she feels like everyone's judging her for weighing more than Lauren London. Even though she's happy with her weight, she's failed the ultimate test: being judged in public. At home, you can be the *Brave Little Toaster*, but once you are forced to step into a room full of skinny Minnie's, you actually see how unflappable you truly are. If timid Miss Thick does get the attention of a handsome man, it will be a player who smelled her fright from across the room. Players prey on big girls who lack confidence. He comes over and spits game in her ear, hooks her, and then goes about embedding himself in Miss Thick's life using either sex or promises. It's all bullshit, but if you have low self-esteem and don't want to lose the only option around, you ignore red flags. The player ends up getting just about anything he asks for, and then jumps ship when you figure it out or run out of things to give him. Half-confident women like that create the "big girls buy you anything" stereotype. Weight has nothing to do with being naïve and weak; it's the lack of self-worth that has these women buying Jordans and cosigning for car loans.

BUILT LIKE A LITTLE BOY

If you don't have ass, you better have titties! I want to attribute that quote to Maya Angelou, but I may be mistaking her with a ratchet Baltimore barber I once had. The hood is a bizarre world when it comes to thick versus skinny because there is this idea in the black community that there should always be some cushion for the pushin'. As a result, there are people who will make a woman feel bad about having the body of an Olympic track star. Forget abs, have ass, or the local hoodlums will go around you to get to the girl with the beer belly just because she has a donkey booty. Growing up, my friends gave me shit because I was a breast man while most of my friends from the block were ass men. I'm going to make a confession: I was neither. I could care less if a girl was as flat as a board in the back and front as long as her face looked like something Catfish perpetrators would steal off the internet.

I met my wife when she was 19 and had no body. One hundred and ten pounds, as pretty as can be, no butt to speak of, and with cups that couldn't hold a can of soda. I thought she was perfect. She later went through a (natural) boob growth spurt that I greatly appreciated, but it wouldn't have mattered either way. Many women, black ones especially, feel left out because they aren't equipped with a huge ass. Unlike breasts, which can be padded and pushed up, the lack of booty can't be covered easily. Most of them have to suffer through the "Noasathal" (no ass at all) jokes, and while that sounds innocent and fun, anytime you poke at what a woman doesn't have, it damages her psyche. All black girls are supposed to have booty and all black men are supposed to be hanging. Not all black men have porno dicks, but that's a secret locked away in their jeans. By the time a girl finds out he's not representing the Mandingo clan, it's too late because he's in the middle of fucking her. Women can't lie on their ass in that same fashion, so there is now this 21st century epidemic of ass implants and Bed Bath & Beyond brand booty pops.

You are not less of a black woman because you don't have a donk. White women have fallen under the big ass spell as well. Plump ass has been the "it" thing since Kim Kardashian sparked the Whooty movement (white girl with a booty), but don't go crazy in the gym trying to squat your way to a perfect ass or find an underground surgeon willing to perform an illegal ass injection. Love your butt or lack of it! There will always be ass men, but that doesn't mean you lose in life if you're unable to get kudos from booty bandits. Give any man a sexy lap dance and I guarantee you his dick will react the same way it would if Nicki Minaj were straddling him. Like name brand clothes, luxury cars, and all the shit that people claim to be must haves—a phat ass does not really matter when presented with something of quality.

For women who have big butts it's a badge of honor, something they find confidence in because like any physical feature that stands out, it draws men in without having to say a word. Salute big booty Judy, don't hate on her. Ass insecurity makes people resent and say every girl with a K. Michelle butt[15] has injections. True or false, it doesn't matter because men don't give a fuck about body enhancements. By stating those things, you shine a light on the jealousy in your heart. Get your face out of her reindeer ass, find your own badge of honor, and highlight the things on your body that make you just as sexy. You don't have to work harder for men to notice you because your cup size is small and your booty isn't as 'licious as others. All you need to do is work what you have with the confidence that no other woman in the room can touch you. Trust me, even the most jaded of men who claim to only want curvy women will double take if you stroll in rocking the right outfit. Charisma doesn't come from

---

[15] K. Michelle is an R&B singer and reality show star known for her ratchet theatrics and ample derrière.

body parts, so stop wishing for something you don't have. Inject some self-esteem and implant some confidence. That's the only makeover you need.

YOU'RE PRETTY FOR A DARK-SKINNED GIRL

Allow me to focus on my sisters for this section. Yes, white women are exposed to ethnic degrading such as, "Jewish girls are like this...Italian girls are like that," stereotypes. However, they are spared the horror of true inner race racism. Even the palest of ginger women don't have to hear rap lyrics that make them out to be second-class citizens. Black is beautiful, but there are those ignorant men who will put an asterisk beside that and point out that lighter shades of brown are more elite. Do not let this ignorance lower your self-esteem. I won't get into a big historical rundown of house niggas versus field niggas, and social brainwashing to think light is right. It doesn't matter why others feel the way they do about complexion; it only matters that you realize how insignificant their opinions are. In black culture "you're black as..." jokes are the norm. I've even heard people make Whoopi Goldberg, *The Color Purple* jokes, when they're the same shade as Miss Celie. It's hypocritical and insane.

Having gone to a predominantly white university, I saw firsthand how my Caucasian friends would marvel at the darker women and not really pay attention to the lighter skin black women at the house parties. My less traveled black friends back home would have been dying to talk to the so-called "exotic yellowbones," but in this world of pale skin, the darker women were the exotic beauties. One of my best friends, Gillespie, was literally obsessed with black women and once made fun of me for talking to a girl with a light complexion. Even though he was a white kid raised in the burbs, he never understood why anyone would want a black woman that wasn't Kelly Rowland dark. That's the appreciation all dark-skinned women should experience. In the African American communities, this beauty is often overlooked by ignorant people. Fuck them. Your shade doesn't define you it highlights your beauty, and any man who would try to make your beauty the exception to the rule, or claim that lighter is better, is a fool! At the same time, don't rage against the machine, or be baited into slandering your lighter skin sisters in an attempt to knock them down a peg. Ignore the ignorance machine and don't allow it to divide. There is nothing anyone can say that will end racism, and there is no discussion that will stop certain African Americans from being colorist. You cannot fight a war for every dark-skinned girl who is told she can't wear red lipstick, blonde weave, or looks good despite her skin. You can only win that battle within yourself each time you're confronted with that negativity. Know that you're beautiful, embrace how you were created, and strut into any room black, proud, and bomb as fuck.

YOU AIN'T GOT NO ALIBI—YOU UGLY

You're probably thinking, "If I'm fat, I can lose weight or rely on my pretty face to lure men in who don't mind a little extra woman. If I'm skinny I can throw on heels, bare some midriff, and work that Anne Hathaway sex appeal...but if I'm ugly, there's no way to highlight not being ugly!" Who decides what's ugly? I decide in my mind, you decide in your mind, and so on until you reach the last person on earth. Yes, there are certain overlapping qualities people can agree on, but there has never been someone universally deemed un-fuck-wit-able. Even Cher's deformed son from *Mask* had bitches. Everyone has something that makes them feel physically attractive; therefore, everyone has something that makes them genuinely physically attractive. Men will always judge and claim they only handcuff dimes, but look at some of the wives of famous athletes, actors, and politicians. Your looks would probably win the Pepsi Challenge over a number of them.

As I said prior, men are not attracted to the physical alone; it's that woman's personality that makes her look like a nine instead of a six. I have two friends who routinely compete with each other in terms of women. My one friend, let's call him Trevor, met a girl off Myspace and proceeded to fall in lust. My other friend, we'll call him Sam, saw the pictures of this Myspace girl and made fun of him for going after someone he decided was weird looking. Sam proceeded to call this girl a tranny, nicknamed her "Baby Amil,[16]" and would insult her with any other derogatory name he could think of. Trevor didn't care and continued to try to court this girl. Ever the asshole, Sam decided to undermine Trevor by inboxing Baby Amil as a prank. Within a month, Sam and this supposedly ugly girl were attached at the hip, and she eventually became his girlfriend for the next year. I didn't forget the jokes and Sam knew it. The first thing he said once it became serious was, "Yo, she's not ugly at all. Those pictures on Myspace were old. She looks real good in person." Did her looks change? Fuck no, his perception changed. Baby Amil turned into *America's Next Top Model* because he had gotten to know her as a person, not a static picture. You can never be ugly if a man doesn't know you. He can judge the cover, but if you were to allow him to read the first chapter, he'd be hooked.

UM...AWKWARD

I'm okay with my physical appearance, but I don't know what to say to boys...I get too nervous. Why are you nervous when talking to the opposite sex? You want them to think highly of your character and approve of your looks. You can roll your eyes and play tough as if you don't care about the approval of others, but when you like someone you want those feelings reciprocated or else you feel foolish. You know how to talk to boys; you've been doing it since daycare. What's holding you back from talking to the men you like is the stress of impressing that particular person. Uncertainty creates fear, and fear causes a reaction where you either keep quiet, talk too much, or overthink everything you say. What follows is an awkward exchange with someone you like where you didn't show the true quality of your character and electricity of your personality. You're not wack, but the five-minute

---

[16] Amil was a female rapper signed to Jay-Z's label whose looks were highly debated.

conversation you just had with that cute boy was wack because you weren't comfortable. Confidence calms nerves and erases awkward behavior. There will always be butterflies, but managing them is the only way to show the authentic you every time you step up to bat. Face your fear of rejection by confronting the reasons why you think he won't approve of you. Women have three main insecurities that make them nervous, shy, or awkward around men:

HE WON'T THINK YOU'RE PRETTY.

HE WON'T THINK YOU'RE SMART.

HE WON'T LIKE YOUR BODY.

I talked about physical appearance at the top of this chapter because that is the foundation that your insecurity is built upon. If you master the ability to love yourself then you will give zero fucks about what others think. Your hair is done, your heels are making you feel taller than Tyra, and your lip-gloss is popping. You're the baddest chick at this house warming, so what man do you have to fear when you look this sexy? Who would disapprove of a goddess in stilettos? I don't care how cute you think he is, once your esteem rises to the point where you need a halo, your nerves will be minimal, and you will be settled enough to talk to him as the real you. That cute guy asking for your number or not asking will not break you down if you are secure! His rejection won't make you feel ugly, have you going home to start a new diet, or make you think about getting a new hairstyle. The difference between a Spartan woman and a peasant woman is that a peasant lets outside opinion, uninterested men, and rejection change how she feels about her beauty. Insecurity doesn't live in a Spartan body because she believes in her presentation as strongly as R. Kelly believes he can fly! You can be as humble and modest as you want when talking to people, but don't be humble in your head, be a cocky cunt with the ego of Kanye West. If you carry yourself like a Spartan Queen, you will feel powerful. Once you feel powerful, you will become comfortable, and then the conversation will flow.

What do you say to him to keep his attention? How about you start with your name and let your swagger carry the rest. Stop overthinking what to talk to men about, there is no right answers when having a general conversation. Do you overthink what to talk to your cousin or co-worker about? No, you just open your mouth and what comes out is who you are without the awkward delay of trying to come off smarter, funnier, or cooler than normal. That filter that you place on yourself is what makes you come off like an airhead because you're trying to screen all of these random thoughts instead of talking your talk. Once you take away the filter, the awkwardness of "I don't know this person," and speak freely as if he's an old friend, you break the ice, and put him at ease as well. The man you're talking to is probably just as nervous, but by opening up, you will cause him to follow your lead. That's what men mean when they say, "She's easy to talk to." Less attractive guys or platonic friends are always easy to talk to for women, which is why your male friends always compliment you as being such a cool girl. They get to experience your blinding personality because you don't have nerves around them. It's never awkward with platonic men because you don't fear rejection or obsess over their opinion of you. Treat those guys you want romantically as casually as you do those you would never fuck, and he's as good as yours.

No matter how a man thinks you look in the privacy of his mind, the more you engage him in conversation, the prettier you become. The more you brush off that shyness and show him how unique and personable you are, the sexier you become. Erase the notion that you aren't someone's type, stop bitterly pointing to hos in tight clothes as being your competition, and be comfortable in your own skin. Living in LA I hear people talk about celebrities they meet, and usually they remark that these people aren't as pretty as they are on camera. They don't need to be perfect to be desired by millions! Angelina Jolie isn't a mega movie star because she has a flawless blemish free face and perfect body.

Angelina has wrinkles, she has body issues, but at the end of the day no matter what role she's playing, her real life charisma shines through and connects with people. Suddenly she becomes sexy, dangerous, fearless, intriguing,—Attractive! Let that charisma shine through no matter your physical appearance. That's the magnetic force that will make it easy to wow any man. Beauty isn't something you are or aren't, it's an evolving perception that affords everyone the potential to be a perfect ten!

There are men out here who are just as shy, depressed, and self-loathing as some women. Those men usually need materialistic things to boost their self-esteem. Luxury car to make up for his receding hairline, Rolex to overshadow his short height, flaunting his bank account to compensate for his weight, and the list goes on. Females don't need those crutches. No matter the package you come in, there are dozens if not hundreds of men who want you the way you are. You're a woman, the most desired thing in the world, which means you should piss confidence! Your vagina is like rocking an Audemars watch while driving a Bentley Coupe; it sends a powerful message! To know you is to love you, but only if you're already in love with yourself. A knight in shining armor won't swoop in and rebuild your self-esteem over dinner, compliments won't give you confidence, and finding a guy willing to have sex with you isn't solving the underlying problem. Every morning you need to wake up and see yourself as the best you there is. There will always be things you can improve and work on, but small flaws aside; you have to fall in love with you first. No one will ever value you more than you value yourself.

18

Approaching Your Dream Man

When it comes time to start dating, what's your first move? No, it's not buying a new outfit or getting a new hairdo, it's selecting whom you will date. You're thinking, "No shit," but most women skip this crucial step, refuse to handpick their men, and simply wait to be selected. When women complain about dating being hard, they're not talking about the actual act of going out and being entertained, they're referring to the selection process. Men wield the power of choice because they are the ones who initiate conversation, stumble through small talk, and finally ask a girl out. Due to generations of "sit, look pretty, and wait to be asked to the ball," women rarely speak first or ask men out on dates. This attitude ensures females give up all power in choosing who they date. You could counter that women have the power to say "yes" or "no," but is that really taking life in your own hands when the only options you have to decide from are fat guy with foul breath or tall guy with acne?

Some women are particular when it comes to giving out their number and will choose none of the above, rather than settle. Nevertheless, these women with standards often end up waiting forever for the perfect man to walk up to them and then eventually crack under pressure. How long can you truly wait to be picked before these lesser men begin to not look so bad? When a choosey woman has girlfriends who are dating or in relationships, she will be attacked from all sides. Her friends want her to find a man because she's the last single lady in the group, so they apply pressure. Once you become the pity or project of that circle, you either start talking to guys who aren't on your level just to prove to your friends you can find a guy, or you allow them to hook you up with some random weirdo who is single for a reason. You can stick to your guns for a time, but eventually your friends will guilt you into going out with any guy that seems nice. Being "nice" becomes the only requirement if you've been on the market too long. Fear and peer pressure will have you looking on the bright side and eventually you will give yourself over to a subpar, very nice, but still subpar man. Ladies, it's time to put an end to settling and start being proactive.

Why don't men approach you? Fuck that. Why don't you approach men? If you're particular about the kind of guy you want, then this waiting game will waste valuable time. The wrong type of guy will keep approaching you because they don't know any better. Men who are too short, too tall, too skinny, too fat, too sweet, too mean, too quiet, too cocky, too whatever you don't like, don't have the benefit of reading your mind, so they assume that they have a shot with you. There is no label on your forehead that says, "Reserved for tall guys that make over 100k a year," or a bum repellent you can spray to stop getting hit on by the wrong types. However, there is something called "balls" that you can grow in order to go after guys who do at least meet your physical requirements. That man you spot from across the room, he's well dressed, smiling, and doesn't have a ring on his finger. He has the look that you go for, but he never crosses over and introduces himself. He doesn't even glance your way no matter how hard you wish for him to, "Look over, look over, look over!" He must not be interested in you, right? The first problem is that you're being a punk by trying to telepathically signal this guy to talk to you. Unless your homegirls are Storm and Rogue, you need to get off your ass and open your mouth because you don't have mutant powers that can make him read your mind. Don't wait for him to notice you, if you see what you want, Spartan up and go for it.

Why are you settling for bad dates with 6's when you could be dating 10's? Many women are shy and see the embarrassment of rejection as a death sentence. Even bold women turn into little girls when it comes to making the first move with a stranger they like. No one is above rejection, but for females who pride themselves in their appearance, that potential blow to the ego isn't worth it. What if he thinks you're ugly? You don't want to come off as desperate. Maybe you're not his type. He looks like he has a girlfriend. You still have ten more pounds to lose. Your horoscope didn't call for love today. All of these excuses are bullshit! Closed mouths don't get fed, and a lot of women would starve if talking to men first were food. If you are not ready to Spartan up and approach the guys you want to date, then here are some things that require less forwardness.

DON'T MEAN MUG

If you walk the food court with the same expression you have while taking a shit, you have a problem. I don't care how pretty you are, no man wants to start a conversation with a woman that looks eternally constipated. Most guys aren't willing to walk up to a chick that has that "first time having anal sex" expression, so they keep walking, scouting for a girl that has a brighter disposition. You don't have to smile constantly, but your blank normal look shouldn't be one of "fuck everybody." The guy you want isn't the YOLO goon in the red fitted hat and skinny jeans hanging off his ass who will talk to you regardless. You're crushing on the guy in the button up shirt who looks as if he actually works for a living. That guy in the button up may think you're attractive, but he's not going to put himself out there and get dissed by a girl who's mugging harder than Fredro Starr. Based off his presumption that you're in a bad mood, he's going to assume you don't want to be bothered, and your opportunity to be approached will pass you by. You don't have to walk around looking cheerleader chipper, but be conscious of the stank face when you're out in public. A smile can be the difference between a man saying hello, or him looking at his feet as he passes you.

HIDING BEHIND YOUR GIRLS

The hardest thing for a man to do is go into a pack of wolves and introduce himself. A guy would rather pull an ugly chick with a big ass because she's by herself than a super dime whose being flanked by her girlfriends. Four Mighty Morphin Power Ratchets are walking together; a guy is by himself, says fuck it, and speaks to the one that interests him. The other three girls are going to feel that he thought she was the best out of the bunch. I don't care if the others are in relationships, jealousy will set in because his actions say, "she's greater than the rest." That may not even be the case. Sometimes a guy goes for the second cutest because the first cutest looks like she's a stuck up. Other times a guy may go for the least attractive because the odds of being rejected by her are slim to none. Females who travel in packs don't think about any of these reasons. They only see a guy disrespecting them by talking to their friend instead. Lord help him if another girl in the group finds the guy attractive, she's going to look at that man with more disdain than Casey Anthony after that pregnancy test turned pink. I've seen girlfriends cock block because they were clearly bitter. These bitter friends will rush the man away as if he's hindering their shopping, get smart with him, or make her friend throw his number away after she takes it. There is a high potential for drama when dealing with a girl protected by a clique, so you can't blame a guy for being intimidated by those odds.

At the same time, it is probably better to meet guys when you are with your girlfriends, provided those girls aren't haters. There is strength in numbers when attracting a guy, especially if you look better than your friends look. However, take into consideration what I just said, and know that he may be unwilling to make the first move if you are in a pride of ratchets. When you are with other girls and you spot a boy you think is cute, do what men do, and have your girls play the part of the wingman. Wingmen or wingwomen are those pals who serve as your mouthpiece if you are shy or run interference if the person you like is with a friend. I had relationships with several girls who I would never have approached on my own, but because their girlfriends called me over and said, "My girl says what's up," it was on and popping. Who cares if having your friends break the ice for you is considered young and cowardly? Nothing is lamer than standing in silence and watching as your potential boyfriend walks away.

DON'T MAKE LOVE TO YOUR PHONE

Social networking has replaced actual networking. I was at a house party and this cute girl stood by the wall playing on her phone the entire time. It's 11 p.m. and you're reading your news feed every five minutes, thirsty to see what other people are doing instead of living your life. That reeks of basicness. In the supermarket, which is a perfect place to catch the attention of normal guys, you'll see dozens of girls looking down at their phones instead of looking up. How can a guy approach you if you're acting like P. Diddy? You're not signing talent and you're not brokering business deals; you're texting back and forth with Shawntae about where you should go to find men. Meanwhile, an eligible man is taking his time in the frozen food section, hoping that you put that damn phone down long enough for him to make small talk. Everywhere I go I see girls talking or typing oblivious to their surroundings. I understand that you may hide behind the phone because you want to appear busy, not draw the attention of certain guys, or maybe having that phone in your hands has become a habit you can't break. Those are excuses. Remember that you don't have to be on the phone every minute that you're outside. You want to make yourself look busy. Well it's working a bit too well because that man you snuck a look at was ready to ask your name, but then he realized you were on the phone...maybe next time.

THE ART OF THE EYE FUCK

Three point five seconds of eye contact followed by a soft smile is all you need to bait a man and see if he is interested. Eye fucking is the most powerful tool for women who don't want to make the first move verbally. While most females know that eye contact is essential, many don't know how to properly eye fuck. There is looking at someone...then there is looking at someone you want to talk to romantically. These are two entirely different glances. I suggest looking at POV porn of Jesse Jane giving a BJ...now that's the eye of the tiger look that makes a man stop his conversation and walk over to you. Three point five seconds of eye contact followed by a soft smile is all you need to bait a man! The next time you see a guy you're interested in, no matter where you are, initiate eye contact. I'm not talking about the act as if you're looking at something else, sneak a peek, and then pretend you didn't look bullshit that little girls do. I want you to look at him until his eyes lock on you, and then hold it for 3.5 seconds. Count it out in your head as if you're in grade school—one one hundred...two one hundred...I know you're embarrassed, and you don't like looking in people's faces, but hold it for 3.5 then end with a smile and subtle turn away.

The hardest thing about eye contact is the turn away. It's always abrupt, and you don't want him to be the one to break it first. At the three-second mark, bite your lip slightly; men have oral fixations, so this takes his eyes off your eyes and shifts his focus to your mouth. Now that he's looking at your lips, smile and find something else to look at. Your eyes should be off him before the 4-second mark. Now he's looking back at you because that was an obvious sign. He's going to wait for you to look back at him, but you don't have to look back. Smile again to yourself, now he will assume, "She's thinking about me." What you just did was tattoo his brain. He may be a shy guy who wouldn't normally approach a stranger, but his fear of rejection is much lower because you two shared a moment. He has the sign that you are interested, which gives him the confidence to walk over and talk to you. If he is indeed into you, he's going to make a move within a few minutes of that initial eye contact. This obvious eye contact isn't strictly for men you meet outdoors. If you're talking to a man one on one and want him to notice that you like him and aren't just making chitchat, use eye fucking to start a sub-conversation. I used to be able to automatically spot those girls who liked me from their obvious lack of eye contact mixed with that moment when they would finally get the courage to look up with that sexy twinkle. That look sets men on fire! Utilize the power of the eyes and always have that sexy twinkle.

DRESS TO ERECT

Why do girls with nice bodies dress as if they're trying to prevent rape? If I were a girl, I would be on my Sofia Vergara swag all day, every day. I wouldn't care if girls hated on me or if thirsty guys molested me with their eyes. You are dressing up because it makes you feel good, and it's the easiest way to show off your best assets. A nice looking woman exudes confidence; men may not care about designer labels, but they go crazy when it's fitting right. I constantly see girls dressed like it's laundry day and they think that's okay because they aren't looking...but they are looking. Those pajama pants wearing chicas who come out of the house moody and pissed because their hair won't lay right are the same ones online filling out dating surveys and complaining that they never meet anyone. This goes back to attracting what you put out! Some men will talk to a girl regardless of how she dresses, but I'm going to go out on a limb and say those aren't the men you want. Thirsty guys who run up on you and don't care if you look as though you have the flu may give your self-esteem a boost, but you know he's full of shit and just looking for a hole.

If men are rocking jeans and t-shirts that are tighter than yours are, you need to reevaluate your fashion choices. I don't care if you're going to the store to grab a loaf of bread and some Playtex gentle glides. Show off! Bum bitches say things like, "It don't matter what I wear, dudes are still going to be on me." Then why are you single and still smashing your ex-boyfriend from a year ago? You're not being approached by quality men because you walk around wearing the type of clothes sexy women paint in. You don't need a lot of money to dress sexy. Show some cleavage, buy some pants that hug your ass, dare to throw some Nair on those rough legs, and wear a skirt for a change.

Your ego may keep beating you over the head with, "Why should I have to try so hard?" You wouldn't if you were proactive, but you're a wait to be picked type of girl; therefore, your presentation is key. Men can afford to be meticulous; they look at women as if they're public transit and live by the mentality that another bus will run every 15 minutes. A man can punk out from talking to one cute girl, wait it out, and then meet another girl who looks just as good by the end of the week. Your objective is to get him to see you as the type of bus that doesn't run every 15 minutes—one he has to run to catch, or he will kick himself for missing it. When you leave a distinct impression by rocking a tight shirt, a pair of fuck me heels, and some sexy leggings, it will increase a man's want to talk to you. Men don't mind rejection as long as you look good enough to risk it. Accentuate your positives and all men will notice, not just the ones you normally attract.

DON'T BLAME IT ALL ON MEN

A popular argument for women who don't like to approach men seems to be placing the blame on the man for not doing "what a real man should." Masking your fear of rejection by challenging a guy's manhood is common practice, but it doesn't solve anything. What are you going to do? Wait until you leave a party, find the car of the guy you thought was cute, and then leave a note saying, "Why didn't you come over and talk to me!?! You're such a pussy, a real man would have asked for my number regardless if I never made eye contact and kept playing on my phone!" Being upset that a man didn't approach you first is counterproductive. If you felt strongly that you wanted him to talk to you, then you should have taken matters into your own hands. Gender stereotypes are just that—stereotypes. A man has the right to be shy just as much as a woman has the right to be aggressive. The truth of the matter is that every man has approached a girl; it's the one thing as teenagers they are dared to do repeatedly. "Go pull shorty over there in the DVD section," is a rite of passage for the fellas. As boys get older, they get less thirsty. Most men don't feel a need to dust off those skills unless she's a rare breed. For less outgoing men or guys who are used to being pursued, a woman has to be worth the rejection. If a man does not approach you, it doesn't necessarily mean you're not special; he's already taken, being lazy, or not a real man. He's just as afraid as you are. In order to get over this fear, he looks for a sign: that eye contact, that smile, or anything that lets him know the chance of rejection is below 50%.

Introducing yourself is the least you can do. The argument that men don't have to do anything these days is weak. After the initial introduction, it's still on the man to ask you out and solidify that there is a connection. The man has to figure out the best place to take you on a date. On that date, he has to work to show you a good time and get a second date. During this period, he has to court you, which means working hard to get you open enough for sex. If you are the type of woman who only sleeps with a guy she's in a relationship with, he has to convince you to make it exclusive. If you are comfortable enough to have sex with him, it's still on him to work at giving you good sex. Once sex is out of the way and he feels even stronger, the man has to work at being a loyal boyfriend. Once you've been together for a time, he has to work to afford an engagement ring, and then he has to work up the nerve to propose. That's a shit load of work that men have to do that women rarely think about! Stop crying about how much effort it is to introduce yourself to a man. Saying "hello" is far from doing everything. I want you to linger on the concept of being proactive because when eye contact, wearing the right clothes, smiling, and getting friends to talk to men for you fails, there will be ONE sure fire way to get the man of your dreams, and that's by opening your mouth.

SAYING THE RIGHT THINGS

What do I say to him? Reread the last chapter on having self-esteem and fully understand that what you say isn't as important as how you say it. The confidence to talk to him casually like an old friend is the foundation that has to be laid before you even go tap him on the shoulder! Remember your Spartan training; know your strengths and weaknesses. Go back and think about the bomb elements of your personality that make you the Wifey type and underplay those bad habits that could make you come off as just Pussy. With that in mind, there are specifics that you can practice and I will throw out some conversation starters.

When you're somewhere like a club, bar, or someone's house party, the easiest thing to do is to make small talk about the quality of the place. I've had girls walk up to me talking about how the DJ sucks, how hot it is in there, how ghetto the other girls are, etc... I'm not the owner. They aren't telling me their concerns because I can do something about it. They were saying "hi" in their own sly way. In crowded places, you can be the most intimate because no one enjoys the overwhelming feeling of being a cog in a machine. He's out in a social setting. That means he is social. His face may look like he's upset, but it's probably him retreating into his shell because he's not having fun. For a man like this, start the conversation with a comment that will quickly tell you his state of mind. Ask him why he's so mad, but don't be dry, use your personality. If you're a funny person, make a joke about him looking like one too many people stepped on his Jordans. If you're the sassy type, be a smart ass and tell him he shouldn't come to gatherings if he's going to mug the wall all night. If you're more of a warm and friendly woman who struggles with creativity, be personable. Walk over and hip bump him gently or shoulder nudge him; touching someone in a general manner like this can disarm them. After that nudge, ask if he's having fun. You know he's not because he's mugging, but it opens up a discussion where you both can break the ice about the quality of the cookout, bar, club, or whatever, and then transition into more personal things like where you're from, what you do, etc...

If it's a stranger out in public who catches your eye, it can be weird to just walk up and start talking, but again, if you have that confidence that you look sexy and talk even sexier, nothing short of having a wife or fiancée will keep him from being hypnotized by you. Remember, eye contact will bait him. Once you grin and he cheeses back, walk over ready to shine. If you see a guy whose attention you can't get or if you just happen to bump into him, you'll have to go in cold without having a sign. That's cool, some people work better under pressure, and after all you are the Queen of fucking Sparta, you need a good challenge to sharpen your skills at least once a month. Your homework is to come up with an introduction excuse for every occasion. Have a conversation starter premade for a man you may meet at school, a new guy who comes to your job, a guy in line at the store, the cashier at the store, the dude who pulls up at a red light, a man who bumps into you accidentally, the guy next to you on an airplane, even the guy who you see on the opposite side of the street and have to figure out a reason to circle back to catch up with him. Create a list of generic things to say to break the ice for any situation you think you will find yourself in like these:

I'm sorry to bother you, my phone's dead. What time is it? (after phone is taken out) An Apple nerd, I should have known.

You don't really need the time or give a fuck about what kind of phone he has but this insult-flirting is always an easy way to get a man talking. Using the excuse of a dead phone also transitions nicely into putting your number in his phone since yours is down and out.

Excuse me, where did you get that <u>insert sneaker/shirt/hat</u> that looks nice. My cousin/brother would love me if I swagger jacked you.

Complimenting fashion or style disarms a man and strokes his ego. Telling him that you're looking out for a family member and not a boyfriend tells him all he needs to know. This is probably the easiest excuse as it can be used practically anywhere.

> *Hey, did you go to State? ...Oh, I'm so sorry, you looked like this boy I thought I knew...a little cuter though.*
>
> Men use the "you look familiar" line all the time, and it can work for women as well. Saying you know him from school, an old job, or as an old friend of a friend, opens the door for conversation.

It doesn't matter what the actual details or situation is, just have a game plan, or default thing to say for most occasions. The key is to get face to face and break the ice. That's not being thirsty, that's being aggressive. There is not a man on this earth who will hold your random flirting against you. Men don't care about how you show them that you're interested as long as it's not creepy like leaving notes on car windows or letters under doors. Be direct! If you don't come away with the phone number of the first man you approach, don't give up. Failure to make a connection is not rejection; see it as perfecting your pitch. By the third time you do this, it'll be like riding a bike.

THE END OF EXCUSES

The ultimate excuse for not approaching men first is, "My friend was approached first, and now she's married." When you point to other women who didn't do shit but sit and look cute, and then say, "Look it worked for them," you're making an excuse so you don't have to change. You're spewing non-facts based on people who are different from you in order to make yourself feel better when you don't Spartan up. If someone tells you most marriages end in divorce, are you going to say "no" to a proposal? If your friends tell you that they had unprotected sex and never got an STD, do you throw away your condoms? Don't live your life based off what happened to the next woman. Treat your situation as if it's unique, because it is.

The man another woman met, the situation where it occurred, and the outcome can never be duplicated. She was at the supermarket and caught a guy's eye; you could hang in that same market for weeks and never even get a glance. Alternatively, you could meet two guys at that market on the same day and both could turn out to be incompatible. The only foolproof plan is to make your own lane! Take your love life into your own hands, let go of your ego, and try approaching men for at least one month. After that month, regardless of if you found someone or not, you won't go back to that outdated way of thinking. Once you realize that you can pull any man you want, you will never settle for just the guys who come up and talk to you again.

19

Getting Him to Commit

Men make their minds up fairly quickly when it comes to shopping. Go to a department store and observe a man by himself. Regardless of what he's looking for he doesn't browse long. There are men who window-shop to kill time or to do research, but the average man in a Best Buy has a shopping agenda. If you see 30-year-old Anthony in the electronics section looking at TVs, the odds are that he has nailed it down to two that he wants after about ten minutes. It will take Anthony more time to check out than it will to decide on that $700 purchase. To relate that to dating, guys always know exactly what they are and aren't looking for in a woman, and only need a week or two to know if she belongs in the Pussy box or Wifey box. Any man who tells you that he's still figuring out what you two are after a month is bullshitting you. Your friend knows exactly which box you go in, and if you get that "figuring it out" response, it's not the wifey box.

How high will you climb up his serious chart has already been determined after the first fourteen days. A fella may not know everything about you, but he knows enough based on your first week behavior to have you scouted. He won't tell you verbally, but his actions will be proof. He either tries to lock you down or keeps you as just his FWB. It doesn't matter if he he's poor, is busy with school, or between jobs; those are excuses that men use to keep you on the waiting list. If he wants you he will have you, believe that shit. When I was dating I couldn't put my finger on these things, but I knew inherently what I wanted. For me to take it from a sex friendship to an actual relationship didn't require deep meditation, nor did it require a girl to jump through hoops to impress me. She didn't have to do shit but be who she was, and that was impressive enough. I didn't care about what you could do for me financially, if you could cook, if you lived at home, or what store your clothes came from. Are you pretty, are you fun, and can I be myself around you? It really is that simple. Every man has a slut side, and every man has a romantic side. Those girls who he simply wants to have sex with do not get a commitment, not a real one anyway; they get numerous excuses followed by sweet talk and more manipulation. In the same way that men no longer have to take women out to dinner for it to qualify as a date; males have also realized that getting sex doesn't necessitate committing. Many women are desperate, which has allowed men to leverage this thirst for love into a buffet of sex. Only after a man sees a woman as unique will he want to commit, not for sex, but for the pleasure of owning that masterpiece.

Each man has a different definition of beauty and charisma; therefore, each woman will be viewed differently. I may see you as the type I would take out for a few weeks, have sex with, and be cool with—nothing serious. The next guy may see you as irresistible, take you out for a few weeks, and then ask if you would be his girlfriend. What determines this deeper attraction? At first, it depends on what a man is looking for physically, but that's superficial, and looking like his ideal women only gets you a seat at the table, not an invitation to stay. What it boils down to is the combustion that happens when a man meets the kind of personality that best meshes with his own. Unlike the physical lusting that a man will have for a music video hofessional, this spiritual connection takes that attraction from lust to genuine adoration. Before you suck your teeth and counter that you have a bomb ass personality, yet you're still single, remember this: Men may not see your greatness because you aren't opening up and SHOWING your full personality due to nerves or insecurity. If he misses out because you haven't put your best foot forward, can you blame him? If you leave *The Mona Lisa* in a cheap frame and lean it against the wall, will a novice art lover appreciate it? We've discussed self-esteem and self-confidence in terms of how they allow you to open up and stop being awkward, but the fear of rejection will once again rear its ugly head if you are too timid to be direct with a man. Today's women don't know how men view them because they're afraid of digging deep. They assume that a guy likes them, that a guy is building toward something, and that a guy respects them. However, these women are unwilling to ask questions that will either prove or disprove her assumptions.

Are you the only girl he's seeing? *Idunno*

Why did he and his last girlfriend break up? *Idunno*

Are you just kicking it or is this exclusive? *Idunno*

He said he works for the state, what exactly does he do? *Idunno*

What do you know? *Why are you in my business? We don't talk about all that stuff...we're just doing us and having fun, damn!*

To realize that she is a placeholder and not his Game Changer can shatter a woman's confidence, so she assumes she's top shelf without confirmation. Everyone wants to feel superior and special, but you will meet men who think you are average and will never commit. How will you know if a man likes you genuinely? You talk to him! One girl vented to me about how she confronted her friend and told him what she really wanted. This was the first time they even talked about relationship stuff and it was already four months into this no titles FWB relationship. He surprised her with, "I'm not going to marry you or nothing. It is what it is." It broke her heart and lead her to email me, but she's not the only one with this story. Women refuse to be that direct because they subconsciously know they are fucking guys who don't like them. Everyone has intuition, gut feelings that allow them to pick up on vibes. The reason you're trying to figure out how to get him to commit four months in is because you didn't use that intuition four months prior.

Most men are not good enough actors to masks their true intentions. I believe that 9 out of 10 women can see through the bullshit and know where they stand with these users, but they blind themselves with hope. The excuse that you can't help who you fall in love with is bullshit! You can help it because it takes more than a week to form that level of affection; therefore, you have more than enough time to consciously control who embeds themselves in your life. The average woman will ignore the little things her boo says and does that are obvious signs that he's not really serious. Hope mixed with desperation causes that same woman to shower him with love and sex in an attempt to erase these signs. When her boo starts to act funny or distance himself, a panic sets in. Instead of this woman tapping out when faced with an incompatible man, she troubleshoots the problem by becoming even more submissive and accommodating. From day one, she knew this man was not that into her, but she continued to try to make it work all under the umbrella of "a good woman stands by her man." The problem is that you're standing by a man that's not really your man and doesn't really want to be your man. Your intuition mixed with asking direct questions would have saved you from being hurt, played, or wasting your time with this indecisive ass fool! It's time to follow your gut, face this fear that he may not want you the way you want him, and transform yourself into a woman who gets a commitment, instead of a dumb girl who gets the run around.

I've talked in-depth about how to build your confidence, be proactive, and check your basic behavior before you even engage a man. It's easier to Spartan up when you're getting into a new relationship where you can flex your power, but there are women who are in the midst of purgatory relationships and have been waiting for their boo to make it official. These ladies are stuck because they can't flip the switch and take their power back. No matter if you're a placeholder whose threats no longer work or the FWB who gave it away for free, there is a way out. You can get a man to rethink that decision, and this chapter will reveal that answer, but only if you're strong enough to follow the steps. This knowledge is for those women who are willing to Spartan up and risk losing that man in order to get what they want.

PROVE YOU'RE DIFFERENT

I ain't like the next chick. You better ask about me! I call your bluff. If I were to ask about you, I'm sure I'd get guys who think you're just as average as the last woman he was with and didn't put a ring on. You talk a good game and brag on your qualities, but what are you doing to prove to men that you are indeed a boss chick? Talk is cheaper than Milky Way Remy, so you need to back up your claims by actually showing him that everything you do is better than the things done by other girls he's met. No, I'm not talking about the way you ride a penis. Contrary to popular belief, you can't sex trap a man into a commitment. "After I put this pussy on him, he's not going anywhere," is the dumbest statement since someone looked at the Titanic and proclaimed, "God himself couldn't sink this ship!" It didn't matter how well built the Titanic was, it's at the bottom of the Atlantic. It doesn't matter how tight or wet your vagina is, if he wants to game you, he will game you, then leave once it expires. While it's extremely beneficial to know how to have sex like a Spartan and not a Corpse Bride, a yanking pussy is not the glue that will bond you to that man or prove your uniqueness. Men love sex, but this isn't the movie *American Pie*. Not all males are horny teenagers who can't keep their dicks out of baked goods. This is the real world and pussy has become so easy to get that it no longer dictates if a man should stay. Ten out of ten girls will say they have the type of sex that would make a guy throw a ring on it...umm it doesn't look like anybody went to Jared and put a ring on your ashy finger. That's not to say you're not good at what you do; it's to say be better than a hole.

The better I'm talking about is your personality as shown through your actions. Every man wants a cool chick who won't flip out when he doesn't answer his phone on a Friday or react to his social media moves with jealousy. In short, a female who's confident enough not to act like a stalker as soon as the relationship starts to get a little serious. You may think that's easy to control, but when you begin to fall for someone, usually after the first few weeks of talking, your emotions become unpredictable. You can be the coolest chick in the world when you're not emotionally invested, but once you begin to open your heart, that coolness can transform into paranoia. Read the chapter on assuming what a man wants again because it's crucial. Understand that the current man you're with isn't like your ex who broke your heart by cheating nor is he your girlfriend's FWB who has been selling her a dream for six months. This man is new, and you can only judge him on how he's treating you during this first month. The honeymoon period of a relationship fades into a rehearsal period where the man you're seeing gets a glimpse into who you truly are. From that rehearsal period comes the ultimate decision of Cuff Her or Bluff Her.

If you're the girl who leaves three texts messages as soon as you don't hear back from him within an hour, that tells him you're needy. If he comments on a celebrity on TV sexually, and you jump down his throat, that tells him that you're jealous and insecure. If you suck your teeth and only give one-word answers after he has to cancel a meet up, that tells him you are a brat that doesn't know how to communicate her disappointment like an adult. That may be exactly who you are but realize that a man stays out of relationships not because he likes loneliness, but because he hates dealing with a shitty attitude. A paranoid, jealous, and clingy woman with poor communication skills is the epitome of a bad girlfriend. No matter how cool you are 80% of the time, showing those dark flaws will keep you his homegirl, just a friend, or girl he talks to, instead of the woman he locks down and throws a title on. Show the maturity of a woman who sees herself as a serious girlfriend, instead of a brat who is jealous, clingy, and insecure. Aggression, Control, and Comfort are the keys to making him see you as a grown woman who could stand beside him for years to come.

Let's begins with aggression, this means taking action, being decisive in that action, and having the confidence to do things when you want to, not just when it's the safest time to take that action. In practice, this means being aggressive enough to call him when you want to call him, not waiting by the phone for him to hit you when he feels like it. Calling too much is pathetic, but not calling enough is just as deadly. Not only should you call, you should have something to say other than, "Whatchu doing? Miss me?" Share something interesting about your day or have a topic you want an opinion on ready to be discussed. Stop coming at him with high school chitchat, not only is it boring, and tiresome, it shows him that you're just like the rest of these dummies. All he'll do is play your game and tell you what you want to here. "I'm chilling. I was just thinking about you, sexy." Men say that shit to get points, then they quickly figure out a way to get off the phone after five minutes because you don't want shit but to hear yourself talk. Prove you're different by coming better than the Basicas who do that. When it comes to dating, you have to be just as forward. If he doesn't want to do anything outside of his apartment, don't give in; be aggressive! Plan what you want to do without waiting for him to give his approval, after the plans are made, dare him to stand you up.

Next up is control, which is just as important because this gives you the ability to check your own irrational behavior. "I'm a girl, we get moody...I can't help that," is a card that females play when apologizing for their emotional behavior. I don't care if you're on your period with cramps as violent as Jodi Arias, you can control your emotions! Exercising control will keep you from getting into petty arguments and saying things you don't mean. Speak up in a direct yet controlled manner when you feel wronged. Don't yell at him as if you're on a reality show reunion special, and don't shut down and be passive aggressive. So many women struggle with their emotions and allow their feelings of anger or disappointment to take over. Ratchet women react with fingers pointed, verbal insults, and threats to fuck someone else. Shy women would rather give the silent treatment than argue. A man needs to see that you are capable of discussing problems. He shouldn't have to try and figure out what exactly is wrong with you based off the response, "You know what you did," or "It don't even matter now..." Act your age, not your weave length!

Let's say you miss him, but he hasn't called you in a day and a half. The little teenager inside of you will get sad and think the worst, "He doesn't like me like that. I knew it was bullshit." Next, you'll get defensive, "Fuck him. He doesn't ever have to call me. It's his loss." Then you'll proceed to write a text proclaiming all of this. Due to your lack of control, you just cursed this man out before you even had a chance to discuss what happened with him. You're falling in love, you're afraid that this was all a game, and the left and right sides of your brain are battling with these negative and positive thoughts. Why so serious so suddenly? Control your anxiety; don't defeat yourself by letting negative thoughts and immature actions win out over maturity and logic.

Okay, let's say you are aggressive and tell him what you want and communicate how you feel. You're also in control and you don't overreact to drama or small situations; you're on the right track. Now comes the last part—comfort. Get comfortable with him and lower your guard enough for him to see the best parts of your personality. I've met girls who have been talking to guys for months and they are still awkward and shy when he's around. I'm not saying fart in front of the dude, but after the second date and weeks of talking, you should start to drop the nice girl act, and open up your true personality. Laugh your laugh, not the fake one you do where you cover your mouth. Eat like you eat in front of your cousins, not like you're at the royal tea party. The mystique of sexiness isn't lost because you act human. My favorite Romantic Comedy, *Pretty Woman* has a scene where Vivian gets comfortable and begins watching *I Love Lucy*, and in that moment of goofy humanity, she immediately becomes sexier than she was whilst rocking the hooker boots and wig. Be yourself, not what you think he wants you to be. Once you're comfortable enough to play fight and tell ignorant jokes, he's free to be just as silly. That's how you get a man, even a tough one, to drop his guard and open his heart.

If you want a commitment, you have to be worth one—not in theory, but in reality. Show him you're special by not falling victim to the pitfalls of basic bitches who thirst for relationships and allow themselves to be boxed in. Make him look at you as a rare woman, one who's cool, confident, and fun. At the same time, if he tests you by acting like he can do what he wants, don't become submissive and let him get away with that behavior, check his ass with controlled restraint and a no nonsense professionalism. After a few weeks of observing how you act, he will see you as special, easy to talk to, low on stress, honest, and far from the typical pushover that would let him take advantage. Now all the, "not like the rest" bragging has been proven. You are now greater than all the other girls he knows. This man will waste little time in locking you down because he recognizes your breed doesn't come around often. If he doesn't notice those things or isn't impressed, then you aren't the one for him and that's something you can't change. Don't waste another week continuing to show an ignorant man the brilliance of the Mona Lisa; he will never get it.

EXCLUSIVE BUT NON-COMMITTAL

Maybe these steps came too late and you didn't blow him away with your personality the first month in order to get that quick commitment. No title was given, but you continued as "friends." You do all the things that boyfriends and girlfriends do, but it's not official, just exclusive—on your end anyway. I call these "Placeholder Relationships," and they are happening more and more often because the knowledge I've shared throughout this book is rarely practiced. Don't feel bad, there is still time to catch up. Why do men beat around the bush when it comes to love and do things on their schedule? You allow that behavior. I don't care how many times you yell, ignore calls, or threaten to leave; he knows something you don't know—you have no one else. You have no other options for love, you don't want to be truly single (although, just having a fromance still makes you single), and you don't want to throw away what you've put your time and energy into for the past several months until you absolutely have to.

The man you're in love with knows that you're hooked and no matter how much you say you're frustrated and one more incident away from moving on, he can smell your indecision. You have proven that you are content with what he gives you, which means he has no reason to change. He's going to take you for granted when he feels like it, not because he doesn't love you, but because he doesn't respect you. He will keep talking to other girls because he knows you will only bark. He will stand you up on date night because he knows you will still let him come over and have sex at 1 a.m. Your friend/boo/baby daddy will come and go as he pleases and talk to you how he wants because you will never truly check his ass. You are afraid to leave him, and that's the chain that keeps you in the placeholder position. The first step in getting a commitment from a man that's already gotten the milk for free is to prove that he isn't your only or best option.

Right now, you're his happy little placeholder. He's won you over, and you are now off the market because you want to see if this will work. You think you're off the market…but you are on the market. No matter how many times he claims you two are "exclusive," without a title it's all bullshit. Having three of the four numbers doesn't make you a lotto winner, and having in house dick doesn't make you a girlfriend. You're playing a role and not being compensated for it—that's called being robbed! You go to work because you want to be paid at the end of the week, right? In these exclusive but not committed relationships, you get an IOU at the end of the week instead of payment. Would you allow your boss to use you with only his "thank you" as compensation? Hell no! You would quit and find a new job. In relationships, even ones that are technically non-relationships, women refuse to go look for something new.

Go back and think about what it would mean to be single again. To go back to the clubs, bars, and parties trying to get noticed must be unbearable if you would rather stay in relationship purgatory. The reason many women stay put is that the search for a new man is often long and humbles her ego. You claim to be the sexiest and most electrifying girl in the world, but then you watch as other women are approached by men instead of you. Being single checks your ego, exposes your false confidence, and makes you feel subpar every time you see a friend's Facebook status update to "engaged."

According to the 2010 U.S. Census 43% of people over the age of 18 are single. If you were to think of being single as being unemployed, that would make over 96 million people romantically destitute. Break it down by race, and the census report shows that black women make up an alarming chunk of that unwed percentage. Because of these fucked up numbers, most women have become desperate to get in a relationship and those who are in one are petrified to break up. It's as if journalists took hold of these raw numbers and tried to scare women into settling for any dick they can get so they won't be left stuck in that 43%. Numbers don't lie, but they do change, and you can't let statistics hold you back from going for what you want. Those women in purgatory relationships aren't even in an exclusive partnership, but they are close enough to the un-single side. Damn if they want to go back to that life of internet dating, friend hookups, and bar hoping. Given that single women outnumber single men, and that only 4.6% of black women date outside their own race,[17] you don't have to be a genius to figure out black men benefit the most. At the same time, other races profit from statistic fear mongering as well. This is a generation that can sit back and half ass it all day in terms of commitment, and because they have

---

[17] Black women were the least likely to marry outside their race at only 4.6% in 2010. 10.8 percent of African American men married outside their race in 2010. Source: US Census Bureau: America's Families and Living Arrangements 2010.

swag, are attractive, or simply approach women first, they thrive. Your would be boyfriend knows you don't want to go back to being a statistic. You are now comfortable, and no matter how much you cry for a title, having him unofficially is better than having no one at all. Getting him to see you differently and treat you with the loyalty you deserve requires you to stop fearing those statistics, stop fearing the dating scene, and stop fearing the single life, period.

I don't care how swagged out your guy friend is or how hard he walks around pretending to be. If a man loses the woman he loves, it will crush him. There is no need to give ultimatums, throw fits, or cry. Here's how you get a commitment right now: *I don't have any more time to waste on you. Call me when you're on the same page.* A man will guilt you with, "You're being dramatic," soften you up with, "Baby, you know I love you," or scare you with, "Fuck you, I don't need your ass anyway." All three of those things are ploys to put you back in place and call your bluff. The funny thing is, women scream, "I mean it this time" but fall for one of those three responses nearly every time. The key to get him to respect you is to mean what you say. If you want to be with him, you must be willing to forgo everything you have with him if things don't change immediately.

How do you do this practically? Before you even have a talk with him, make plans to get him out of your life. If you live with your non-boyfriend, start seriously looking for a new place to stay. I'm not talking leads. I mean see the place and even pay for a credit check as if you are going to move out at the top of the month. If you don't have much money, go to a friend or a family member and tell them what you are planning to do. Most of you ladies don't live with your would be boyfriends, so it's much easier to cut him off…in theory. Start by getting yourself ready to delete his number. This means removing your personal items from his place or vice versa, so you'll have no reason to call again. End any kind of weekly arrangement you two have like social group gatherings. Most importantly, you have to toughen yourself up mentally by accepting that this relationship will soon be over. Visualizing breaking up and taking all the steps that lessen his impact in your life before actually breaking up will help you deal with his tears and cries for you to stay. When it comes time to have the talk, the bridge should already be on fire. He can talk to you seriously and see where you're coming from or he can continue to give you the same old excuses about money, work, and not being ready for the next step. You're asking to be exclusive, not for a ring, how the hell is he still not ready for this level of commitment? If you hear the same shit you've been hearing, set fire to the rain, and let that bridge burn by walking out of his life that night. Having done the prep work you won't have any reason to call him or come back over, this is true radio silence, which means he won't just brush this off as just another blow up from which you need time to cool down.

Don't feel a need to explain yourself, argue, or cry it out with him. If you create a dialogue, it will allow him to kiss ass and snake his way back through guilt or false promises. He thinks you're a weak bitch and is simply acting out for attention. Remember, stringing women along comes with a price; it means that the man doing the stringing is also an on-call firefighter. Every so often, he has to put out the flames when you show out. Don't allow him to calm you down like some Bottom Bitch with nowhere else to go. This is the crucial step in making him respect you because men know when a woman is bluffing as opposed to being serious about moving on. If you walk out on him with no conversation and don't answer his calls for the next month, he knows it's real and will come back ready to work something out...that is if he gave a damn in the first place.

Most of you reading this are thinking that's easy. Some of you have tried to leave and know how hard it is. Remember, this is the man you are in love with. Can you take him crying like a baby on the phone, sending you love emails, buying you gifts, or talking about how he would die without you? Most women can't withstand and they buckle at the first text that ends with a smiley face. Remind yourself that he didn't cry when he was coming and going as he pleased. He wasn't talking about suicide every time he told you that he wasn't ready for a serious relationship. Don't give in to his sudden need to be with you because it's not genuine. This only works if you actually follow through. If you confront your guy friend half-heartedly trying to get him to say, "Okay we go together now," then you will never get what you need! A man will lie to you in order to calm you down and then you're back where you started. An empty "we're exclusive" is bullshit. You don't need him to just say it; you need him to live it!

In order to keep you, a man should say the words, and then prove it over the course of the next few weeks. I'm talking taking you out to dinner, updating his Facebook status, allowing you to tag him in post, going over to his parent's home, agreeing to hang with you some nights instead of his boys, give you a key to the apartment, and most importantly opening up his heart about all the reasons that kept him from committing during the first month like a normal man. The title alone means nothing unless it comes with the trust, dedication, and communication of a real relationship! Honesty and quality time are things real girlfriends get. Therefore, you must demand those terms before you take him back. I repeat, the key to making this work is to follow through. A lot of women last a few weeks being tough then they go soft, get scared, and let him back into their lives. Stop being afraid to lose a man you're comfortable with and embrace the fact that you have the right to redefine the rules of this arrangement. Come to grips with the possibility that he may be like, "bitch, bye" and that you may have to go join the 43% back in the world of the single. Some of you will try this on men who were just using you and those men won't come running back. That means he revealed himself as a user. Be thankful that you didn't waste more time chasing someone who never wanted you. It will never be easy putting your foot down, but either get a commitment or accept being single, never settle for the in-between!

REGAINING YOUR POWER

Let's say you're not strong enough to walk away just yet. You would rather try to show him that you aren't basic and impress him in the manner you should have when you first met. How can you make your man hit reset on the relationship and see you as more than used pussy or a Bottom Bitch? The first step in regaining your power is to stop being accessible. People take for granted those things they don't have to work to acquire. A man will expect you to cater to him if all you do is cater for the sake of catering. Appreciation will be a foreign concept to this man because he got your best effort without any effort. He wants to talk to you about his problems, so you're there to listen. He wants sex at night when he's done living his life, so you come over. He wants to go out with his boys, not out on a date, so you happily find a girlfriend to accompany you to that movie. You cannot be that accommodating to a man that refuses to go all in. What motivation does he have to upgrade you if he's getting all the benefits now? Learn to say "no," and say it often. Most men will complain, but they respect a challenge, and if he's truly into you, he will compromise or do things on your terms once you show him you're not a joke. That's not being a bitch to get your way. That's using your leverage to make him respect you.

Live life on your terms, be selfish, and make him come to you. Demand to go places you want to go. Have sex when you're in the mood. Don't respond back after every text message. This is the only way you can redistribute the power in the relationship. This isn't something you have to do all the time, just until he gets the point that you aren't afraid to lose him. Once a man knows you don't jump when he says "how high," then a mutual respect forms. You are no longer a girl. You are a woman and that's how he has to see you in order to take you seriously. You may be thinking, "I don't want to force him to be with me. He'll just start creeping with a new girl who is submissive and doesn't pressure him." No man does anything he doesn't want to do. Don't think the fear of losing you is forcing him into a corner where he does something against his will.

Forced relationships don't last because a man who honestly doesn't want to be in a relationship will always find an out. If you show him that you don't need him and he doesn't want to make that commitment, then he will let you go. However, there is usually one final bluff-calling test a man will give his former slave. A manipulator will let a woman walk out, then take actions to make her jealous or remorseful. Most women can't handle being jealous or lonely, and they will reluctantly return to the plantation. I remind you, don't take him back until your conditions of being an actual girlfriend are met. Not all men are going to let you regain that power, not because you're doing it the wrong way, but because you've gone too far down the weak bitch path. You know how some older friends of the family still see you as a young girl despite being grown? Men can be so caught up in you being the old subservient slave, and they will never be able to look at you as a grown woman who means what she says. To these stubborn men, you're always going to be Pussy because you allowed too much time to pass and that box to become permanent.

By striking fear in a heart of a man who does love you, but is afraid to take it to the next level, you are giving him a needed push. A man who truly cares for you will appreciate that push, take you out of the box, and remix your relationship. Men do not always give into their true feelings and handcuff a woman. This reluctance usually comes from a male who was hurt or played in a previous relationship. A divorced man, a guy who was once engaged and had it called off, or any man that's been betrayed by a woman he loved, will give you a hard time. Pushing a man like this helps him face his own fears. Let's say that he has been your "friend" for six months, and he keeps dodging that relationship status. You walk out of his life and now he realizes what he had. You showed him how easy it is to lose you, allowed him time to realize how incredible you were, and then gave him a second chance to fix things. That's how you reset the relationship, not on his terms as soon as he calls crying, but on your terms. Not only will he step up and appreciate you more the second time around, he will also realize that being handcuffed isn't awful.

Men fear being locked down because they don't understand what a good relationship is; only the negatives they've seen or experienced. A good relationship isn't a cage where he has to keep his eyes to the ground when other women walk by, be in the house by 10 p.m., and have stale sex. Once you have the title, show him the benefits. Reward him by getting a little freakier in the bedroom than usual. Let him have even more space with his friends and prove that you aren't going to turn into a prison warden now that you have the commitment. Continue to tighten that bond by communicating more. Pick out a day each week where you two can have alone time as a couple and talk. The only way to earn his respect and keep his respect is by flexing your power! Sex on demand, yelling when he hurts your feelings, being submissive, transparent threats to leave, or attempts to make him pay attention through jealousy are wrong turns that lead back to the same bumpy road you're currently stuck on.

20
50

When Is It Time to Move On

That's all bullshit. A bunch of generalizations that your know-it-all ratchet girlfriends or aunts tell you to elicit head nods and the classic Basica response of, "I know that's right!" You can't go by a check off list in real life. Red flags are never actually red! Warning signs don't come blinking with sirens in actual relationships. If it were that easy to point out a bad man, then there would be no single women. You can have a thousand examples of things that men do that would make you leave him, but until you're in that situation with your heart on the line, you can't say for sure that you would actually leave. Someone on the outside looking in will see just one of the above examples and tell you to leave. If they see two, they label you a dumb bitch. The hard truth is that unlike those judging, you see him as a human being with various sides…some parts of his personality make you cry and swear that he's the devil, other parts make you smile and thank God for him being in your life. You worked so hard to get him to commit to you, you're finally out of that 43% single group, and there is no way you're going to break up at the first few red flags. I understand that mindset, and standing by your man through the good times and bad is what defines being in love. However, now that you've gotten to the level where you two are in a committed relationship, you can't unconditionally love a man who constantly takes advantage of your loyalty.

Women are stubborn. They think they can save any man with enough love or transform his potential into her perfection with enough time. That mentality mixed with the fear of losing all she has worked for will always keep her holding on to a bad relationship. There is always that woman who huffs and puffs about how she would never be with a man after he cheats on her. When it does happen, she changes that tune and makes an excuse for why she's still with that cheater. You swore you had to have a man with a job, now here you are in love with a person who is constantly unemployed. You called your friend stupid for letting a man hit her, now here you are using cover up after the love of your life knocked you around, holding on to claims that you hit him first. If you thought "friends" put up with a lot to get the title, actual girlfriends will walk on hot coals to keep their men. Guys know the right mixture of false promises and sex will cause a girl to put up with things she swore she would never put up with just a month prior. Everyone will experience relationship difficulties, but the messiness that some girls go through is beyond growing pains. Real love isn't a roller coaster it's a fucking tank. If you loved yourself, you wouldn't be constantly allowing someone to hurt you. If a man really loved you, he wouldn't be making the same hurtful mistakes every few months. There is no true love in bad relationships, only a sad dependency that makes women hang on in hopes of a miracle.

There comes a breaking point in most relationships when two incompatible people should split, but they don't. They continue because they're comfortable with each other, afraid to find someone new, or are downright delusional. Everyone around you can see that your relationship is weaker than Gandhi doing a chin up, but because you think he's the best boyfriend ever (and only real option) you stay. In a few months, you'll look back and say to your girlfriends, "I can't believe you let me stay with him so long. What was I thinking?" Then a week later, you will relapse and go back to him. I've compiled a list of various types of men that are littered with red flags. Study these men, take an honest look at your life, and if the shoe fits, make him wear it on the way out of the door.

> "People tell you who they are, but we ignore
> it because we want them to be who we want
> them to be." – Don Draper

THE CHRIS BROWN

Girls do not know how to Chris Brown proof their vagina. Of course, I'm not talking about the real Chris Breezy. I use Chris Brown as the metaphor for the one guy who looks exactly like your fantasy man, and be honest; every female has a fantasy man. The Chris Brown type is that guy who at first sight makes you scream inside, turns you on, and gives you butterflies as if you're a high school girl giggling near the lockers all over again. There are women who pass judgment on other girls who are "whipped" or in lust with no good men. These ladies think they are smarter than the average female and believe there isn't a man built that could make her go dumb for dick...then "Chris Brown only a little darker" comes along, and she forgets everything she thought she knew. Men like Chris Brown, Idris Elba, George Clooney, and that wolf from *True Blood* are considered default panty droppers. Meaning 90% of women left alone with them will give up the ass. Don't be ashamed, women are human beings too, and human beings are sexually charged. Your body wants what looks good, and no amount of praying to Jesus not to get moist will change those sexual desires. Take a man with great, not just good looks, add the gift of game, and he becomes a nightmare for even the smartest of women.

Women do look past the physical; they've been bred to believe that being a provider is more important than being a looker. Often you may hear a woman rant about, "He takes care of his responsibilities. That's the biggest turn on." They aren't just saying that to look on the bright side, that quality is inbred. Let's face it, if every woman decided to wait for the best looking guy in the village, the battle royal over that penis would put *The Hunger Games* to shame. Since civilization began, women have been pursued by men that were less than handsome and have learned to look at what matters most—his heart and ability to take care of her. Despite the tradition of marrying a provider, the female eyes have not devolved; they still widen at the sight of handsome men. Let's keep it real, women lust after good-looking men the same way men lust after beautiful women. Enter the Chris Brown type. He looks exactly like the man of your dreams, but he's in your face giving you attention and you're dripping wet at the thought of a man like this being yours.

Some women who get into a relationship with a Chris Brown type will try to control their jealousy with lies, brainwashing themselves to think, "He ain't that cute." However, for most girls, this is their first time being with a ten and they can't handle the mental pressure of having a man that's wanted by 90% of the women he meets. These women crack, and paranoia leaks out; now they're hopping gates to see the fool, doing drive-bys at 1 a.m. to make sure he doesn't have company, and Googling "how to track android phones" because she's afraid of the competition. When females stalk, fight, and commit property damage over guys, it's not because the man has a bomb personality, it's not because his dick is dipped in fairy dust—it's because of LOOKS! Looks make everything better. It makes his jokes funnier. It makes his dick go from six inches to eight. It makes his Dodge Neon look like an Audi A8. Perception is a motherfucker. Instead of becoming suspicious the moment he doesn't answer his phone and losing all self-respect because you fear never finding another man as fine, you have to take steps to control your paranoia.

One girl left a comment on BGAE saying, "I expect a sexy guy to cheat at least once; it's only natural." Basicas give into that "accept it" mentality. Spartans don't think on that primitive level, they demand loyalty no matter how good that man looks. Admit that he's fine internally, do your little dance of joy when you're alone, but when you're face to face treat him like you would any other man. Rock hard body, pretty eyes, or killer smile, none of it matters because you're still the prize that's trying to be won over and kept happy in this relationship, not him. Pretty boys know they're pretty; they are used to special treatment. Be the one woman who doesn't give him that level of attention and leeway. Having money often allows a man to put a woman in this, "bitch, be happy to be along for the ride" state of fear. Good looks do the exact same thing, and when a vain man meets an overly impressed woman, the fear of losing him will box her into a corner. Men will jump ship when they want to jump ship, and if your Brad Pitt tires of your Jennifer Aniston, there will always be a Super Spartan like Angelina Jolie there to take him off your hands. There is nothing you can do to keep a man who doesn't want to be kept. Let him know that he's free to go be with those girls who dick ride him online, at school, or at work, but while he's your boyfriend, there will be no special treatment. Hold this good looking guy up to the same standards as any man who stops communicating, keeps lusting after other woman, and disrespects your relationship. Looking good is not a pass to act out. The moment your Chris Brown type feels it's his right to entertain other women, entertain your right to delete his number. You attracted one dime; you can do it again. Trust.

HOT AND COLD GUY

He's so nice, then he's so mean, then he's nice again, then you're back to fighting. Stop trying to play *House MD* and find a diagnosis that explains why he has the right to treat you like crap. He's not bipolar, he's just an asshole; accept it. Hot and Cold Guys act extremely distant and then act extremely sensitive for no apparent reason. These guys are skilled at attracting girls because when they're nice, they're really nice. A woman can be involved with this ticking time bomb for two months, and everything will be perfect. He's affectionate, not afraid to share his feelings and thinks of you first. Additionally, he won't let you boss him around like a wimp and calls you out on your shit. He's everything you've ever wanted, a sweetheart with a spine. Nevertheless, once he becomes comfortable with you, out comes the Diana Ross diva. Everyone's out to get him and no one cares about his feelings. When it comes to Hot and Cold Guy, it's him against the world for reasons he will never truly explain. Next, you're feeling guilty, and you don't even know what you did wrong. Why would a woman want to be with a man who's more emotional than she is? Every little thing starts an argument with the Hot and Cold Guy. You can be eating Chinese food and grab the last fortune cookie, and it sets him off. Two minutes later, you're in P.F. Chang's being yelled at for being selfish. "You know I needed that fortune cookie. I told you how my mother never let me have them when I was little," and he's dead serious. The Hot and Cold Guy has severe baggage from childhood, ex-girlfriends, and life in general that causes him to lash out.

The Hot and Cold Guy will always apologize, you two will make up, and everything will be perfect for a few days...then you decide to go out with your girlfriends instead of hanging with him, and he's back on his emo shit. Next, he will accuse you of cheating or call you a lesbian because he's paranoid and insecure. Hot and Cold Guy has issues that your love can't rectify. A man like this may be perfect for a few weeks, but he will never last because he has issues that only a therapist can sort out. Do you want to go through years of walking on eggshells in an attempt to keep him from erupting? He's not bipolar or depressed; he wants attention and pity. Pack his bags, hand him a box of tampons, and show him and his menstrual cycle the door.

THE PUSHOVER

Women love the Pushover at first. He's not argumentative, he does nice things for you, and when he tells you that he loves you, he means it. On paper, a Pushover looks like the guy you marry, sweet, giving, and communicative. The problem is no girl wants to bump vaginas with her boyfriend. Women like excitement and a challenge, not a man who jumps at the chance to go get a biweekly mani/pedi with her. This woman sent me an email asking the best way to break up with her pushover boyfriend who had done her no wrong. Her boyfriend would bend over backwards, but she couldn't take any more of him overdoing the romance and agreeing with everything she said like a puppet. Although she wasn't fulfilled by this relationship, she was afraid to tell him that it was over. Once she told him, "You smother me," and he nearly committed suicide, so she stuck with him. Here she was nearly a year later, still miserable. I told her that she was ruining her life by being polite. If that man is at a point where he honestly doesn't want to live, you can't save him by pretending to love him. The glue of a fake relationship will eventually crack and leave him even more depressed.

Being real and being nice don't always go hand and hand. A man who peer pressures you into settling for him is just as dangerous as a player who uses lies to hook you. Don't feel guilty and don't imprison yourself. Just because he's a nice guy, doesn't mean he's the right guy. Breaking up is always going to be hard, and when you're the one who's doing it, you will have second thoughts. People are taught to treat others as they would want to be treated, and no one wants to be pitied. The longer you stay in a miserable relationship the more likely you are to cheat, abuse that person, or become depressed. It's better to end a mediocre relationship with a good man than to continue with a relationship that will make you into a bad woman.

THE RUNNER

People break up and get back together all the time. There is nothing wrong with second chances. However, some people break up so much that you wonder what the point of them being together in the first place is. Just like the Hot and Cold Guy, The Runner relies on spurts of good times to hypnotize a girl. He's a loving boyfriend, but as soon as drama happens, he runs. All it takes is an argument or a situation where he doesn't like how you're acting and he disappears. He doesn't want to talk and figure out your problems. He has a secret weapon to end any dispute. It's called "bitch, try being alone." Sometimes it doesn't take a confrontation or disagreement, The Runner may vanish because he's bored or looking for a new pussy fix. On cue, he will run back when he's done hanging with the homies or when the new girl he was trying to sleep with rejects him. Regardless of how abruptly he left you or what he did when you were supposedly "on break," he knows that you will take him back. The Runner preys on relationship girls because these women will always cave in when threatened with abandonment. You want love and the idea of "my man" so bad that you open yourself up for this exploitation. The Runner doesn't stay gone, he will run back, and all will be forgiven without you ever bringing up the reason he ran or holding it against him.

The majority of unhappy women are in love with The Runner, and as a result of this treatment become The Bottom Bitch. So much energy is wasted trying to deal with those periods when he leaves you that eventually you stop arguing. Instead, you give him virtually anything in an effort to keep from doing something that may cause him to run. You no longer have the heart to deal with the pain of your boyfriend vanishing for weeks at a time, so you become a docile pet who barks but is afraid to bite. That's the game The Runner is playing from the start. He's training you like a dog so he never has to answer for any of his actions after you are housebroken to accept them. This type of boyfriend knows that you're not going to let him walk out of your life, and the fucked up thing is, you know it too. After a week of being alone, you will start sending texts or passing messages through mutual friends that you're not mad anymore and that it's okay to come back. A question I get often is, "Why did he leave only to come back?" Who cares? Why did you let him come back? Better yet, where is your fucking self-respect? Stand up to this man, and the next time he runs off to his mother's house rather than have an adult conversation, change the locks.

EMOTIONALLY UNAVAILABLE

When women put walls up after being hurt, they become emotionally guarded Tank Girls. This usually leads to these women being alone and miserable because it's only so much lack of affection a man can take before he's on to the next chick. However, when it comes to these emotionally unavailable men, their defensive armor doesn't stop them from getting female affection. It actually helps to be emotionally distant because there are so many women that want the glory of saving these kind of troubled men. Emo Eddie is in one corner telling you how pretty you are and trying to take you out for a meal, yet he's seen as being too thirsty and that turns you off. In the other corner is Iron Man Stark who never calls you first, doesn't want to go anywhere that isn't a room in his crib, and makes you work around his schedule. He's showing you his ass to kiss, and what do you do? You kiss it! The emotionally unavailable guy is a challenge. He doesn't need you, and that turns you on. It took a minute, but you have managed to get this man to make it official. You think Mr. Emotionally Unavailable will now open up, tell you his life story, and explain what's going on in his head—wrong!

Having a guarded boyfriend is something many women complain about, but trying to get him to open up often transforms into this strange masochistic rush. Your maternal instincts are in overdrive, you want to take care of him by giving him a shoulder to lean on and a vagina to rest in. None of that affection will break down his walls! If anything, it has the reverse effect! The moment Mr. Unavailable feels as if he's getting too comfortable or that you're getting too close, he's going to back off from the relationship. Emotionally unavailable men will go to extreme measures to keep you at arm's length. This can include flipping out for no reason, wanting to take a break just for the sake of taking a break, and even using other women to make you jealous enough to leave. You think you can unlock the hurt in his heart and save him, but you can't as long as you play by his rules.

The first thing you do to win emotionally unavailable men over is to establish who you are. You're not the girl that broke his heart when he was in 11th grade. You're not one of the hos from *The Maury Show* looking to creep with his best friend or brother. Most importantly, you're not the girl who's going to give everything and receive nothing in return. You cannot be too nice to emotionally detached men. If you handle these guys with kid gloves and let them get away with murder, they will continuously use and abuse you because they have no respect. If you force this guy to open his eyes and see that you aren't out to break his heart and shove his face in the fact that he's being a coward, then his armor will begin to crumble. Now that his guard is down, and that like he has for you will start to grow into love. Next, he's attached to you as if you were his own flesh and blood, and those sappy Drake lyrics he hated now make sense to him. He wasn't emotionally unavailable; he was being immature. All he really needed was a strong woman who refused to play his immature game. Don't accept that he is the way he is. If he can't drop his wall for you, then why would you drop your panties for him?

LET IT BURN

These are only a few types of men, and not meant to represent an overarching category that all males fit in. Immature men and players are ever evolving. Some take a little from column A and a little from column B, and come in ways that you may not recognize until it's too late. A woman who only knows how to guard against one or two types will probably be caught off guard. When it's time to break up for good, it should be legitimate or else you'll stress over if it was the right choice and this indecisiveness mixed with being lonely will drive you right back into his arms.

Don't go off a list of actions or react based off one mistake. Observe his overall character, that will tell you if he's worth another chance or stuck in his ways so deep that he will never truly change. Your job is to study the behavior of every man, and keep these red flags in mind. It's not enough to just Chris Brown proof your vagina, also make sure that when he hits you with the Hot and Cold routine that you see exactly what's going on. Smart men combine hustles! Don't live in denial and become so deep in love with a broken man that you'll sacrifice your sanity to fix him.

Every time I hear some wide-eyed Basica regurgitate, "Love is worth fighting for," I want to laugh. You're the only one fighting, fool. What you have isn't love, it's dependency. Forgiveness is a privilege, not a right, and just because he's better than the last two guys you met, doesn't mean he deserves a second chance. One more chance turns into two more chances followed by one last chance, and then you're old and broken down, your entire prime wasted on a bum. How many times do you need the same person to piss in your mouth before you figure out urine doesn't taste good? Breaking up isn't fun, it isn't easy, and no matter how strong you think you are, it's going to hurt like a motherfucker...for a long time. Deal with it. The world doesn't laugh behind your back every time you fail at love. Everyone experiences defeat, but your goal should be to know the warning signs, recognize the type of person he is, and be able to exit before the storm hits again. The difference between a girl and a woman is the maturity to recognize what you need in your life as opposed to what you want. You want a man, but you don't need one who hurts you on a weekly basis. A woman recognizes when her kindness has been taken for weakness and is strong enough to walk away no matter how infatuated, in like, or in love, she is with that abuser. What do you need that only he can provide? Dick, companionship, looks, and money? That shit isn't as rare as you think if you actually got off your ass and met people. You don't need him; he's just convinced you that you do. Letting a bad relationship burn is not a choice—it's your duty.

21

Cheaters, Cheating, & Revenge

C heating is the most complex issue any person will face. The outside consensus seems to be if someone cheats on you, it means that they never loved you, and you should end it immediately. Cheating is never cut and dry, and rarely does it mean that a person doesn't care about you. If your boyfriend cheats on you, it points to a lack of discipline in him, and a lack of excitement in your relationship. Every man has a wandering eye. As much as I love my wife, I still look at other women and admire…when she's not around of course. It is impossible to stop having sexual thoughts about the opposite sex; it's as much a part of the human genome as blinking an eye. The thing that differentiates The Cheater from the average person is discipline. I once wrote that a man should have Jedi like control over his penis and stay out of tempting situations. I'm a realist that knows most men crack when they're placed in a room full of hos, no matter how in love they are with that woman at home.

Some women may think it's as simple as "no thank you," but the discipline to turn down what you have been taught to go after since you were a little boy takes years for a man to master. The Cheater has yet to reach that level of maturity. Take a malnourished homeless person who has been on the street for ten years and set his tent up in a buffet. Even if you give him as much as he wants under a set schedule, it would take a while for him to understand that he doesn't need to take extra. The Cheater either doesn't understand that the struggle is over and it is okay to slow down, or doesn't want to chill because the hunt for sex is in his veins. Instead of knowing his limits he will flirt past the point of innocence with another woman. Next, he will talk in secret to that woman. Finally, he will do everything in his power to complete the goal of having sex because once you start down that road, it's impossible to stop.

When I was younger, I was The Cheater. For every actual girlfriend I had, there was always a girl on the side, literally. Morally I never felt guilty because my reasoning was airtight. As a young man, I figured that I wasn't getting married anytime soon, so I had to get it in while I could. As a side note, there is something to be said about men competing to have the most sex. Getting notches on the belt by bedding women is a male tradition that few females completely understand. I wasn't chasing a number, just trying to experience as many different types of women that I could. No matter how much I liked these girls, I wasn't going to marry them, so that meant I was still free to act single. The response to this logic is, "Why make her your girl if you're about having fun?" Even the most unfaithful man has a need for companionship, safety, and convenience. To have a girlfriend means that he has someone to talk to intimately and be affectionate with on a level that the girls he sees as side pussy don't deserve. Understand that the girl a man is cheating with is rarely a girlfriend type; she's usually the wild party girl or nasty submissive girl. Unlike his girlfriend, this side girl wants to laugh instead of talk, fuck instead of cuddle, and stay in instead of go out. These kind of low maintenance women appeal to a man's immature side, while his regular girlfriend appeals to the affectionate mature side. Having the best of both worlds lulls him into a sense of comfort, and if it feels right, he will think it is right.

When dealing with The Cheater, you have to know the severity of his problem. Let's keep it real; women rarely leave a man after the first time he cheats. There is no excuse for cheating, yet the promise never to do it again usually results in a second chance. It's not enough for him to apologize, you have to face your fear and find out the reason why he ran off. What was it about this side chick that made him step out and risk losing you? If you're agreeing to give him another chance, you can't be foolish enough to think it was a onetime thing. The Cheater will give you a list of easy excuses, but you have to be smart enough to bypass the, "I was upset, drunk, or caught up in the moment" bullshit. There is still some kind of need or insecurity inside of him that he refuses to open up about, and it's more powerful than his love for you. It's fascinating that when a woman cheats on a man it becomes an obsession. A guy becomes Clive Owen in the movie *Closer*. He wants to know what position you did it in, for how long, and if you came or not. It may sound weird, but that competitive nature in a man demands that he figure out how to improve and outdo any man. Women in comparison, tend to black it out, pretend as if it never happened, then bury it so they won't break down emotionally over the fact that she somehow wasn't good enough.

Stop burying your head in the sand and face the problem head on. Who was she? How did they meet? What did he like most about her? Knowing these things may not stop him from cheating again, but it will help you see the signs that he's going to repeat the same mistakes even before he knows he's about to creep again. Know your man's type. Don't be naïve and believe that you are the only one he has eyes for or foolishly think that your love will keep his dick from getting hard for another woman.

TWO CAN PLAY THAT GAME

Women cheat...a lot. At least once a week I receive an email from a woman who is stepping out on her boyfriend and confused on her next move. Although women aren't above finding love and affection elsewhere, females are still grounded by a sense of loyalty that quickly transforms to unbearable guilt. Sex for many men is just a physical act, sometimes it may bond them to that woman, but for the most part, it's the things she does outside of the bedroom that makes a man love her. Some women will openly proclaim, "You can have sex with her, but don't let me find out you were giving her my money" because they realize that getting his dick wet is often just a release, not a meaningful act. To take the woman on a date, buy her things, etc... shows a deeper connection than just sticking a penis in a new vagina. Physical and emotionally cheating are equally hurtful, but there seems to be this unsaid 50's housewife rule that men are free to roam if they keep it discreet and purely sexual. When the tables are turned, there is no unsaid rule for female cheaters. Men don't look for excuses to forgive a woman; her disloyalty is cause for an immediate break up, violence, or relentless verbal abuse.

The Cheater never imagines that two can play that game or that his woman will become fed up and look to the arms of another man. If he even suspects that his girlfriend would stoop to his level, the relationship would end, and all of the talk of second chances that he begged for when he cheated, he now refuses to give to that woman who did the same thing. It's a double standard that you can't get around. You may rationalize that he cheated on you, you cheated on him, two wrongs don't make a right, but it was sweet revenge. That logic is not going to stand in the world of man. Your boyfriend's reaction to you giving up his pussy will be nuclear. When speaking to women who have engaged in revenge cheating, I tell them not to confess. Will your man forgive you? Initially, but most likely it won't be for very long. The male ego is sensitive and giving away his pussy, mouth, or even flirting with a man as if you're going to do those things, cuts extremely deep and destroys trust.

So what's a woman to do? Does she put up with The Cheater, forgive him, and never think about it again or does she start creeping and get love somewhere else? Many R&B songs are driven by the theme of, "if you don't treat me right, the next man will." However, the next man isn't the guy you meet after the breakup; he's usually the guy you meet at the bar on a night your boyfriend pissed you off. Women need to feel loved and appreciated. Some will suck it up and deal with an unfulfilling relationship; others will mix and match. By mix and match, I'm referring to keeping the man you're in love with, but seeking out another man to fill in the places where your man is weak.

Let's say you and your boyfriend don't have fantastic sex. He's a five-minute bust and snore, never considering that you want to cum too. Months or even years of that can drive a woman to long for what she used to get or what other women are getting, and because of this need for a sexual release, she becomes vulnerable. Maybe she won't seek out a new man, but being a woman she doesn't have to search for sex. Men are always looking to flirt and see what a woman's relationship status is. The concept of once you have someone, everyone wants you, is legit. If you're throwing out an unhappy vibe, it only takes one guy who looks the right way or talks the right way to get you open. Your loyalty to your boyfriend isn't as strong as it once was, so you take his number instead of dismissing him. Those nights of falling to sleep wet and angry have changed you. While your sexual frustration isn't big enough to break up with your boyfriend, it is big enough to add a new member to the team. Next thing you know, you and Mr. New Dick are in a hotel room, and since you're new pussy to him, he's super hard and digging tunnels in your coochie like he's trying to reach China.

For the first time in a long time, you are experiencing good sex. Maybe you can go back to your man and be content or maybe you keep Mr. New Dick around in secret for those times when you need that sexual release your man can't give you. That is what I call mix and matching. It doesn't have to be sexual. Some women aren't looking for good sex; they just want appreciation. Other men will buy you gifts, pamper you, wine and dine you, etc... Name a spot where your man is weak, there is another guy waiting to give you that missing piece. Many of the women I talk to mix, match, and think it will run its course, but cheating never runs its course. It usually stops when you are caught or caught up, and the damage has been done. Two can play that game, but one will always lose.

IF YOU'RE GOING TO CHEAT...

Women are skilled at creeping. Unlike men who get lazy and forget to cover their tracks, a woman will always go to extreme measures to keep her secret. While I don't condone cheating, here are a few things to keep in mind. Never tell your girlfriends that you're cheating on your man. I don't care how sympathetic to your pain your bff may seem, cheating is an extremely sensitive topic for women. She may resent you for stooping that low and let something slip. With any news of that magnitude, there is always a chance "I promise I won't tell," ends with, "I only told one person." The next thing you know, seven people know your secret. All it takes is for one of them to want your man or be upset with you, and your secret is out. Additionally, sisterly love is often on-and-off in nature. Most women go through spots where they stop talking to their girlfriends; some even become bitter enemies. If her loyalty fades, and she has dirt on you, your secret fling, even if it happened a year ago, will be exposed. I love how Rose on *Titanic* never told anyone how she was fucking Jack the hobo while engaged aboard the ship. Not even her future husband years after the fact knew that she was cheating with some guy she met after a day. "A woman's heart is a deep ocean of secrets," therefore keep your skeletons submerged at the bottom of the ocean floor!

The other way women are caught is that the jump-off man becomes attached, and he no longer wants to play the side dick. Sex without emotion is easier for women when they have a man. Unlike the FWB situations, she's not projecting her want for love onto the guy...she's just fucking him. Her man is the love while her side dick is...well, the dick. However, that sideman who's being used as a piece of meat may start to want more than just sex. It's man's competitive nature, and while it was fun at first to say, "I'm smashing another guy's girl," it usually evolves into your sideman not wanting to share with your main man. I don't have to go into detail on how explosive two men fighting over the same woman can be. This won't be a case of keying a car or posting something on your Facebook wall like a scorned side ho would. When men fight over a woman, it's often deadly. Don't add drama to your life. No matter how adept you are at cheating, it's never worth it. Have dignity not to sell yourself cheap. Have the strength to take the woman's way out of a relationship, which is, "I'm not fulfilled — bye." Not the cowards way out which is, "I can creep. He won't find out." No love is worth compromising your body or your morals. Walk away, and find a new man you deserve, instead of creeping on one that doesn't satisfy you.

CONFRONTING THE CHEATER

No matter how angry you are, do not go tit for tat, and don't give him more than one opportunity to redeem himself. When you find text messages or get a phone call that your man is seeing another woman, it will feel like a punch in the stomach, don't run from that hurt, remember it. You need to measure that pain against the joy you get from him before you make your next move. The first instinct is to make him feel that hurt by doing the same thing, but if you make him feel that hurt, he's going to leave you. If you numb that pain and try to forget, you blind yourself to those signs when he's about to hurt you again. Risk versus reward, that's what you should focus on. Is this man at his best worth what he's just put you through emotionally? Consider the mess factor: if he had another girl in your bed, calling your phone, or got her pregnant, it tells you all you need to know. Not only did he cheat, he did it in a manner that had no regard for your health or feelings. Additionally, a man who confesses his sins is still capable of repeating his infidelity just like the man who was caught. It's up to you to weigh the pros and cons of your relationship before deciding if he's worth a second chance.

Everyone has problems, but if you spend more time crying than smiling then you already know it's time to leave The Cheater. *He's the one for me. We talked about getting married. I never had someone who I felt this strongly about. I know this time will be different.* If he was really your soul mate, he wouldn't be trying to mate other souls, he wouldn't lie about any and everything, and he wouldn't be trying to fuck the same girl you forgave him for trying to fuck last year. You didn't do your homework and you chose the wrong man. It happens, and mistakes are a part of growing wiser. He can have several positive traits that you love, but they will never outweigh two negatives: dishonesty and disrespect. Cheaters apologize more than drug addicts do, and it's usually insincere. He'll buy you an engagement ring, a car, or say he's ready to start a family, but those things are out of guilt, not love. Remember that a ring on your finger doesn't end the drama in your life, and bringing a baby into your toxic relationship won't make him keep his dick in his pants.

In the end, there is no secret way to keep a man from cheating. Your job as his woman is to treat your boyfriend the way you want to be treated in an ideal relationship. This includes having good sex, doing exciting things together, and being there for him emotionally when he needs to talk or express himself. Outside of those duties, you can't really give any more of yourself to make him happy. The decision to abstain from chasing new pussy is something that he has to control on his own. The only way to combat The Cheater is by allowing him the room to sink or swim. Too many women ramp up security once their men cheat. Hack into emails and Facebook accounts, pop up on the job, start monitoring his friends, etc… That won't save you. If anything, that kind of paranoia upsets him. You forgave his infidelity, now here you are showing little to no trust. Like a rebellious teen whose mother checks under his mattress for drugs, he's going to resent you for this. If he's going to be accused of cheating, he will just do it. Let the dog off the leash, and allow him to show you his true nature. If he runs off and sniffs the ass of the first bitch he meets, his affliction is beyond repair; he's a cheater, and nothing you can do will ever change him. Allowing him to show you that he's a dog a second time will give you the strength to accept that he will never be the man you want him to be, and make it that much easier to walk away. If you let him off the leash, and he behaves himself then there is hope. Most women will be cheated on; the only shame in this is allowing it to happen twice.

22

How to Get Over a Breakup

*I*t's *not the end of the world. You'll get over him. Everything will be okay.* People love to shovel that kind of bullshit down the throats of folks who are going through a breakup. Let's be honest, it is the end of the world as you know it, and contrary to popular belief, you will never truly get over that person. Ending a relationship is the closest thing to death there is, and just like losing your first puppy via vehicular homicide, a kernel of that pain stays with you for life. No matter how many times you go through breaking up, the cut feels just as deep as the first time, if not deeper. The only answer is to suck it up and deal with the pain, but this is a culture that desperately needs a morphine type prescription, something to gently numb the pain until the wound heals. A teenage girl being dumped by her first love, a woman in her twenties being told it's not working out by the man she thought she would marry, and a married woman who decides to file for divorce after finding out that her husband's been carrying on an affair. Out of the three, who hurts more? The logical answer would be the married woman, but honestly, no heart aches more than the next once a person has fallen in love.

A married woman going through the embarrassment of a divorce is life shattering. She has to deal with the legal ramification, the permanent scar of having to tell new men that she's a divorcee, and the constant fear that another marriage will end the same. Not only is a married woman faced with the emptiness of being alone, she's forced to confront the outside perception that she is the one to blame and wasn't good enough to make a marriage work. Add children to the mix and the new world of co-parenting with the enemy, and it's enough to drive even the strongest woman mad. A teenage girl also has to deal with unbearable pain after she has her heartbroken. When you're a teenager, you don't understand what heartbreak truly is and for a 17 or 18-year-old girl it's such a shock that it often leads to suicide attempts. That physical sickness, the sudden anxiety attacks—no one tells you that those hit you like a truck and that crying is the easy part. For young girls, losing that first love usually signals the end of their innocence. Parents can't console a teen with "you'll forget all about it, you're still young" because there is no minimum heartbreak age. It's just as insensitive to brush off an unwed woman's tears by saying condescending things such as, "Oh well, you two didn't have any kids" or "be thankful you didn't marry him." You don't need a ring or a child to fall completely in love. Regardless of what level your relationship reached, the sickness you feel in the pit of your stomach will always be unbearable. However, there are multiple ways to combat those feelings of loneliness, regret, and anger.

ACCEPT, DON'T REGRET

"Fuck him, I can do better," will quickly turn into "...maybe I was being unfair." The funny thing about heartbreak is that it turns everyone into a revisionist. The explosive arguments that you had suddenly become trivial and those annoying habits you hated aren't as frustrating in retrospect. The more you want an ex-lover back in your life, the more willing you are to blind yourself to the past. Instead of having Jiminy Cricket on your shoulder giving you the confidence to move on, you have a mini Rihanna telling you that it's okay to go back: "Tings' weren't that bad, gal, that punch didn't even hurt. You two shined bright like a diamond!" What's happening is that your heart is attempting to rewire your brain, blocking out crucial events so that you don't feel guilty about trying to give him another shot.

It does not matter if you were dumped or did the dumping; you have to be aware that your heart is overriding your brain during the first several weeks following a breakup. If you broke up with him for X, Y, and Z—hold on to that. Do not allow nostalgia to erase that alphabet. It kills you not to be talking to him and you want to change everything about yourself in order to make him want you again. Were you that bad of a mate, or are you looking for a desperate solution to a hopeless situation? I've talked to women who proudly took the role as scapegoats in the relationship. Last week her ex was a liar and cheater with a little dick and no money. Leave her alone for a week with only her revisionist thoughts and suddenly he's not bad at all. Her ex is now honest, loving, has a wonderful penis, and money doesn't matter. It's sad, but understandable. Your brain is in defense mode and attempting to rationalize why you need him. If you think of him as irreplaceable, then you will do anything to get him back. The brainwaves are saying, "Once you have him back, the heartache will stop, and you will be cured." It's a false solution that will not solve your problem. You two broke up for a reason and repairing that issue that caused the rift is the only way you two can get back together. Caving in to your depression, waving the white flag, and taking the blame for not being what he wanted is a fool's medicine. Two adults rarely break up over something small, so that issue that couldn't be fixed probably can't be fixed—accept it; don't excuse it.

If you are dealing with an ex who moved on and is now happy with another woman, you can't see this as merely a competition and attempt to prove yourself. A heartbroken woman is already thinking erratically, add another woman to the mix, and jealousy makes her that more desperate. Now you want to lower yourself and do things that you would never do in order to prove you're better. This isn't *Flavor of Love*; you can't win a man back by competing in a series of basic bitch events! Bribing him with sex is a temporary solution; you're acting out in order to prove that his new girl can't keep him faithful. What's the point of getting him to cheat on that girl? He had sex with you, then goes to have sex with her the next day…and he takes her out to dinner because he feels guilty. Who's winning? Everyone but you! In the end, his choice to come back will be based on his missing you, not a result of whoring yourself out to win him back. If anything, you damage his image of you by being extra thirsty.

Your girlfriends will tell you that you look better than his new girl does, and that you can easily take him back. It does not matter! Being more attractive, intelligent, or having more money than his new girlfriend will not make him break up and rush back to you. The only thing you can do is accept that he found someone else who he thinks is better for him. Embrace that idea, not because she is better than you are, but because in his world, he believes she is better. The more you dwell on his relationship, the harder it will be to let go and heal enough to start your own relationship. Don't hold back the tears; cry it out of your system. After the tears stop, use his happiness with someone else as ammunition to start the next chapter in your life. I repeat, let him go. Do not allow his new relationship to fill you with depression and desperation. He moved on and so can you.

GETTING HIM OUT OF YOUR SYSTEM

Let's say your boyfriend wasn't there for you when you needed him, he ran the streets with his friends and put you second or even third at times. Despite your complaints, he never tried to make things better. No more apologies, no more talk of change, you showed his ass the door…this is the part where you're supposed to feel great but you don't. If this were the movies, you would be sipping wine and dancing the night away…but in real life, you're crying, tired, and have zero appetite. Breaking up isn't the hard part it's only the beginning. You are supposed to feel like shit! Few women, regardless if their men were great or horrible, feel happy a week later. Some ladies see this pain as proof that they should be back with him (as if the human body wouldn't hurt if the breakup was justified), but if you loved that person, you will always suffer from separation anxiety, right or wrong. The following weeks are crucial. Breaking up is like kicking a drug addiction: most are strong enough to say no more at first, but few can go cold turkey and stay clean.

After a few weeks of being single, the loneliness sets in and your heart will try to take control of your brain. Instead of remembering those nights he left you home alone in tears and using that trauma to reaffirm that you did make the right decision, you begin to obsess over the good times. Your heart warms at the handful of instances when he did take care of business and treat you like a queen...the good sex, the one or two gifts you received, and the times he told you how much he loved you. Those memories begin to push the negativity out of your system. A week later, you have forgotten how sad he made you, and you're now holding on tight to this image of a man who was perfect for you. He wasn't selfish after all; you were the dumbass who made unreasonable demands like, "spend time with me," "take me out," "stop texting your ex," and "answer your phone after 11 p.m." Again, this is that revisionist historian known as your heart, taking control of your mind. Now you're leaving Facebook messages, texting old inside jokes, and debating on if you should go see him. Nothing has changed except your willingness to shortchange yourself.

That man is still the same one you left for a better life or the one who left you for a better life, but you're in denial. Your heart is clouding the facts of the breakup and giving you the easy solution of "go back to him." The more you feed into the myth of your ex-boyfriend, the more likely you are to take him back or try to win him back. Stop being a revisionist and start being real. Get a pencil and write down all the things you love above him. On the next page write down all the things you don't like about him. Go through each one of those negatives and ask yourself if you addressed those with him. I'm going to assume that you tried to make it work, and your list of negatives were things he didn't want to change about himself. Hold on to that list, tape it on your bathroom door and read it every morning. That list humanizes your ex-boyfriend when you heart's making him into a god.

Do not attempt closure through communication or explanation. Women have this obsession with saying goodbye or having one last talk about what went wrong. There is no true closure when you break up! You can have one last roll around in the bed, talk about the good times over one last dinner, or hug each other for an hour in the middle of the street, but the pain will not disappear. The most telling question about breakups I receive is, "Should I call him and tell him how I feel before I delete his number?" Hell no. By texting or calling in order to say, "By the way, I won't be calling you again," you're trying to give him one last chance to tell you he's sorry and say you two should work it out. Don't try to be pretend that you have to get something off your chest. This is you being sneaky and trying to give him a window to come back. Cutting him out of your life does not require notice that you're cutting him out of your life!

Another mandatory breakup rule is to avoid social network stalking. I once heard some woman say that it was immature to unfriend an ex on Facebook. What's truly immature is torturing yourself just to put on a brave face for the rest of the world. Some females can handle online interaction; the majority can't, especially when the wounds are still fresh. You do not want to know what girl in a tight dress he likes on Instagram, see a timeline full of dates he's going on, or why he's suddenly Twitter flirting with the girl he said was just his little sister. He's not your concern anymore, which means erase him online the same way you erased him offline.

HE ENDED IT WITHOUT WARNING

What if the decision to call it quits wasn't yours? Let's say he was the best boyfriend you had, there was nothing you could complain about, and then unexpectedly he decided to break up. How do you accept the fact someone you were so happy with doesn't want you? You know you're a decent person, and if he would just open his eyes, he would see how perfect you two are for each other. You don't think you should accept his idiotic decision; you should fight for what you want and go down swinging for your man! Stop sipping the Crazy Capri Sun and evaluate the situation logically. Why did he break up with you? Few things come without warning; you did something, said something, or were getting on his nerves way before you had "the talk" ...or these days, "got the text." This can be difficult to pinpoint because men can be particularly aloof about why they don't want you anymore. Most of the time, they're trying to spare a woman's feelings, so they give you a bullshit reason for the breakup. It's bad enough that he's telling you the relationship is over. He doesn't want to rub salt in the wounds by laying out the reasons you suck while you're in the midst of crying—you have a shitty personality, attitude problem, corpse bride coochie, not as pretty as the new girl I met, etc... Since most guys won't point out your faults, it is up to you to research the events that lead to the breakup and determine what made him leave.

What did you fight about the most? All couples argue, be it big or small, your job is to go back and think about what subjects you two clashed over that never were resolved. What things made him pull away and not want to talk to you at times? If he stood you up, or didn't answer your calls, think back to his reasons. The things you two had issues with may have been stupid in your mind, not your fault, or just a misunderstanding. However, if he broke up with you, those small things could hold the key. When men break up it's not the result of one big fight, few guys are going to explode and make a rash decision like that, unless it had something to do with cheating or betrayal. If he gave up the comfort of in-house coochie, it had to be a problem that was growing and becoming unbearable. Stop thinking of yourself as perfect, your relationship as air tight, and look at it from his point of view even if you don't want to admit to these flaws. Don't be surprised to find out that you were demanding, you did call and text too much, you were jealous, and there were times you chose your friends over him.

You may think it doesn't matter why he broke up with you now that it's over, but the only way you're going to get another shot with him or avoid those same things with the next man, is to learn the exact things you do that turn men off and push them away. On the flip side, maybe he simply grew away from you or had eyes for another woman. Those kinds of revelations are out of your control. Too often, women beat themselves up because they couldn't keep a man. It's not your job to keep anyone. It's a partnership, and no matter how great he is at his job, eventually Batman loses one Robin and has to find a new one. Don't beat yourself up and regret not being everything he could have ever wanted. You are a woman, not clay to be molded at the will of some indecisive man. Not being affectionate, nagging, or pressuring him for things are traits you can address and should correct. However, not looking like the girl he just started dating or not spoiling him like his mother isn't something you can fix or should attempt to inject into yourself.

If your soul searching reveals that you just weren't the type of girl he wanted, accept the fact that you put your all into the relationship, treated your man the best way you knew how, and he didn't think it was good enough. If you backtrack and realize that your unfair actions are responsible for the breakup, then it's up to you to tackle those things internally and start improving those areas that you think are flawed. The theory that a good man will love you regardless of faults is a bullshit excuse. A man who genuinely wants you will accept you for who you are, but that doesn't mean he will stick around and put up with those ways forever. Men have an almost inflated sense of self-worth that will not allow them to settle for less. Guys value comfort and happiness above all, which is why they have an easier time being selfish than women. If men are unhappy, they go find happiness elsewhere, end of story. A romantic would call this giving up on love, but a realistic person would call this loving yourself enough to do better. If your relationships have ended multiple times for reasons that you don't quite understand, it's not him it's you. Being serial dumped is an obvious pattern you have to investigate starting from within, no matter how painful it may become.

MEN AREN'T THE ANSWER OR THE ENEMY

If a building is on fire, common sense dictates that you don't throw gasoline on it; so, why would you try to heal a broken heart by jumping into another relationship? Being vulnerable isn't an excuse for making poor decisions. After a breakup, you have to slow down and focus on self. You may have spurts where you feel like the old you and think you're ready to hit the single scene, but let's be honest, something isn't right. Breakups are traumatic. Stop pretending you are fine, and take the time to ease back into life. Being in love felt great, but that doesn't mean rush out to find that feeling with someone else a month later. Friends will try to hook you up with someone because they ignorantly believe that companionship will get your mind off "that person whose name we no longer say." You don't tell a cocaine abuser to start shooting heroin to take their mind off blow. Jumping into a new relationship or restarting an old relationship with the guy you were with before your last ex isn't healing; it's swapping one compulsion for another.

Get out of the house and do things. Heartache, anger, and frustration mixed with an internet connection will cause you to relapse. All of those friends you probably stopped hanging with because you were so in love with your boo, it's time to call them up and start being social again. Go shopping, go to the movies, or take up a hobby. The one thing you must avoid is dating. Going on a date with Greg the new guy to get your mind off your ex can easily lead to rushing things. You're so afraid to be alone with your thoughts that you want Greg to come over, you want to talk to him all the time, and eventually you try to force this man into the role that was once filled by the person you're still in love with. Instead of dating like a normal woman, you're more like the psycho woman who's lost a child, so she takes to dressing her cat like a baby girl. I repeat, let your heart heal. Men love rebound women. You would think a dude would be frightened by the prospect of a clingy emotionally fractured chick trying to make him her boyfriend too fast, but it's the opposite. Some men grab these rebounds with the fury of 90's era Dennis Rodman, knowing that it's much easier to have sex with someone who's looking for love in all the wrong places. She's sad, wants to believe that nothing was wrong with her and that it was the man who screwed up; therefore, she eats compliments like chips and begs for more. Men who are trying to win a girl over lay it on thick anyway, but having gone through the wringer, a rebound woman isn't as quick to dismiss that type of ass kissing. She usually falls for sweet talk because her esteem is low and ends up dating someone who will manipulate her, discard her, and lower her spirits that much more. The solution is to distance yourself from romance. It's fine to go out to eat or share company with a platonic male post breakup, but don't fool yourself into thinking you can handle the advances of a guy trying to fuck you. There is no shame in not being ready. If your friends constantly cry for you to see other people, inform them that they're being insensitive by trying to play cupid. How do you know when you're ready to date again? You're ready exactly two months from the moment when you first think you are.

Some ladies have the opposite reaction. Instead of trying to use a man to fill that hole in her heart, she takes to hating them. Any woman who's been burnt by love has some animosity toward men. It's okay to harbor a little resentment so long as you don't let it overwhelm you. Going Anakin Skywalker[18] and giving into your anger won't help you sleep at night; it'll guarantee that you'll be sleeping alone for a lot longer. Men do horrible things...correction—some men do horrible things. Your fear of being hurt will probably save you from making the same mistake twice, but generalizing an entire gender makes you emotionally detached, overly guarded, and paranoid. By the time you meet a nice guy who isn't trying to get in your pants or play you, he'll be so turned off by the cold shoulder that you won't have a chance to open up and explain your past. Yes, men who actually see

---

[18] Anakin Skywalker let the emotions of love, fear, and anger transform him from a loyal husband, friend, and Jedi into the villain known as Darth Vader.

something special in you will try hard to peel those layers back, but they won't try forever. Every man that has broken your heart, or who will break your heart is a unique individual and do not represent all of mankind.

GETTING BACK WITH HIM

A few months have passed, you are now thinking clearly, and you understand where your relationship went wrong. This is a new you, and it's time to show your ex how much you've grown. Going backwards is not always a terrible thing. The hope that you can regain what you lost is a powerful motivator, and to take that away would be unfair. With the right amount of work, two people can break up, and then come back together stronger than before. A high school couple who weren't mature enough for a deep level of commitment four years ago can reunite and have a storybook ending if they both were able to grow during that time apart. That wife who files for separation can rekindle that fire to the point where they save their marriage. That woman who was engaged and called it off because she wasn't sure, can take the time to learn about herself over the course of several years, reconnect with the man she ran out on, and finally walk down that aisle. Know that the odds may be against you but the chance exists. Nevertheless, a few months away followed by make-up sex do not complete the journey back. Anytime you take a break from a relationship and give that person space, you go through a cool off period. After you cool off, you two are able to talk cordially and because the tension isn't as thick, you think your issues are solved. Being friendly and being fixed are not the same. Your problems are on hold, and far from solved.

Taking a short break to solve your problems is like going on vacation because you hate your boss. The first few weeks back to work after the vacation will be wonderful. You two will shake hands and play nice, but you two never talked about your differences, you simply swept them under the rug. How long until you're having the same problems, burnt out again, and thinking about quitting? I shake my head at those couples who are on and off five times in one year. You're chasing that feeling of love like you had in the beginning, but things are so bad that the only way you can reach that passion is by breaking up then coming back to each other. Breaking up to make up is a false high that can't last because neither one of you has changed or talked out the real problems. The first step to getting back with your ex for real is to build that friendship again. Just because you know each other like the back of your hand, doesn't mean you can pick up right where you left off. Rebuilding takes discipline because the natural instinct is to dive back in and show how much you've missed each other. Be strong and keep the reunion affection free. The moment you start kissing, you get horny, and you have sex. Sex brings back all those old memories, and now the two of you are cuddled up laughing instead of talking about the issues that separated you in the first place.

Start with phone calls. Keep it light at first and then build to the past. If you felt like it was you who did things that were unfair or that you reacted immaturely due to something he did, own up to it. Instead of playing the, "you did this, so I did that" game, be an adult and let go of that petty shit. It's not about you apologizing or him apologizing, fuck placing blame. You both need to understand what you did wrong and find a solution going forward. Acknowledgment is the only path to forgiveness and growth. Women can be extremely stubborn when it comes to being done wrong and although they can claim to be over it, they rarely are. You don't have to forget, but don't throw the past in his face when getting back together. If you don't think you can trust him, then why are you considering taking him back? With no trust, there is no relationship. Any time that he whispers on the phone, you're going to think that he's seeing another girl because the paranoia is eating you alive. Any time he doesn't text back for hours you're going to relapse and think he's hoing again. You can't hold a grudge and be in love at the same damn time. If the trust is that badly damaged then he can never repair it. For your peace of mind and his, let it go and find someone new.

After you two begin talking again, begin dating. This step is often tossed aside because men don't want to spend time courting something they've already swam in. Guys would rather go from promises of a new relationship to you coming over the crib and having movie night and dick dessert just like old times. Again, that's ill-advised because you're putting the cart before the horse. You spent a few weeks talking on the phone, ironing out issues, but how will you react out in public with him. Being out on dates can't be practiced; the conversations go in all sorts of directions. It forces you to react to real world situations, and let's face it, most relationship problems stem from things that happen outside the house. Go out for a month or so, and then once you feel comfortable that it can work, make it official again. The time you spent talking and going out helps you get over that happy to see each other high that causes others to break up a month later after they realize nothing's changed.

Not all people are going to get back together. Don't hold out hope that he needs time to cool off, his new girl will break up with him, or that you just need to try harder to win him back. If you break up with a man because he made you miserable, no matter how much he's claimed to have changed, do not go back down that road. Alternatively, if a man breaks up with you and makes it clear that he doesn't want to get back, respect that. Too many women ask how to get their ex back, but these men clearly don't want them back. Remember, men don't play hard to get. If he's brushing you off, get the damn hint. You can have sex with him, go kiss his mother's ass, or get his friends to try to talk to him about you, but when a person realizes they're happier without you, it signals the end of that relationship forever. Not all good things come to an end, but all bad relationships do, one way or another. If you're not together, maybe it was never as good as you remember.

RELAPSE

A woman will see her ex calling her phone and lament, "…what does he want," yet she still picks up the phone. Sex with your ex is a hell of a drug. It represents a return to normalcy, and for the 20 minutes, he's inside you it's like stepping back in time. Don't waste the months you spent healing by sampling that throwback penis. Casual sex isn't casual when you and that person have a history. Having sex with a man you were/are in love with does several things. It gives you hope that maybe it can work out again, it reminds you of the good times, and it makes you comfortable. Maybe you're the type of woman who won't let it bother her and will continue to live her single life while having sex with her ex. That discipline is rare. Assume you will relapse if you're close to your addiction and avoid that drug completely. You will think to yourself, "One more time and I'm done," but one more time will become two, five, even twenty more times.

The thing I realized about most of the girls I've been with was that just because we broke up romantically; it didn't mean we had broken up sexually. I had an ex who fucked like a champ and gave the kind of head that would have made Homer write an epic poem crediting the gods with bestowing her with that level of Fellatio skill. I had to cut her completely out of my life in order to move on because I knew that every time we were alone in a car or a house we were going to have sex. My willpower is amazing, but my fully erect penis was no match for the fond memories I had of her vagina. I made the tough decision that if I wanted to get serious with other girls she had to go. The final step in getting over a breakup is having the strength to stay away even after all has been forgiven. A part of you may see the past as water under the bridge and want to bring your ex-boyfriend back into your life as a friend, but what's the point? *My ex understands me! We've been through so much.* Who cares what you've been through; it's about where you're going!

Do not let your ex hover around as if you two are platonic friends. Two people who have 69'd can't be platonic. Let's be real. The friendship you form with your ex is conditional, that condition being: he still gets the benefits in case of emergency. Once a man realizes he can't sample your latte anymore, or sees that you have a new man, he's not going to want to be your platonic friend. The boundaries of what you can and can't do as exes will always be murky because women will bend the rules as soon as they make them. I had an ex tell me that we could talk on the phone, but we weren't allowed to see each other out of respect for her new boyfriend. One day she must have been bored because she asked if I wanted to go get something to eat with her. Yes, we ended up having sex. As a man, I'm going to be an opportunist when it comes to sex, and the moment she wanted to see me, it let me know that she wasn't 100% committed to the new life she was trying to live. This weakness for what we used to have, gave me an opening that could have ruined everything she currently had. This woman is now married to the man she stepped out on, but she risked that future for old times' sake...even though old times weren't even that awesome. Think about that the next time you're tempted. Exes are not repackaged friends. They are a drug habit waiting to hook you and take you back to the place you swore you would never go. Just say no!

23

Dating After a Breakup

I don't know where to start, I haven't dated in forever. No matter if you were in a six-month or a six-year relationship, the anxiety of getting back out there can be overwhelming. The breakup was hard enough, the healing stage is ongoing, and now the pressure to continue your romantic life is mounting. Where do you start? That's simple: start at the beginning and with the basics. Regaining your confidence is step one. No matter if you were dumped or did the dumping, you have to get Barack Obama cocky. Brush your shoulders off, look in the mirror, and tell yourself that you are the best option in your city. It doesn't matter how you get your mojo back. Some women chop their hair off, or get tattoos, while others hit the gym and reshape their bodies. While going to extremes isn't necessary, it is a good idea to do something to psychologically distinguish the old you from the new you. Don't dismiss this step and just get back on the horse with a half ass opinion of yourself. Men smell low self-esteem from a mile away. If you walk into a room reeking of doubt, you will be eaten alive and end up hurt all over again. Work on regaining confidence before accepting any dates. Remember, you're not on a time limit.

Being inadequate is the biggest fear women who have been out of the game have. One woman confessed to me that after being married for two years, she felt as if she wasn't skinny enough, hip enough or wild enough, to interest today's men. Any woman who was in a long-term relationship is at a disadvantage, not due to the time away, but due to the relationship comfort that spoiled them. You didn't have to entertain your ex-boyfriend with new things to talk about, dress your best, or even wear makeup. You most likely spent most of your time indoors, and the conversation came easy because you two knew each other intimately. The new men you are going to meet won't share your inside jokes and you will probably struggle through the "getting to know you" conversation. Think back to the example I wrote in Chapter 17 and constantly remind yourself to loosen up and talk to this new friend as if he is an old friend. Repeat to yourself several times before you meet up, "he's just a man," and those butterflies will subside and allow you to talk freely and act in ways that allow the real you to shine.

Remember to dress to erect, not because you're out for sex, but because looking good makes you feel good. You can't just show up wearing whatever, even if it is a casual get together. Loose clothing with your hair in a snatch back ponytail can't possibly make you feel like a new woman. New suitors, unlike your ex, haven't seen you at your best yet; therefore, they will judge you for looking mediocre. You can't afford to be overly shy, elusive, or plain when attempting to get back into the world of dating. Keep in mind that you aren't the only woman looking for a man. Once again, you're back in a world where you have to prove that you're Wifey and not Pussy. You know you're not ordinary, but now you have to prove it all over again. You are in direct competition with hos who dress like sex, know how to strike up a conversation, and don't mind doing body shots. Take the time to build your esteem to the point where you aren't afraid to talk to any man in the room and always focus on yourself, not rival females. Your swag should be so untouchable that the sight of another beautiful woman is as rattling as seeing a fly on the wall. Once the nerves and insecurity diminish, competition with other women won't enter your mind because you will be convinced you have no competition.

BE SELECTIVE

That past relationship is now in the past. You may sometimes think about the guy whose name you won't mention but you have accepted it as a closed chapter in your life. You took the time and worked on your flaws. You are happy with what you see in the mirror, know your value, and followed the earlier steps on getting outside of your comfort zone when looking for new friends. You are now on your way to a Spartan life where you will attract the quality men you deserve, but you have to be patient and meticulous. There are several men you should avoid at all costs.

Friend Zone Buddy: Women constantly complain that they don't know any men when there are a good eight that she interacts with on a daily basis. Correction: you don't know any men you would want to be with romantically. If those people weren't on your radar back then, they don't deserve to be on your radar just because you are on the rebound. Friend Zone guys feast off women who go through breakups, and are so vulnerable that they are now willing to settle. Keep your standards! Giving out pity fucks and sympathy relationships are not going to make you happy. Unless that Friend Zoner is going to introduce you to some new guys you've yet to lay eyes on, don't agree to go out with him. This sneaky male pretends to be your platonic friend, yet is overly excited that you're single again. He will be there to comfort you at first, and then once your guard is down he will make his move. "Chill, you're like my brother" used to work, but now you may be so desperate for male affection that you give in — beware.

The Stalker Co-worker: The same goes for the men at work who have been stepping up the compliments since they found out you were back on the market. You can think about giving Brandon from the stock room a shot, but weigh the pros and cons before you accept his offer. This isn't just one date to see how it works out. This is a date where you have to see him the next day…and the day after, no matter if the date goes wonderful or horrible. If box mover Brandon was your crush for a minute, and you know how to keep it professional, then go for it. If he's just someone you think is "okay" but is showing attention when you're in dire need of it, don't give in, keep it moving. Remember, when you only have a few males in your life, you will project romantic feelings just because you're in need of that type of affection. Override this habit of creating a fantasy love life just because you see him every day at the job. There are numerous men out here for you to choose from, don't get lazy and settle for the convenience of Work Dick.

The Homegirl Hookup: Your friends are constantly being asked by men, "Do you have any single friends?" Now that you're on the rebound, she can finally hand out your number. Don't do it! Yes, it is possible to meet some great guys who are friends of your friends. However, will these men be outside of your comfort zone? If your girlfriends are ratchet, they're going to introduce you to ratchet men. If they're freaks, they're going to introduce you to guys who think you're just as slutty. Just because your bestie recommends good Netflix movies doesn't mean she's good at cosigning men. Look at who's doing the hooking up before you jump for joy at the promise of a blind date.

FIRST DATE TIPS

Once you select the right man to go on a date with, you have to keep your neurosis in check. Your job isn't to worry about if he likes you as a girlfriend or just as a sex object. You know you can't jump in his head but since you have been hurt before, you're overthinking everything he does. The biggest self-sabotaging a woman can do is to confuse being cautious with being paranoid. Relax and keep an open mind, take a mental note when he does or says something you see as a red flag, but don't shut down mentally and determine it's not going to work the moment he does something that reminds you of your ex. For example, if the waitress is attractive, he may sneak a peek or smile extra hard. There is not a man alive who has not given the once over to a hot waitress while in the company of another woman, but some have better poker faces than others have. If you see him do this, coming from a relationship where you were cheated on or had your boyfriend try to get at other women, this is going to send a message to your brain that this new man is a dog just like that old man. The moment you associate the old with the new, you become turned off and the date will not go smoothly due to that underlying resentment. Again, file that away in your mind, but give this guy a little margin for error. After all, he is single and even though he's taking you out, he's still in that looking mode. If he gets out of pocket during the date and any of those red flags become too much, then that tells you this man has no discipline and isn't ready to seriously date. That's great to know. This way, when he calls you up for date #2, you can decline (or ignore his calls) without feeling guilty or obligated.

It's important to understand that going through a breakup is the most educational thing that can happen. That old relationship allowed you to see certain things that men do up close and personal and now you know what you can deal with and what really is a deal breaker. By the time you're on this first date, you should know after two hours if this new man is worth your time or if he shows too many incompatibility signs. That's called the gift of romantic clarity! This may be the only date you've had since you became ready to mingle again, as well as the only one on deck, but so fucking what! Don't forget what I said about letting limited options pressure you into poor decisions. If this man doesn't impress you, make this the last date.

Back to the beginning of the first date, while you're sitting across from this new guy, remember that you're the ringmaster. I hate to see girls looking over the menu, struggling for a topic to bring up that won't make her seem idiotic. You're not on a date with him; he's on a date with you. You're the Diana Ross, and this fool is The Supremes. You are in control, so take charge and just go for it without overthinking. What does a man want to hear about on a date? He wants to hear that you're not crazy, possessive, or carrying baggage from the past. Men don't care if you want to talk about celebrity gossip, world news, or the last vacation you took, they just want to have fun and feel engaged. Treat him like your girlfriend and talk about the shit you enjoy no matter how trivial you may think your interests are. Men know who Kim Kardashian and Kanye West are. Your trivial subjects don't have to take up the entire date, the point is to talk about topics you are into until you become comfortable enough to truly open up and let your personality and intelligence shine through. As the ringmaster of this date, your main goal is to uncover as much information as you can about him without talking too much about yourself. Coming from a heartbreaking relationship, your first instinct will be to vent, not because you're proud of the breakup, but because you think it serves as a warning of what he shouldn't do. "My ex used to order for me. I hate men who think they run shit. I hope you're not like that." Are you high? You're on the first date. It's too early for all that drama. Never talk about your ex-boyfriend.

If he asks why such a pretty lady is single, shrug it off, redirect, and answer, "What makes me so pretty? Maybe other guys don't see it." You know you look good, but instead of getting in your feelings about your ex, and coming off as bitter or pathetic, you turn it into flirting. Now instead of spilling your guts on why you were cheated on or how you didn't feel loved by your ex, your date is easing your mind by letting you know that he thinks you're attractive and his reasons why. Any negative past experiences should be omitted. This is a date, not rehab, keep it real but don't show all and tell all just yet. Furthermore, control your motor mouth. Girls talk a lot because they have so much bottled up. The first few dates or phone calls with a potential boo is not the time to unload a year's worth of stress, hurt, and anger. This man will listen to you and pretend to understand, but take it from someone who has been on the other end of the conversation, men tune out, and eventually he will figure out a way to stop talking to you if you come off like a bitter Basica who mistakes dating as therapy. There will be a time to explain your past, for now focus on your present.

When it comes to asking him questions about his ex-girlfriend, you have to be stealthy. Most men are up on game enough to sidestep questions about their past relationships. They will either ignore or give short answers that make them seem perfect. You don't want, "She just turned out not to be the one." That answer tells you nothing and sells you a false image that he's a good guy who's looking for his soul mate. Bullshit! Make intelligence gathering into a game. Learn to read between the lines, and never take what he says at face value. I heard a woman say that she asks a man if he believes in marriage during the appetizer because there is no point in sharing a meal with someone who doesn't want a long-term relationship. That's the thirstiest avenue you can take. Asking a man if he's ready for marriage or kids when you don't even know his life's story, sends a message to him that you're ring chasing or sperm trapping. Things like this will lead him to judge you as desperate, and put you in the Pussy box. A veteran of the game will lay it on thick, drop hints that you are the type he could marry and that you'd make a good mother. It's the first date, he doesn't know you from the waitress, so he's telling you what you want to hear based off your thirst questions. By asking an extremely personal question like that so early, you overplayed your hand and that man will use that to his advantage. A non-player will tune out as well because you're scary. What sane man wants to be in a relationship with some weirdo who asks those things to a virtual stranger? You sound like a woman whose biological clock is ticking, not someone who wants to build a legitimate partnership.

There is a better way to find out if he's into marriage, kids, commitment, and a quality man without being so rude and random. Ask him hypothetical questions that tell you about his mentality, without him feeling as though he's on trial. For instance, a woman should state, "I can see why some men cheat. Some girls just don't get the job done." That's a perfect bait statement. His answer will tell you more about his mindset than, "Why did you break up with your ex," will ever reveal. Direct questions are easy to deflect because men think about what you want to hear, and then tell you what you want to hear. If you transform questions into point of view statements, it will throw him off his game, and he will answer more in tune with what he actually thinks. Write down a list of statements to spit out on the first date similar to these:

> **I haven't been to church in a while, my mother guilt trips me all the time:** This leads into his views on faith without the fear of you jumping down his throat about being non-religious or too religious.
>
> **...aren't you a gentlemen. Did you learn that from your father or did you pick that up from teaching your own kids:** Half joke, double whammy question. You ease the mood by getting him to laugh, and then the response will be either that he doesn't have kids or that he does. The follow up will get him talking about his family life. This way you can see if he comes from a two-parent household or if someone else raised him.
>
> **I bet you've dated a lot of girls who start telling you their wedding colors on the first date. Girls are so hard up:** This baits him into talking about if he's ready for that step and his experience with women who want a commitment. He's more likely to tell you that he was once engaged or married from this statement.

Again, create your own bait questions based on the things you feel are important to know about a man, and then practice with a friend or by yourself until it's conversational and natural. You're not 19 years old just looking for a warm meal and company. If you want a legit relationship, put in the work before you even sit down at the table. If you're creative enough with your bait, you should leave that date knowing exactly what kind of man he is. If he gives answers that you don't agree with, don't argue or get upset, just keep the conversation flowing. If you start debating, he's going to stop being honest, and tell you what you want to hear. Instead, take mental notes, and base whether you go on a second date with him on those responses.

GIVE HIM SPACE

I trust you didn't start dating too soon after your last breakup and aren't projecting your need for love redemption on this new guy. Either way, the first two weeks of getting to know a person is heightened, it's lust on steroids, and that shit feels a lot like love. This guy is extra fascinating because his stories are new and different from your ex. He's sexier because your kitty's been caged for months and horniness is making him seem that more attractive. He's returning your advances as if he's already trying to lock you down, but this could just be wishful thinking. Give yourself time to stand back and see if this is your hormones lusting after something new or if he's a legitimate contender. Take your time! Someone asked if dates should be back to back on consecutive days. Before you laugh, understand that many young women come from bad relationships where they skipped dating. A man will want to take you out as much as he can because he's probably just as in lust with you, but take a few days in-between or wait a week. At the same time, don't over or under call/text him during this time. I suggest talking once a day during the first week, no more no less. The second week you can add an extra text or call in if needed, but it's important that you save something for when you actually meet up. This keeps you from putting too much of your time and energy eggs into one basket, and protects him from feeling smothered by clingy actions.

GETTING SERIOUS AGAIN

Getting back on the horse doesn't mean hop on the first jackass that gallops your way. Coming from a failed relationship you should know exactly what you're looking for, and the selection process should be so thorough that it nets you a thoroughbred. Remember to entertain multiple men, not sexually, but romantically. If you can attract one, you can attract another. When you limit yourself to dating one man at a time, you waste time. You just got over a breakup that left you depressed and confused. What sense does it make to throw all of your attention at the first cute guy who offers to take you bowling? The average bullshit relationship where a man is just trying to have sex or gaming you for other things lasts two or three months. That means by dating two of these type of men back to back rather than at the same time, you're going to lose half the year and be back at square one—hating men, and wishing you had stayed in the relationship with your ex-boyfriend aka the devil you know. Dating isn't reserved for men you already think of as serious nor is it a sprint to find the first guy who wants to get your phone number. Dating is a process of elimination! Options keep you honest, and while he doesn't have to know you are dating someone else, the fact that you can compare and contrast these men will keep you from getting comfortable with a subpar man.

The most important step is becoming the *Bachelorette*, which means just like on that show, you utilize the power to choose the man you want to be with by telling him verbally that you're ready to take it to the next level. There will come a point where you really like one man more than the rest and you stop talking to the other boys in order to focus solely on Mr. Could Be Right. The moment that you want to be exclusive with a man be transparent and communicate those feelings. Your last relationship was probably one where you waited for the man to choose you, and that old way of doing things didn't end well. What do you have to lose this time around? Open your mouth knowing that you have reached a point in your maturity where you won't be heartbroken by a man's rejection. A decisive woman will always get a decisive answer, be it "yes" or "no."

By knowing exactly what you want and having the balls to say it, you either get started in a real relationship with this new man or get started erasing his number so you can start looking for someone else who is on the same page as you. Grown women aren't in a rush, but not rushing doesn't mean you are in a state of waiting! The fun and games of being a single woman looking for sex and a good time are over. Your goal is to find a life partner with whom you can build a foundation. Date only the men you feel a connection with, not those who simply pop up and are good company. Research the men you date carefully by asking the hard questions most women are afraid to ask, be creative when getting him to talk about sensitive information, and give him the time and space between dates to show his true colors. Once you feel like this man has more positives than negatives and doesn't exhibit behavior that conflicts with your personality, then *Pokémon* that ass—choose him, and let it be known that this is serious. If he's on the same page as you, this will have landed you a well-scouted boyfriend who earned his spot through actions, not by default. Now comes the final task: seeing if your boyfriend has what it takes to grow into a husband.

24

Is He the Hubby Type

There was a disturbing poll I once read which stated that 67% of women who have been dating their boyfriends for less than a year would say yes to a proposal. Think about that. Less than a year into a relationship and you would give your life to this man. No one truly knows another person after a year; they may think they do, but both parties are still learning each other. Yes, you can fall in love fast, but you can't grow together any faster than one day at a time. Marriage isn't just the next step after boyfriend/girlfriend; it's the last stage of your romantic life and should be treated as if you're writing the final chapter in that book. Still, there are women who irrationally walk down the aisle because it's expected after a long-term relationship. You are at the point in your life where you are done playing house and being Pussy. You want something legitimate—great. Now is the time to truly dissect every part of your boyfriend and be sure if he is built for the long run and worthy to have you as a wife. Being in love isn't enough to say "yes." There are factors in his life and your life that determine if a marriage can work. "I love him, we have our issues, but God will see us through" is the wrong mindset.

You shouldn't be jumping as soon as he gets on bended knee and then praying that it's the right choice. Choosing a husband is like buying a car with no warranty: you can fall in love with the exterior, drive it around the block, love the way it handles, but if you don't pop the hood and see what's underneath, you're making a horribly uneducated decision that has the potential to leave your ass stranded. You're on the highway of life and it's your job not to let an unchecked desire leave you broken down, embarrassed, and full of regret. Get over the ego stroke of being asked to be married, and review all aspects of your relationship before you agree to put on that ring or start asking about marriage in the first place. Has this man shown you in the years of being in a relationship that he can carry the weight of matrimony? Being married isn't just the same shit with a different last name; you have to be able to trust him, live with him, deal with the bad, and reward the good—24/7 365. It's an exhausting life and love alone won't see you through, you need to be prepared for surprises!

Knowing if your boyfriend has a lazy mentality is crucial. If he's the type that does just enough to get by when he's at work, and then coasts until it's time to clock out this tells you that he's going to be the type that gets married, kicks his feet up, and lets you cater to him and the household. I know several women who may as well have gotten married to themselves because they do all the work. One of my friends had a man that literally did nothing but hang around and watch ESPN while she put forth the effort to keep the romance going, bills paid, and her perfect world out of the divorce court. How could she have known that he was a moocher? Simple, he showed those signs in other aspects of his life. A man may not show you all of his cards when he's trying to impress, but over the course of a long relationship, you will see all of his tricks. Pay attention to how he lives his life in general. Knowing that he has bad work habits, hustles friends, likes to manipulate family, etc... will help form a complete picture. That bad behavior may not affect your love life with him, but once you're married, those traits will start to spill over. Pop the hood early and often, and get to know that man's character on multiple levels, not just the romantic side.

Do not base your decision to get married on age, money, pressure from relatives, or see this as a chance to floss on your unwed girlfriends. Many women say yes to the ring, not the man. They cry tears of joy thinking about the wedding, not the lifetime spent with that person. Today's marriages seem to be more about the status of marriage than the bliss of matrimony. In the African American community in particular, there are conspiracy theorists who haven't finished getting their GED, but are quick to tell black women that all the good black men are either married, gay, or in jail. When you add that 43% unwed stat to the mix, it causes a panic the moment a woman finds herself single again. No woman wants to be alone, so she will race into a serious relationship hoping that the man she's found is decent, instead of taking the time to play Devil's Advocate and prove that he is decent. When you rush, you make mistakes. Even if you've been with a man for years, that race to get to the altar will cause you to ignore all of the problems you two had over the years that have yet to be resolved, and rely on simple hope. Some of my readers in Atlanta feel disheartened over the ratio of men to women in that city. One told me that her friends are so thirsty for men that they don't mind paying all the bills, letting them get away with lies, and generally compromising their values so they can be one of the few Atlanta women that has a man that's not in prison. In those scenarios women don't want to be Spartans, they don't care about power over men or getting the best partner available. They are driven by fear of being the last unmarried woman on earth.

There seems to be two prominent schools of thought once a woman becomes desperate for a ring. Settle for Mr. Just Okay because you're tired of waiting for Prince Charming or latch on to Mr. Turn Me On, who's wrong for you on so many levels, but can be fixed...or so you think. Neither man is worth your time, but once again, not knowing your own value and a refusal to date more than one guy at a time has penned you in a corner with only one romantic option, so you try to make it work. For instance, a 34-year-old woman is turned on by a tall, dark, rugged looking guy who has a very aggressive attitude. She doesn't care about his job, how many bastard kids he has, none of the important things...she wants what she wants because she wants it. Her new boyfriend is no different from the bad boys who have broken her heart, but she's getting older and won't be denied what she thinks is her last chance at love. This kind of woman wants a husband, and no matter how much he doesn't fit into that role, she is going to FORCE him into it. You don't get a dog and expect it to shit in a litter box…you get a cat. If you take a noncommittal man and force him to put a ring on it, you will become a part of a worse statistic than being a single lady—being a divorced one.

Being a Spartan is about getting what you want, but never should you focus your desire on attaining something unworthy. You can get any man, but that doesn't mean you can transform any man into a compatible one. Having the power to attract is worthless if you lack the wisdom to pick the guys that best suit you emotionally. If a doctor were to tell you to cut out sugar from your diet or die, would you be that hard up for a cupcake that you would risk your health for a taste? Maturity equals discipline and self-love demands self-preservation. You know in your heart that this man is wrong on more levels than he is right for you. Even if you have a diamond ring in your face and he's on bended knee, show discipline and don't say "yes" until you know if this guy is a project or a partner. If you realize your relationship has been messy and he's not compatible, don't have faith in God to see you through this potential shit storm. Have faith that you will attract someone better, and turn that ring down. I find myself often giving advice to women who went against their intuition and gave the benefit of the doubt to the wrong men, and one of the common regrets is, "I knew he wasn't right for me." No shit.

Is He Just Dick

Some women are just Pussy, yet hard up men still try to make them into Wifey. Divorce lawyers have made millions off simple men who dared to ignore Pussy signs and put a ring on it. Women make those same mistakes when confusing Dick with Hubby. Not only will a female ignore the signs, she embraces them and swears, "It's nothing. I can straighten him out!" Ego, pride, and the desire to be loved will fuck you over every time you undertake the pointless project of transforming Dick into Hubby. How do you know if your boyfriend is just Dick? Dick is a man who is immature, selfish, controlling, and deceitful. Dick is also passionate, affectionate, smooth, and sexy. Dick uses the power of manipulation to convince you that he's the man you've been looking for. He uses the hypnosis of good sex to convince you that he's worth the headache. Furthermore, Dick uses your own desire to be saved from the world of single in order to crawl so deep into your heart that you will forgive just about any infraction. The easiest telltale sign to look for when attempting to spot the Dick in your life is that his potential has stopped, and you're often asking, "Why doesn't he act like he did when we first met?"

Hubby is that man who grows, matures, improves, and learns. That makes him the perfect candidate for marriage because that's a union based on one's ability to compromise and work together. Dick doesn't want to work together in harmony or do better, Dick is content with who he is and expects you to do things his way. Dick's sole purpose is to settle with a woman who he can dicknotize into catering to his needs for the rest of his life...or until he finds a better candidate. Yet another wolf in sheep's clothing; he accessed your heart then revealed his true form like, "Gotcha, Bitch!" You can go to couples therapy, talk to the Deacon after church, and try every trick in the book to get him to revert to that perfect man who first asked you out, but he's not going to act like that nice man you first met because that was all game. This flawed and problematic person is who Dick actually is, and the only change in behavior you'll see from a man like this will be temporary. Dick is incapable of true change, but will do just enough to prevent his lady from moving on for good. Dick's ultimate trick is to keep a woman in check with the promise that one day he will give her what she wants—The Ring. I call this, The Commitment Carrot.

"Break a woman down mentally as if you can do better, and it will mind fuck her until the true problems of the relationship become nonexistent. Make her compete for both your time and penis by pretending your time is precious and your penis is coveted. Use your attraction to other woman as a leash, and yank it whenever she gets out of line. Remind her that she is just another fish in the sea, and that you are a man capable of reeling in better trout. Her threats of finding "the next man" are hollow; she doesn't want the next man, she wants you, and will always welcome you back. She does not want to be single. She does not want to start from scratch. You represent comfort. Although you are flawed, you are all she has."
— The Dick Handbook

THE COMMITMENT CARROT

Here's a secret, not as shocking as the existence of the Illuminati, but just as revealing: most men do not respect the intelligence of women. Many are raised by women they love to death, yet mothers are seen as less deserving of respect than fathers. She carried him for 9 months, fed him from her tit, and showered as much love as possible, yet the son will flat out refuse to do what she asks unless he's threatened with his father's or uncle's wrath. It's not the physical fear of a man hurting him; it's the respect of an adult male that puts him in check. Little boys learn early on that they can get away with things because they think mom is weak. Other kids in school or older boys will even tease a boy for listening to a woman, making it an act of bitchassness to bend to the authority of a female, be it his teacher, classmate, or mother. While a strict mother can instill the fear of punishment in a son, getting a switch off the tree does not make a boy think of her as equally intelligent. Males take compassion for weakness and from that early age proceed to lie, yell, and threaten their mothers into doing what they want until they are adults. Mom is the most powerful female figure in a man's world, and if she can be manipulated and proven one-step behind him in the smarts department, he will view all women as inferior.

Women in relationships are often baffled that their boyfriends, who were raised by loving mothers, still treat females like shit. All men come from a woman's womb, yet this world is extremely misogynistic. All men can love women, but some have yet to mature to the point where they can break those bad habits and stop trying to play their girlfriends in the same way they played their mothers. There are exceptions to the rule, such as those mama's boys who respect every aspect of their moms to the point of worship. These men tend to grow up with a great appreciation for women, yet they turn into pushovers because they overdo it. For women who are used to submitting to aggressive men and turned on by their level of confident roughness, this type of mama's boy adoration is unattractive. There are other men who are more progressive, maintain their manly nature, and see women as equals. Still, the majority of men you will come across will be Dick, and Dick thinks he's smarter than you are. His goal is to prove this theory by promising you the ring but giving you the run around. I know each one of you are MORE INTELLIGENT than Dick, but love or the thought of it, has dimmed the lights of common sense. It's my duty to shine a spotlight on the manipulation game so you can see firsthand that your boyfriend is Dick and not Hubby.

Certain men play the Ike Turner game where they beat you down mentally in order to convince you that you will never do better, can't get better, and should never leave. Men know that a weak mind is easily influenced. All it takes is that one negative poke from a man whom a woman has feelings for, and her confidence buckles. It doesn't have to be exaggerated yelling, it can be tiny pot shots that he drops innocently, such as what girls were flirting with him at work, how you put on weight, or jokes about finding a new woman that will do x, y, and z better than you do it. These are called "bitch checks": a self-esteem draining tactic to keep his bottom bitch at the bottom, his basic bitch content, and his ratchet tatted up with his name on her arm.

Smart men realize that a girl doesn't need to have daddy issues for him to pull an abandonment hustle. People always ask, "What exactly are daddy issues?" Here's a shortened version of what it means. A little girl feels unloved because her father has gone off and found a new family or never comes home at night. She covets the memory of daddy holding her and boosting her confidence by calling her "princess" or "beautiful," and without daddy around, she doesn't feel special. This little girl is too young to understand what's really going on between mommy and daddy, so she blames herself for his lack of interest. If only she could change something about herself or do something extra to make daddy love her again. That's a daddy issue, but it also relates to any woman who has abandonment fears or don't think they measure up enough for a man to love them.

Men are well aware of a woman's desire to be not only loved, but to be the only one he loves. Girls want to be told they are special and they need to feel like they are special. All women lust for a man who only has eyes for her, who will claim her as his woman, and then seal it under the eyes of God and the legal system with marriage. Wedlock is the ultimate safety net and ego boost that will make a woman feel superior. Men know this is the driving force behind many of the choices females make. Some men will be careful not to lead a girl on solely for sex, but Dick doesn't care about leading a woman on and will use her want to be special for his own benefit. Like a donkey chasing a carrot on a string, a woman follows and follows. As soon as she figures out this man is full of shit and she's not going to get the prize, she looks for the door. The man reacts by dangling the carrot closer or by threatening to give her carrot away to another woman. The realization that she's close to getting what she wants or the fear that she's going to lose everything she's been chasing to another woman puts her back in check. That's the Commitment Carrot. It's insanely genius, tragically cruel, yet easy to stop.

FOR SPARTANS ONLY

I saved this section for last because this book truly is a system that relies on overcoming the negative customs of your old life in order to regain your power. To rule over her romantic kingdom, each Queen needs to understand the kind of woman she once was, the mistakes she's made in past relationships, and most importantly that there is life after breaking up. Until you master the art of recognizing your own basic behavior, confronting your insecurities, and finding that inner Spartan, you will not be able to see past Dick and go after Hubby. You have to study past mistakes that you've made and that others have made in order to know when Dick is trying to play you. You have to open your mind and think progressively so you don't play yourself by adhering to unjustifiable rules that serve no purpose, such as waiting for a man to speak to you first, only dating one person at a time, or torturing yourself for ninety days before you have sex. Finally, you have to become confident in your ability to attract men, yet also be mentally tough to the point where you can walk away from any man who doesn't give you everything you deserve, no matter how in love you are.

If you are lacking in any of these areas, stop and re-read this entire book starting with Chapter 10 until those lessons are as embedded in you as the alphabet. You can't solve being single unless you commit fully to this way of thinking. It's not enough to read it and take what you want; you have to put this Spartan training into practical use every day of your life. This power isn't just something you release on the weekends or in those situations where you feel comfortable. This invisible armor has to surround you every day! Failure to commit to your own empowerment will lead to failure across the board. The moment you come face to face with a guy you like, you'll forget everything I've laid out and go back to trying to do things the old way. If that happens, you're back to being just like the rest of these undervalued women who play the victim and rely on being chosen. There's no such thing as learning to halfway swim. You either learn fully or drown.

DECIDE WHAT YOU WANT

Having mastered your Spartan training, you now understand that getting any man takes an equal mix of self-confidence, insight into the male mind, and a working knowledge of your own self-worth. That's the easy part. Once you are in a relationship that's made it past the four-month honeymoon period where you usually expose guys as incompatible, your love life gets much more complicated, and it could be difficult to see if this is a love worth working on or a love that's run its course. If you've reached this point, then it's time for the end game.

There are women who enter into relationships and see it as just something to do. They treat love like a part time job: it's not really in their career field, but it pays the bills so it'll do for now. The man you're with may be incredible, but if you were to keep it real with yourself, he's not the type you see yourself marrying. He's just a good man who provides you with love, affection, and attention, so he'll do for now. Why settle for part-time when you want full-time? A mature adult relationship is not an exercise in waiting to see where it goes, it's the most important interview of your life. If you're merely going through the motions of being girlfriend and boyfriend, stop right now and decide what you want. If he hasn't impressed you enough for you to want to one day marry him, what's the point? He's not going to change that much more from the man he already is. In the meantime, you're lulling yourself into a sense of comfort that will lead to settling for what you have, instead of getting what you need.

Spartans don't have time to waste with things that do not benefit them. If you just want dick in a Taye Diggs package, you're powerful enough and disciplined enough to find a good-looking boy toy to scratch your itch. If you want attention and companionship, you're charismatic enough to make friends, go on vacations, and enjoy your youth. Anything you want in life you can have without settling down with a man. I assume the reason you're reading this is because you do want more than just fun and sex, you want a deeper connection, and you want to get married. Say it. Admit it. Focus on it. Little girls shrug their shoulders because they aren't sure what they want. Spartans point their fingers knowing exactly what they want, then take it!

On the flipside of this are women in relationships that know the man they are with is the one and want this boyfriend/girlfriend exercise to end in marriage. Bra-fucking-vo, you have become a decisive woman! However, instead of being proactive, you will sit by and wait for that man to pop the question. Spartans do not wait, they are constantly moving toward their goals. I will not give you hints or ways you should go about letting him know you are ready to be proposed to nor will I recommend buying him a ring and asking for his hand in marriage. A Spartan does not need to drop fucking hints that she's a wife. Her man will know that she is a wife because every day that they are together she will communicate and act like someone worthy of marriage. Do not ask, "Where do you see this going?" That's for weak bitches who are at the mercy of their man. Tell him where you see it going and then wait for his response. People call this "the talk." Men don't like the talk because it usually comes out of nowhere. Your relationship goal is to be the wifey type from the moment you agree to be exclusive. Unlike Basica's who sex trap or spoil a man in order to secure a hollow relationship, your bond is based on respect and appreciation. You two should be on the same frequency before you even consider marriage; this isn't "the talk," it's more of "the confirmation."

During a romantic dinner or while spending time together, you need to tell that man that you appreciate him, that he means a lot to you, and then finish with this: *I see us growing old together, and that's from the heart*. Those exact words are all you have to say! His reply will tell you exactly how serious he is about you being in his future. By this point if you've communicated as I've described constantly in previous chapters and aren't afraid to read his vibes, you will be able to pick up on if he's sincere about wanting to be with you, merely telling you what you want to hear, or if he's honestly unsure. If he responds with similar sentiments, then you two can continue that talk, and honestly open up about marriage and how close you are to that goal. If he's lying through his teeth trying to appease you, no need to check him, you already know what must be done. If he sounds unsure about the prospect of marriage, don't get an attitude, have a conversation about his hesitation so you can both come to some sort of understanding going forward. You've done your job by stating clearly that you are in this for life, now the rest of it is on him.

TAKE YOUR TIME

So when is your ring coming? Some people are engaged after months, others years. Remember that the time it takes you to get engaged is not a reflection of how good or bad you are as a couple, it's a reflection of the rate you two are growing. Money, family, jobs, distance—they are all factors that come into play. If you have been in a four-year relationship with a man who is just now finding steady work, you can't honestly expect that he is ready to take care of his duties as a husband. It's not about the money it's about the mindset. Even if you can cover the bills while your man tries to advance his position, he won't be mentally ready to give you his all. Understand that guys who aren't bums or users will never be happy with you carrying the load. If your boyfriend is frustrated with his own shortcomings in life, he will need time to fix himself before he can shift his focus to marriage. The excuse of not being able to afford a good wedding ring is a front. Most of the fellas who say this are more ashamed that they can't afford to give the woman they love a proper wedding or purchase a home after they walk down the aisle. These men use the cost of the ring as a metaphor for not being able to provide, and as a partner, you have to understand and help him get over this phobia.

You can point to other couples who got married with ten dollars in the bank, but you can't expect your situation to mirror theirs. Some men don't care about money; they know they'll find a way to make it work. Your man may not have that kind of faith and his pride may not allow him to hit up the Justice of the Peace for a "let's get it over with" ceremony. The solution isn't to wait until he's totally on his feet; instead, you have to get him to express everything I just wrote aloud, so you can tag team this problem. Stop asking about when your ring is coming! Show the maturity of a wife by unselfishly asking your partner about his insecurities. Get him to open up about the reasons why you two need to wait, and then together you can discuss the ways you two can accelerate the process as a team, instead of you selfishly resenting the time it's taking to walk down the aisle.

Some women have lofty goals, but their dream of being a Mrs. overtakes those ambitions the moment a man asks for her hand. You should be willing to give your man time to get closer to his dreams, but don't forget to do the same thing for yourself. If getting married means moving somewhere else or compromising a part of your life that you aren't ready to concede, then let him know, don't just give up on your dreams. Take your time and have faith that a man who loves you is not going anywhere! If you were approved to buy a home, would you take out the loan knowing that your current job is temporary and that your student loans would leave you with barely enough money to eat each month, or would you wait until you found a permanent job that pays enough to afford your bills and new mortgage? A smart woman would not rush into that kind of decision just because she wants to say she owns a home. She realizes that what she wants will still be there, and goes about getting her life in order so that she can buy that home and still live life comfortably. You must have faith that you will get what you want in the manner you most deserve it! Keep that in your mind and you will be immune to rushing into an ill-advised engagement or shotgun wedding. Any man who threatens to abandon you if you don't jump at his proposal proves his incompatibility. Again, take your time.

ARE YOU READY TO BE A WIFE...SERIOUSLY?

The most important part of knowing if he's the right man is becoming the right woman who is prepared to be a wife. You have to grow within the relationship, live within the relationship, and thrive within the relationship. Poll any woman over the age of 25 and they will swear they would be the perfect wife, yet they haven't even mastered the art of being a good girlfriend. Don't put the Wifey crown on when you're still stuck in pussyville. In order to grow with this man to the point where marriage makes sense, you have to put being partners into practice.

Cooking dinner and watching TV together aren't real life moments. How much do you two know about each other's bad habits or faults? Does he know you pay two of your bills late and need a little extra help? Does he have credit problems that are keeping him from doing certain things, and if so what's his plan to fix it? You both want children but how responsible is he at this point in his life? You love the thought of being a mommy but how do you truly feel about adding a third party to your current lifestyle? It's not enough to say, "I think I know," or "We'll cross that bridge when we get to it." Communicate and live life as if you're already married! How you two react to the stress and pressure of bills, bad health, and professional setbacks, are character-defining things that you have to get familiar with now, not later. Your relationship can't be contained to the bedroom where you small talk about your day and then forget your troubles by laughing and making love. If you two refuse to communicate about your real life, and just escape to each other's affection, you are not preparing for marriage nor are you doing the proper compatibility research to see if marriage could even work. To love him is to know him and vice versa. How much do you know about one another during pressure situations? You are constantly learning more about that man with each new curveball. Additionally, you are learning about your own level of readiness the more you expose yourself to solving your joint issues, instead of accepting them in the name of love.

You can't fall asleep because the finish line is in your sight. The man you've fallen in love with may have proven that he's more than just Dick, but he can still have incompatibility issues that make him unfit for marriage. Do not be afraid to continuously examine his worth and character because constant examination may uncover new truths. You cannot be scared of what you may find. This is no longer a college boyfriend; this is potentially the man you will be with forever, therefore, you need to know the whole truth even if that truth leads to you breaking up. Better to know two years in that your boyfriend has deep seeded issues than end up like one of these clueless wives on *48hrs Mysteries* who are shocked that their husbands were capable of horrible things ten years later. I don't care how many people expect you two to get married or what you rely on from him to live. With or without him, you will survive, and as long as you're breathing, that reset button is always at your disposal.

Marriage isn't about walking down the aisle and taking bomb-ass wedding pictures. It's about the life you have to live once people on Facebook stop liking those pictures. Prepare, take your time, research, and then make your decision based on how high he scores, not how huge the diamond is. For those women who find themselves still waiting with no end in sight, I ask again, have you talked about being married or are you just talking about getting married—there's a huge difference. The root of most relationship problems boils down to not being strong enough to express yourself to a man. I'm not talking about saying "I guess I want to get married. I guess I want kids. I guess I want a house." I'm talking about expressing what your ultimate goals are and how you plan on reaching them together. Basic bitches take the shy route and talk around their men when it comes to plans for the future while ratchets take the angry route and yell at their men when the next step is taking too long to reach. Neither of these women are showing the mature qualities of a woman who deserves to be a wife, thus, they leave their fate in the hands of their indecisive boyfriends who secretly know they can do better and don't want to get married. Spartans communicate and guide their own destiny. Constant and deep communication takes the guesswork out of getting married. He will play his cards close to his chest because he wants you to be surprised when he pops the question, but by staying on the same page, he knows what you want and you know what he wants. At that moment of harmony getting the ring stops becoming a fantasy that you're wishing for and transforms into an imminent reality that you've earned.

...AND ONE LAST THING

There is no exception to the rule when it comes to men and marriage. All men want true love, and each one of them is capable of recognizing a woman who embodies that so long as she is presented in a powerful package made up of confidence, understanding, and exceptionality. Guys are overly cautious, but that caution evaporates when presented with a special woman who shows him a side that other women were too average to get across. Every man who you have met from the playboys, to the emotionally unavailable, even the losers, as well as the cheaters, will find a Game Changer. The Game Changer will be that woman who not only impresses him but also knows how to handle him. Regardless of how unsure or cautious a guy is, his brain will override his old way of thinking and make him recognize that this type of woman is rare and must be treated as such.

Bitter women look at old flames who got married and remark, "Hope she knows he ain't shit." That's what the negative mind of a hater wants to project in order to mask her own failure or incompatibility. The truth is that someone's "ain't shit" usually transforms into someone's great husband. Don't be closed-minded and think that it was the man who finally matured and snatched the first woman he could find. More times than not, it's the woman that came along at the right time and made that man want to mature. Each and every one of you reading these words has the potential to be a Game Changer, but you have to change your own life for the better before you can begin to change someone else's. For those of you who need to apply this to a relationship that you're already in, the transformation will be difficult at first. A man, especially one who sees you as dumb, weak, and inept, will not let you Spartan up. He will either laugh in your face or roll his eyes the moment you try to lay down the law and change the status quo, but you must stay strong! Do not retreat to the bathroom and cry like you don't know what to do. If you have read these chapters, then you know the path you have to take. *"I didn't ask for this,"* doesn't live here anymore. You did ask for it! You allowed that man to set the tone, and now it's time to pull the rug out from under your friend, boyfriend, or fiancé, and reestablish balance. Your words are no longer squeaks from some soft bitch; they are thundering commands from a powerful woman who isn't so in love that she won't back up her threat to leave. A Game Changer will get the highest level of commitment from any man if that's what she chooses. The time has come to stop feeling sorry for yourself, stop looking at the statistics, and stop allowing indecision to keep you from rising to Game Changer status.

Finding true love is not about getting a ring. It's about finding a man who succeeds where others have failed, who can grow with you, and who sees you as an equal in all respects. Do not stress over the search for a man, you set your time limit, not society. Have fun! Once you turn it into a laborious hunt, you will rush and make a critical mistake. At the same time, do not sit on your pretty ass and wait for the universe to drop a man in your lap. The universe rewards those who understand that effort is more than prayer, it's your desire turned into action that will cause opportunity to knock when you least expect it. All you have to do is live your life normally with the insight that I have shared, the awareness of your own pros and cons, and the proactive power to approach every situation with the intelligence and determination of a Spartan, not the hopeful desperation of a lovesick little girl. Fully embrace the lessons in this book and reread these chapters until you have supercharged your confidence and erased fear from all aspects of your mind. Once you have conquered the indecision, nervousness, and self-doubt that are byproducts of fear, you will have unlocked not only your power over men, but over LIFE. At that moment, you will have mastered the art of being a Game Changer! No longer will you be the girl who settles for what a man is willing to give, you will have grown into a woman who gets exactly what she demands.

ABOUT THE AUTHOR

Born in Baltimore, MD, G.L. Lambert is the creator of Blackgirlsareeasy.com and a screenwriter who has produced works for the likes of Kelsey Grammer, Brett Ratner, and Walt Becker. He currently resides in Los Angeles, CA.

Made in the USA
Charleston, SC
08 March 2014